To John and Eric,

Hope you find
the story of the
boat interesting!

Shelley Wachsmann

The Sea of Galilee Boat

An Extraordinary 2000 Year Old Discovery

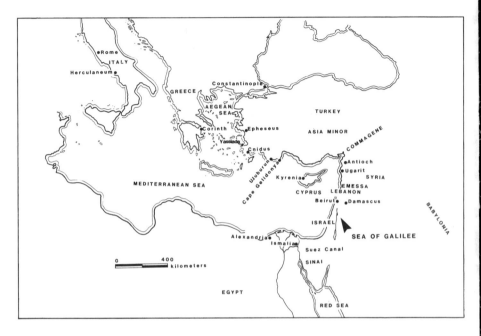

Mediterranean region

The Sea of Galilee Boat

An Extraordinary 2000 Year Old Discovery

SHELLEY WACHSMANN

PLENUM PRESS • NEW YORK AND LONDON

Library of Congress Cataloging-in-Publication Data

Wachsmann, Shelley.
    The Sea of Galilee boat : an extraordinary 2000 year old discovery
  Shelley Wachsmann.
      p.   cm.
  Includes bibliographical references and index.
  ISBN 0-306-44950-1
    1. Tiberias Lake (Israel)--Antiqities. 2. Underwater archaeology-
  -Israel--Tiberias Lake. 3. Ships, Ancient--Israel--Tiberias Lake.
  4. Excavations (Archaeology)--Israel--Tiberias Lake.   I. Title.
  DS110.T62W33 1995
  933--dc20   95-5896
                                                                  CIP

The quote which appears on page vii is from the lyrics to "Life Is a Rock" by Paul DiFranco and Norman Dolph. Copyright 1973 Crushing Music, Crazy Chords Music. All rights reserved. Used by permission.

ISBN 0-306-44950-1

© 1995 Shelley Wachsmann
Plenum Press is a Division of Plenum Publishing Corporation
233 Spring Street, New York, N.Y. 10013-1578

10 9 8 7 6 5 4 3 2

Printed in the United States of America

For Karen

At the end of my rainbow lies a golden oldie.

From "Life Is a Rock"
PAUL DIFRANCO AND NORMAN DOLPH

Preface

This book concerns a unique and exciting treasure: the first ancient boat ever found in the Sea of Galilee. It is both an adventure story and a whodunit. It is not a report solely of the facts. Many of the descriptions that follow are also of feelings and impressions.

It is a story as seen through my eyes. Others who participated in this undertaking would no doubt describe their experiences differently, for each and every one of us perceives reality in his or her own unique way.

Acknowledgments

No book dealing with the Galilee Boat can begin without first paying tribute to the many men and women, organizations and groups, who gave their time, effort, and money to this venture. This was a team effort, but it was undertaken by individuals, without whose dedication the endeavor never would have succeeded.

The rescue excavation of the Galilee Boat was a project of the Israel Department of Antiquities and Museums (IDAM; now the Israel Antiquities Authority, IAA). A. Eitan, the former director of IDAM, made the courageous decision to excavate the boat, despite considerable odds against a successful outcome. I am grateful to him for his unstinting support throughout the expedition. I am also indebted to A. Drori, the present director of the IAA, for permission to present the story of the boat here.

Additional members of the Department's staff gave significant assistance to the excavation: Deputy Director Z. Yeivin and District Archaeologist G. Mazor helped with the many administrative aspects; Claire Epstein served as a liaison in the initial stages; Orna Hess handled the extensive media interest; E. Kazaioff and Y. Majar transported supplies and personnel; A. Kligman and E. Kohai, who were responsible for logistics, kept the expedition well supported; M. Feist, V. Shor, and Y. Vatkin, the Department's surveyors, mapped the site; Y. Stepansky was instrumental in notifying me of the boat's discovery and was very helpful throughout the excavation; at night the excavation site was guarded by IDAM's Anti-Looting Unit: I. Ben Yehuda, T. Frank, M. Katz, and Z. Levi.

My thanks also go to Ruta Peled, the IAA's chief curator. It remains Ruta's concern to find and allocate the funding for the boat's various needs—a difficult job, but one which Ruta carries out with distinction.

The members of Kibbutz Ginosar adopted the rescue mission and made it their own. Without their unbridled enthusiasm and dedication, the boat would never have made it. M. and Y. Lufan, the two brothers who discovered the boat, continually exhibited an exuberance and ingenuity that sustained the excavation in times of doubt and difficulty. Y. Abes, D. Ronen, and Y. Amitai, the "Ginosar Fiberglass Team," built the frames and supports. And special thanks are due to kibbutz members S. Edri, Nurit Gofer, Y. Gofer, G. Klop, M. Lipnik, I. Lufan, Aliza Paz, O. Sabag, Y. Rotem, and E. Shalem.

Providentially, the boat was found near the Yigal Allon Centre, whose staff and administrative resources unceasingly supported the excavation and continue to support the conservation phases. A particular debt of gratitude is due to Nitsa Kaplan and I. Rotem.

Members of Moshav Migdal contributed considerably during the excavation. I want to thank S. Karasanti for the use of his mechanical backhoe, as well as Z. Malach and G. Horowitz for their valuable assistance.

The safety of the boat during the excavation was a particular concern, given the unceasing press of visitors. The site's security was directed by E. Janet, who was responsible for security in the Kibbutz Ginosar region. In this task he was assisted by I. Rabinovitch, M. Tayar, M. Lieberman, U. Kach, Y. Even, and the border guard station at Tabgha.

Ambassador T. Pickering and Alice Pickering are keen amateur archaeologists, and through them, the American Embassy came to play a major part in the project's success. The travel expenses for Professor Steffy to take part in the excavation were processed through the United States Information Service in record time. I am indebted to public affairs counselor H. Lane and cultural affairs officer R. Petersen for what amounted to a bureaucratic miracle. Ambassador Pickering and Science Attaché A. Rock also secured the donation of forty tons of polyethylene glycol for the boat's conservation process. I am also indebted to embassy family members Karen Sullivan and Nan Leininger, who participated in the excavation.

The challenge of protecting the site from the rising waters of the Sea of Galilee and keeping the groundwater that welled up inside the excavation pit at bay was a task admirably accomplished by members of the Kinneret Authority. For this assistance I thank the Authority's chairman, Z. Ortenberg, S. Bahalal, and staff members L. O. Bakish, R. Gada, and I. Gal. The Tsemach Fire Station donated the sandbags used in the dike.

Faced with novel problems, we searched for innovative solutions. Israeli experts called upon for advice gave freely of their time and knowledge. Special thanks are due to engineers A. Aharonson and I. Yakobinski; G. Shamir of the Haifa Port Authority; A. Halamish of Kibbutz Ma'agan Michael; M. Gophen of the Kinneret Authority Laboratories; D. Shenhav of the Israel Museum Laboratories; and Y. Ziv, director of Israel Chemicals.

The success of the excavation was largely due to the unceasing dedication and perseverance of the expedition staff; indeed, it is difficult for me to envision a better one. Conservation was a major component of this project. Orna Cohen, the boat's conservator, shouldered a heavy burden throughout the excavation, transfer, and conservation phases, the last of which continues to this day. It fell to Orna to find solutions to protect the fragile hull during excavation and to move it to the conservation site. Orna eventually found innovative solutions to each problem.

D. Syon (Friedman) faithfully recorded the excavation with his cameras. Some of the fruits of his labors illustrate the following pages. When not occupied with photography, Danny took on the often backbreaking job of stringing and tagging the boat's timbers. Later he assisted diligently in the process of removing the polyurethane foam from the boat once she was in the pool. I asked Edna Amos to help out as registrar temporarily when she visited the site on the first day of the excavation. She remained through

The crew. Front row (left to right): Gadi Horowitz, Danny Syon, Eti Shalem. Center row: Yisrael Vatkin, Orna Cohen, Aliza Paz, Karen Sullivan, J. Richard Steffy, Shelley Wachsmann, Hani Efroni, Zvika Malach, Edna Amos, Nitsa Kaplan. Back row: Yaron Ostrovski, Shalom Edri, Yossi Amitai, Gill Klop, Kurt Raveh, Moshe Lufan. Absent: Yohai Abes, Nurit Gofer, Yaron Gofer, Eliezer Janet, Moshe Lipnik, Yuval Lufan, Israel Lufan, David Ronen, Isaac Rotem, Yaakov Rotem, Ofir Sabag.

out that first difficult night and stayed for the rest of the project, which greatly benefited from her skills and dedication. K. Raveh assisted considerably in the initial probe of the boat and during the excavation.

Volunteers came in droves from all over Israel and from all walks of life. Each person contributed in his or her own way to the success of the project. I thank B. Azraf, L. Baron, A. Bolodo, M. Cohen, G. Efroni, M. Gallon, H. Ilan, Y. Ostrovski, and D. Pearl. Those who had artistic abilities were employed in recording in freehand drawings the boat and the related finds as they came out of the mud. Hani Efroni drew the boat's interior, while R. Malka sketched additional remnants of hulls found in the boat's vicinity.

The excavation received much unsolicited coverage by representatives of the media, two of whom deserve special recognition: the late Z. Ilan, archaeological correspondent for the Israel daily *Davar*, lost a "scoop" but gained my deep respect for his sense of responsibility; M. Ben Dor, cameraman for one of the large American networks, provided considerable help during the excavation.

Support, both financial and in-kind, came from a variety of sources, all of whom deserve recognition and thanks: Sachaf, Ltd., generously donated a steam shovel to excavate a channel to the lake; Orna Fraser, editor of *IsraEl Al* Magazine, secured a flight for Orna Cohen to consult with conservation experts in England, while Orna's stay there was made possible through a contribution from the Anglo-Israel Archaeological Society. Dow Chemical Company donated forty tons of polyethylene glycol for the boat's conservation that was kindly processed by R. Jacobsen of Jacobsen Agencies, Ltd. The Israel National Tourist Company committed funds for the heating-circulation system required for the conservation process, as well as for the preparation of a short video presentation shown to visitors to the boat. Private donations came from M. Hatter, B. Lewin, and Irene Sala.

Israel's number one "Kinneretologist," M. Nun, played an indispensable role at the time of the boat's discovery and subsequently was a valuable participant in the excavation. His vast knowledge of the Sea of Galilee, its history and archaeology, has been an invaluable source, which he has willingly shared.

I owe an enormous debt to J. R. Steffy, who studied the boat's construction under the harsh conditions of the expedition. His knowledge of ship construction is unsurpassed, and his advice on problem solving was an incredible asset. I was privileged to work with him on this project and appreciate his willingness to add one more project to an already considerable work load.

In researching various aspects of the boat and its milieu, I received much welcome assistance from a variety of scholars. I thank L. Casson for his valuable comments on the enigmatic craft prepared by Vespasian's forces for the battle of Migdal; G. Foerster for our discussions on Byzantine mosaics; and Y. Meshorer for bringing the Caesarea Paneas coin to my attention and for many other valuable insights.

Much—although by no means all—of the research for this book was initially carried out in preparation of the excavation report, which appeared as Volume 19 of the Israel Antiquities Authority's English journal *'Atiqot*. In addition to those already named, I owe a debt of gratitude to the following scholars, who gave their time and knowledge to prepare contributions for the report: D. Adan-Bayewitz, Y. Carmi, H. Gitler, Y. Nir, Claire Peachy, A. F. Rainey, I. Roman, Varda Sussman, Ella Werker, R. White, and J. Zias. The report benefited considerably from the editorial skills of Ayala Sussman and Inna Pommerance.

The concept for a book dealing with a "behind-the-scenes" look at what can only be described as an exceptional discovery and a hair-raising excavation first came to me while I was preparing a popular account of the project for the journal *Biblical Archaeology Review*. I have always felt that there is more to the story of the boat than just a report on artifacts.

In this, I have had much welcome help. I owe a considerable debt of gratitude to Regula Noetzli and R. Wertime, who were instrumental in making this book a reality. I thank Linda Regan of Plenum Press for her valuable comments, probing questions, and insightful advice, which helped keep me on the straight and narrow while preparing this manuscript. I am grateful to Herman Makler and Trudy Brown for seeing the book through production. Thanks also go to Melicca McCormick for her assistance. I appreciate the administrative assistance given to me by Claudia LeDoux, Becky Holloway, Patricia Turner, and C. Reese.

Readers of the manuscript—or parts thereof—have made valuable and insightful comments, from which the manuscript benefited considerably. I thank V. Bryant, Orna Cohen, W. H. Charlton, B. Crouch, Y. Hirschfeld, P. and S. Sullivan, and J. Zias. Thanks also to F. M. Hocker and D. Johnson for their illustrations, and to Kyra Bowling for preparing the maps and many of the accompanying illustrations.

I wrote this book while serving as the Meadows Assistant Professor of Biblical Archaeology in the Nautical Archaeology Program at Texas A&M University. I am grateful to G. F. Bass, the Meadows Foundation of Dallas, the Institute of Nautical Archaeology, and Texas A&M University for making this possible.

SHELLEY WACHSMANN
College Station, Texas
September 1994

Contents

Prologue

I have a word to tell you,
  a story to recount to you:
the word of the tree and the charm of the stone,
  the whisper of the heavens to the earth,
   of the seas to the stars . . .
Come, and I will reveal it.

From *The Baal Cycle*
AS TRANSCRIBED BY ILIMILKU[1]

It was a fine February day, with an azure sky and the nip of winter in the air. We had spent the day surveying the Mediterranean coast opposite the Carmel Mountains, south of Haifa, Israel. As the resident nautical archaeologist for the Israel Department of Antiquities and Museums at that time, I had been called upon by a geologist friend to help in measuring the depth of an ancient well for a study on sea-level changes in antiquity. The four of us—the geologist, an American volunteer, my assistant, and I—had finished the task and were heading back to our base in a jeep.

I drove the jeep down the bright beach, splashing the wheels in an otherwise silent sea. Tide marks still left patterns in the sand far inshore; here and there lay flotsam spewed on the beach like so many Jonahs.

We neared Tanturah, a lagoon created by a necklace of small islands. Tanturah serves the local fishermen as a modest harbor. Brightly colored boats—their green nets secured into canvas bundles—danced lightly at anchor on a crystal bed of sparkling water. I was so engrossed in the scenic splendor that I nearly drove the jeep over two large objects buried in the sand.

The peaceful scene was a far cry from the murderous storm that had rampaged up and down the coast during the previous week. One old-timer had assured me that this had been the worst storm he could recall. The storm had finally been subdued by a *sharkia*, a bitterly cold wind that comes howling down off the Syrian desert. When the *sharkia* blows, it blows mightily. Particularly pronounced along the Carmel coast, the wind cascades down the mountain range onto the sea.

I had often walked alone on the beach, pushed along by an unseen yet powerful *sharkia* as it drove flurries of loose sand into

3

the sea before it. In these circumstances, the sea is absolutely flat near the beach, but a short distance from the shore, whitecaps begin to curl. Indeed, a few miles out to sea, a storm can be raging. It was this wind that was most feared by biblical seafarers.

But for now, the Mediterranean was serenely smooth. It seemed almost apologetic for having ranted and raged. Only modest wavelets approached the shore.

Before the storm had hit, the fishermen had diligently hauled their boats well up the shore and turned them over, like so many stranded wooden turtles. For further protection, they had dragged their rusty-red grapnel anchors farther up the beach.

The sea, however, had other ideas. It had stretched out its watery arms and gulped down two of the vessels, only to regurgitate them back onto the beach, and then, finally, to bury them upside down beneath a thick sand blanket. It would be rough going for the fishermen to dig them out.

Karen, the American volunteer, stood by me and looked at the boats.

"OK, what omen do you see in this?" she asked, her voice a challenge.

"Oh, I don't know," I told her jokingly. "I guess it means that we'll soon be finding an ancient shipwreck or two."

Shortly thereafter we returned to our base, located in a nearby old glass factory. Someone had left a telephone message for me on my desk. The note, from our head office in Jerusalem, was scribbled on a crumpled bit of paper torn from the corner of a notebook. It began, "Shelley, a boat, possibly ancient, has been found in the Sea of Galilee. Please investigate . . ."

It is fascinating how often seemingly inconsequential objects and events—a chance meeting, a missed bus, or even a scribbled note—can completely turn a person's life around. Little did I realize, as I read the note in my hands, that it was an invitation to the adventure of a lifetime, one that would consume my attention for years to come.

Chapter 1

The Boat That
Made Rainbows

I have a feeling that people do not "discover lost civilizations"; but rather that, when the time is ripe, lost civilizations
reveal themselves, using for the purpose whatever resources
and people are to hand.

From *Looking for Dilmun*
GEOFFREY BIBBY[1]

T he message on my desk was the immediate and direct result of actions taken by two brothers from Kibbutz Ginosar, a communal agricultural settlement located on the northwest banks of the Sea of Galilee.

A particularly harsh summer in 1985 and a subsequent lack of rainfall in the fall of that year had created a drought in Israel. Parched fields required irrigation. Water was pumped from the Sea of Galilee, which, despite its name, is actually an inland lake and now serves as Israel's primary reservoir of fresh water.

As time went by, the skies remained clear and bright, the water flowed south, and the level of the lake took a nosedive. In areas where the shore is fairly steep, this was less noticeable. But in regions where the shore was relatively flat—and this is most of the lake—vast expanses of the "seabed" became mud flats.

The lake looked dismal and dirty. Israeli newspapers carried editorials lamenting the diminishing water reserves and predicting dire outcomes if the situation were not reversed. It seemed as if all Israel watched with furrowed brow as the country's water supply dwindled before its eyes.

Well, almost all of Israel.

Two Israelis were absolutely delighted with this new turn of events. Moshe and Yuval Lufan, brothers in their midthirties, saw in the drought a remarkable and marvelous opportunity. "Moshele" and "Yuvi," to use their nicknames, are avid amateur archaeologists. They are imbued with a love of the past and a longing for the adventure inherent in uncovering it. As if Providence were on their side, they also have a remarkable knack for finding things. Growing up on the shores of the lake, they had

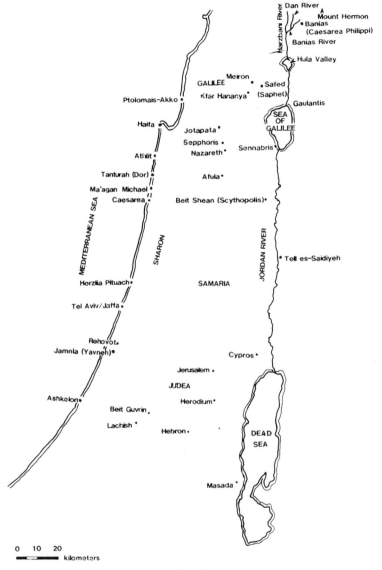

Israel.

long dreamed of finding a special boat—one that had plied the waters of the Sea of Galilee in antiquity.

Normally, organic materials, such as wooden boats, decay rapidly in warm, freshwater lakes like the Sea of Galilee. Thus archaeologists, myself included, had never given serious thought to finding the remains of ancient vessels in the Sea of Galilee. No one had told the brothers this, however, so they spent their free time on the quest for an ancient boat that any scholar probably would have explained to them could not, and did not, exist.

Neither of the brothers knew how to dive. So, for them, the lowering of the lake's waters seemed an incredible stroke of luck, as if a silent wish had been fulfilled.

As Yuvi explained to me later, "It was as if the lake had raised her skirt and, with a wink, had invited us to take a peek." Yuvi still remembers how, as a child, he would watch the members of Kibbutz Ginosar play soccer on the mud flats. But with the construction of the dam that controls the outflow of the lake into the Jordan River, the level of the lake went up and the land was submerged. No one ever imagined that it would reappear.

The brothers decided to take advantage of the lake's "immodesty." At the time, Yuvi was working as Ginosar's *sadran avoda*, the person responsible for assigning work to all the members of the kibbutz. Needless to say, it is a thankless and difficult job, one that kept Yuvi busy enough.

Despite this, he would find time each afternoon to go "boat hunting" with Moshele along the shores of the lake. Like oversized storks, they searched the mud flats, their eyes focused on the ground at their feet. In this manner they began systematically to survey the exposed lake bed, each time choosing a different sector for scrutiny. They began by examining the area around Capernaum. This, however, proved unprofitable and soon their attention was drawn closer to the region south of Kibbutz Ginosar.

As the mud flats dried out, local people had begun to use the terrain as a roadway. For the most part, the ground was firm enough to support vehicles. Some spots were weaker than others, as at least one driver had the ill fortune to discover. He spun his back wheels in the mud in an unwise attempt to get free. Eventu-

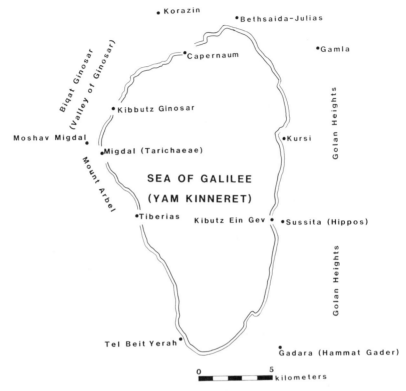

The Sea of Galilee and its environs.

ally, he was able to extricate the vehicle, but only after his back
wheels had carved out two deep ruts.

One day, the brothers decided to inspect the lake bed opposite
Migdal, the ancient home of Mary Magdalene, located several
kilometers to the south of Ginosar. On that day, Moshele walked to
Migdal along the beach while Yuvi rode his bicycle on the highway. When they met, it was obvious that Moshele was excited. He
showed Yuvi a handful of green corroded bronze coins.

"I've found a place," Moshele began, "where ancient coins are scattered on the surface! The place is 'dead.' It's in the middle of nowhere, with no land site and no harbor near it."

Yuvi followed Moshele back to the site. They saw the deep tracks that the trapped vehicle had left in the mud. In attempting to escape, the vehicle's spinning wheels had tossed out coins, which until now had been safely buried just under the surface of the mud.

The coins drew the brothers to the spot. They began to narrow their hunt to the immediate area, each day searching slightly to one side or the other of the location where they had found the coins. Each day they would come back with some piece or other of metal bric-a-brac.

This search continued for about two weeks. Then, one day they found a large iron nail. Next to it lay a second nail . . . and a third . . .

"That's when we noticed a faint 'line' of wood in the mud," Yuvi explained later. "It was little more than a curving arc of wood, flush with the surface of the ground, but we immediately realized that this was the uppermost plank of a boat that was entirely buried by the mud."

The brothers had in actuality discovered the boat of their dreams. They were ecstatic. On the way home they agreed, for the time being, to keep their discovery a secret.

It was a Wednesday, and Yuvi, as he does on every Wednesday, went folk dancing in the kibbutz dining room. He wore his most festive clothes. When friends asked why he was so dressed up, he only smiled. But silently, he thought to himself, "You have no idea how wonderful I feel."

In the days that followed, the brothers ruminated on their boat. The first question that had to be resolved was this: How old was it?

This question they put to their father, Yantshe Lufan, who had spent much of his life fishing in the Sea of Galilee and had dragged nets over just about every nook and cranny in the lake. He had even sunk some boats himself in the local disputes that had erupted between the fishermen at times over fishing grounds. (Fishing is still an important source of income for Ginosar.) If the boat were modern, his sons decided, surely Yantshe's nets would have caught on it. Moshele and Yuvi swore Yantshe to secrecy and took him to see their discovery.

Yantshe studied the imprint of the boat. He had never been as fascinated with the past as his sons. Still, it was obvious to him that this was a very old boat. His nets had never been caught here, and furthermore, how could the depth to which it was buried in the mud be explained if it were not ancient?

The father's pronouncement elated his sons. After much soul searching, and not without some difficulty, Yuvi and Moshele

Yuvi, Yantshe, and Moshele.

came to the recognition that, no matter what, it was their duty to turn the find over to the authorities. They realized that they simply could not keep it for themselves. First and foremost the boat belonged to Israel.

But whom to call? This was not exactly like finding a wallet on the sidewalk. They couldn't just report it to the police.

Kibbutz Ginosar had recently donated some of its waterfront land, directly south and adjacent to the kibbutz, for the establishment of a museum in honor of an Israeli statesman and soldier, the late Yigal Allon, who had been a member of Ginosar. In the spirit of its namesake, the museum was to be a living tribute to the possibilities of peace between Jews and Arabs, and to the panoply of cultures that had coexisted in the Galilee.

When the brothers found the boat, the Allon Centre was nearing completion. The person in charge of the museum was another member of Kibbutz Ginosar, Nitsa Kaplan. Nitsa is a human dynamo, full of energy, and, the brothers knew, very knowledgeable as to outside authorities. Surely, Nitsa would know whom to contact.

Previously, when construction of the center had just begun, Yuvi and Moshele had tried to convince Nitsa that it should contain some antiquities. Nitsa would have none of it, adamantly insisting that it was to be an educational center dedicated to the present and future, not the past. Certainly it was not a proper place to exhibit ancient artifacts.

Friday, January 24, 1986, is the first definitive date that can be fixed in connection with the discovery of the boat. It was on that evening, just before the festive Sabbath eve meal in the kibbutz dining room, that the brothers approached Nitsa.

Taking her aside, they excitedly told her about their discovery. Nitsa didn't have to think twice. She immediately called Mendel Nun.

Mendel Nun is a member of Kibbutz Ein Gev, on the east side of the Sea of Galilee. He began his lifelong love affair with the lake during the many years that he plied its waters as a kibbutz fisherman. During that time he collected information on the many facets of the lake—from archaeology to zoology—becoming in the process Israel's foremost expert on the lake and its history. Surely, if anyone could say anything about the boat, it was Mendel.

On Saturday, Mendel showed up with an archaeologist who was accompanying him on a tour of the ancient harbor facilities of the Sea of Galilee. The latter was pessimistic about the boat's antiquity. After a cursory inspection, he pronounced the vessel to be modern, or at least very nearly so. It certainly couldn't be more than two—at most four—hundred years old. In Israel, with its rich memory of history and culture, this was tantamount to saying that the boat was as recent as an old Coca-Cola bottle.

Yuvi kept pressing Mendel to say something about the boat, but Mendel repeatedly maintained that he had no expertise in ancient ship construction and simply could not answer their questions.

Moshele and Yuvi were crestfallen. Their great discovery had turned to ashes. The brothers passed the next few days in a deep depression.

Before Mendel left, however, he offered to put the brothers in contact with the Department of Antiquities. Soon thereafter Mendel notified Yossi Stepanski, the Department's regional inspector. The next day Yossi visited the coast with the late Dr. Zvi Ilan, an archaeological reporter for the Israel Hebrew-language daily newspaper *Davar*. They were unable to find the boat, however. That day, Yossi sent a message to notify me nonetheless about the discovery, which led to the note on my desk.

ℓℓℓ

The following day was Wednesday, February 5. The weather had turned cold and ugly. As I assumed that the boat had been found underwater, my assistant, Kurt Raveh, and I hoisted two scuba tanks and our dive gear into the back of my jeep and headed out to the Sea of Galilee.

On receiving the message, I had been surprised that anyone had been able to find anything in the Sea of Galilee. In my experience, diving in the lake is anything but enjoyable; her waters are about as clear as pea soup. In fact, visibility is often so poor that my outstretched arm would disappear at the elbow into the murk. More often than not during a dive, I had to "walk" around on the seabed, blindly feeling my way with my hands. And then there was the time that my movements had raised a dark curtain of fine silt that so clouded the water that I could barely see my watch in front of my mask's faceplate. Losing all sense of direction, I had been able to determine which direction was up only by following the bubbles from my air exhaust.

No, I was definitely not looking forward to diving in the Sea of Galilee.

Near the city of Tiberias we descended into the Jordan Valley. Kurt pointed to a sign next to the road that indicated that we were now descending below sea level.

"If we excavate this boat," he mused, "it will be the deepest shipwreck ever excavated."

I laughed at this thought, although I had to admit that he was right. The normal water level of the Sea of Galilee is over 200 meters (656 feet) below sea level.

We drove to the east side of the lake to pick up Mendel at Ein Gev and then headed back to Ginosar for the Lufan brothers. Mendel had arranged that they meet us at Nof Ginosar, the guest house owned and run by Kibbutz Ginosar.

After Mendel made the introductions, Yuvi came straight to the point. "How can you tell if the boat is ancient?" he asked.

"Oh, that's easy," I said.

I explained that, while we knew nothing about how watercraft had been built on the Sea of Galilee in antiquity, a great deal of research had been done on shipwrecks in the Mediterranean Sea. From their excavation and study, we knew that in antiquity ships were constructed in a method quite different from that in use today.

In modern times, when a wooden ship is built, the shipwright will first lay the keel and then attach the stem and sternpost to it. Following this, the shipwright attaches the frames (ribs) to the keel, forming a "skeleton" framework to which the hull planking is then nailed. This form of construction—not surprisingly—is known as *skeleton-first technique*.

However, a shipwright building a ship in antiquity would have gone about his task quite differently. After laying the vessel's keel and posts, rather than attaching the frames, he would have added the hull's planking directly to the keel and built up the "shell" or the ship's hull. Only after much of the hull was already in place would he insert the frames into the ship's hull. Normally, he would not even connect the frames to the keel. This is termed *shell-first construction*.

But undoubtedly the most unusual part of this construction technique was that the hull's strakes (planks) were joined to each other not by metal fasteners, but by wood carpentry. The planks were edge-joined by means of pegged mortise-and-tenon joints. The mortises—narrow rectangular cavities—were cut into the narrow top edge of the strake. Then a flat, tight-fitting hardwood tenon (dowel) was driven up to half of its height into each of the mortises. Opposing mortises were cut into the bottom edge of the next strake, and the two planks were joined, somewhat like an extension leaf inserted into a dining-room table. Following this, holes were drilled into the tenon on either side of the seam, and wooden pegs were hammered in, locking the tenon—and the planks—in place.

I pulled out a napkin and drew a diagram of a mortise-and-tenon joint. "All we have to do is to scrape away some of the mud from the uppermost strake. If we assume that the shipbuilding traditions on the Sea of Galilee followed those of the nearby Mediterranean coast and we find evidence of pegged mortise-and-tenon joints on your boat, the vessel can't be less than 1,400 years old," I assured him.

We finished our coffee and headed out to the jeep. Only when Yuvi saw the diving equipment in the back of the jeep and asked why we had brought it did we find out that the boat had been found on land. I must confess that the idea had never occurred to me.

The four of us piled into the jeep and bounced south down that flat, featureless lake bed until, about a mile north of Migdal,

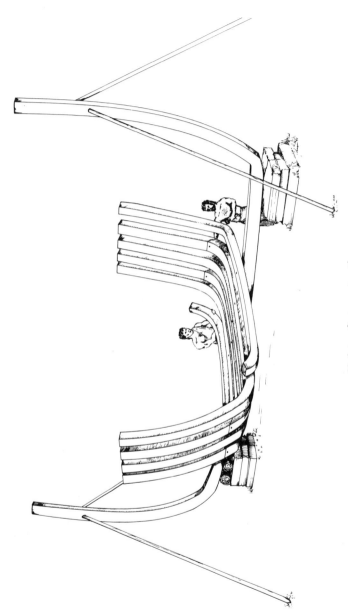

Skeleton-first construction.

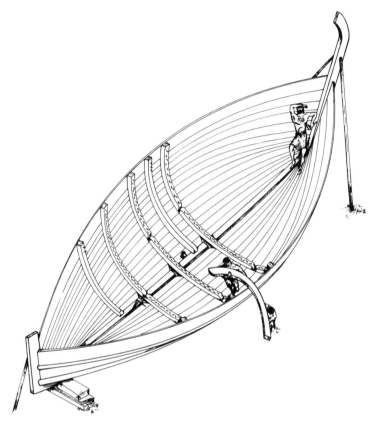

Shell-first construction.

Yuvi told me to stop. Threatening clouds covered the sky; the heavens were a dull, dark gray. Getting out, I searched for signs of a wreck. Shipwrecks that I had surveyed in the Mediterranean had normally had some distinguishing characteristic—a pile of ballast stones, a load of amphoras (pottery jars), frames sticking up with comblike fingers—that called attention to themselves. Here there was nothing but a long stretch of muddy land.

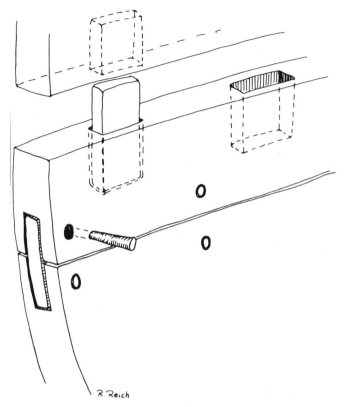

R. Reich

Pegged mortise-and-tenon joints.

"Where is the boat?" I asked.

Yuvi smiled and pointed to the ground. "You're standing on it," he said.

I slowly looked down, all the time wondering if Yuvi was pulling my leg. There at my feet arced the dark red edge of a boat's strake, no higher than the mud around it. I had never considered the possibility of an ancient Sea of Galilee vessel being preserved by the lake sediment's burying and protecting it. With growing

Where is the boat? Yuvi stands on it.

anticipation I cautiously scraped away the mud from a foot-long length of the outer side of a timber. To me this procedure seemed to take an eternity to accomplish; it probably took all of two minutes. I carefully washed away the mud clinging to the soft, spongy wood with some of the groundwater that had filled the shallow cavity. The narrow rectangular shapes of mortise scars came into view, and beneath each of the evenly spaced scars was the dark, round head of a locking peg.

"Here are the mortise-and-tenon scars and the round heads of the locking pegs," I said matter-of-factly, pointing them out to the others. "This boat is definitely very, very old."

And then, slowly, what I had said sank in. I was staring at the first ancient boat ever to have been discovered in *the Sea of Galilee*.

Ohmygod.

As Mendel was aptly to describe it, "It was only then that we came to the realization that we were discovering history and, at the same time, making it."

How did we feel? I cannot speak for the others, for I find it difficult to describe how I felt at that moment. I guess it was an even mixture of awe, joy, and intense excitement. I felt as if the air had been knocked out of my lungs, like the feeling you have standing on a very high and steep snow-swept mountain, with bright sunlight reflecting in your eyes and cold, dry air burning your lungs.

I was awakened from my state of awe when a heavy raindrop splashed on my nose. Moments later, all four of us were dashing for the jeep as sheets of rain came pouring down. It was as if the heavens had opened up.

Minutes later, the cloudburst ended as abruptly as it had begun. The scent of ozone filled the air. In the sky, as if a movie director had ordered it, a brilliant double rainbow shimmered as it cascaded into the lake. Spielberg himself could not have done it better. We stood there staring at it in disbelief.

"Well, now we know who the boat belonged to," someone said.

"Who's that?" I asked.

"She's obviously the longboat from Noah's Ark."

We all laughed. But nervously.

There was something remarkable about the whole experience. We felt both elated and humbled at the same time. Years later, Yuvi told me, "I took the rainbows to mean that we had been 'given permission' to excavate the boat."

I remember standing there with my mouth open. Had this been a movie script, I would have thought the whole scene was much too farfetched. "This is not really happening," one part of me kept repeating. But the other part of me, the one that knew better, just said, "Why not?"

As the colors began to fade, I rushed to the jeep for my camera, and we took turns posing with the rainbows in the background. I felt that it was important to record them. I wondered what was the likelihood of a double rainbow's appearing in conjunction with our identification of the boat?

I still wonder.

ℓℓℓ

When confronted with a newly discovered shipwreck in the Mediterranean, our normal procedure was to spend several days examining it. This preliminary investigation was to determine the vessel's approximate age, its state of preservation, and its archaeological significance in order to recommend to the Department of Antiquities what further steps, if any, should be taken.

Thus, the next two days found us carefully digging sections along the visible planking of what now turned out to be the boat's starboard side, at the bow, amidships, and at the stern. At the bow—the side closest to the lake—we discovered that the keel was resting on part of a buried tree trunk. The keel at this extremity terminated in a tenon; the post assembly or "stem," to which it had been attached, was missing. On the first day of the probe, Mendel, who was working in this section, discovered a ceramic cooking pot lying face down in the mud, adjacent to, but outside, the hull.

Amidships (near the center of the hull's outline), we opened a two-foot-long section and were able to determine three different

The cooking pot.

strakes before the groundwater came up to meet us. To accentuate features for photography, we fastened lengths of white electrician's wire to the planking seams, and circles punched from bright red fabric were pinned to the heads of the pegs locking the mortise-and-tenon joints. On the port side, Nitsa, who had joined us, found an oil lamp lying within the outline of the hull, but near the surface of the mud.

At the stern, as at the bow, I was surprised to find that the post was missing. The strakes on both sides of the ship, which should have been nailed to the post, instead simply ended in the mud.

Although we eventually collected a variety of sherds (fragments of pottery), the cooking pot and the oil lamp uncovered on those first two days were the only complete ceramic artifacts that we were to find. Even in the field, it was clear that both of these artifacts dated roughly from the early Roman period, that is, between the late first century BC and the first century AD. The fine tuning of their dates would come only later.

Linking the pottery to the wreck was a problem, however. They were clearly not part of a cargo. Indeed the boat appeared to lack a cargo, and thus the cooking pot and oil lamp theoretically

The oil lamp.

could have been washed in by the sea. The boat had clearly spent many centuries buried in the silt on a shallow shore. In the Mediterranean I had seen numerous cases of artifacts being shifted around by violent storms and vicious currents. One of my favorite photos is of a soft-drink bottle that I found lying inside a sixth- or seventh-century AD Byzantine amphora.

Despite these considerations, the pottery artifacts indicated that human activity had taken place in the immediate vicinity of the boat during the Roman period. This in itself hinted at a similar date for the craft. Additional evidence would be needed to date the boat more accurately.

On the afternoon of Friday, February 7, we concluded the probe examination. We filled the opened sections with mud and reburied the boat, taking care to camouflage it. Because it would be impossible in the coming days to prohibit access to the public beach or to guard the site indefinitely, we were concerned that the boat not be rediscovered by anyone else.

There was also a real danger of vehicles driving over it. Moshele and Yuvi brought a tractor from Ginosar and placed a variety of flotsam and jetsam around the site in a manner that would dissuade any driver. They then drove south several hundred meters and dug two more "decoy excavations."

"These should confuse anyone who might look for the boat," Moshele explained.

Preparing a report for my supervisors in the Department of Antiquities, I recommended that an expedition be mounted and that the boat be excavated—eventually. A great deal of fiscal and organizational preparation is required to conduct an archaeological excavation. Also, it would be wiser to excavate the boat when it was underwater again, allowing us thoroughly to study and record the craft while its waterlogged timbers were protected from the air. I wanted to keep the discovery secret until the rising waters of the lake had safely hidden the find. Only then, when strangers would be unable to locate the boat, would it be possible to announce its discovery and organize a proper excavation.

The following Sunday I was in Jerusalem at the Rockefeller Museum, a venerable showcase of antiquities from biblical times. The Rockefeller also houses the offices of the Department of Antiquities. Orna Hess, the Department's contact with the media, whom I had just alerted to the discovery, came toward me, a newspaper in her hand and a concerned expression on her face.

"You'd better take a look at this," she said.

The boat's discovery had been leaked to the press. Tucked away on page seven of one of the Hebrew daily newspapers was a tiny notice describing the boat and noting that it might date approximately to the time of Jesus's ministry on the Sea of Galilee. I went ballistic. But there was nothing I could do other than hope fervently that no one would pay attention to the article. What actually happened, however, was the far side of a worst-case scenario.

We had invited the Israel Television Authority to film the probe excavation with the understanding that it would not use the footage until the boat had been made public. Once the story was out, we could not prevent the Authority from airing the footage.

The next day, all the local newspapers had front-page stories about the "boat of Jesus." Never mind that there is no mention in the New Testament that Jesus actually owned a boat, that indeed, to the best of our knowledge, there was no such thing as "the boat of Jesus." The media had a field day with it; the hype was overwhelming.

Adding fuel to the fire, the Israeli Ministry of Tourism—facing a lull in tourism due to Gaddafi's most recent terrorist antics—delighted in the possible "Jesus connection," hoping it would draw more pilgrims to Israel. In Tiberias, Ultra-Orthodox Jews, fearful that excavation of the boat would be used as a springboard to promote Christian missionary work in Israel, demonstrated against it. At modern Migdal, the Moshav Migdal council demanded that the boat be placed in their agricultural settlement because it had been found adjacent to their fields. What had started as a remarkable archaeological find began turning into a political and religious free-for-all.

It was truly amazing what intense emotions those few waterlogged planks were able to generate. It was also exceptionally dangerous for the well-being of the boat.

More complications arose when the boat was rumored to be full of gold coins. Every body of water, I am sure, has its myths of a "treasure wreck." In the Sea of Galilee, stories have been making the rounds for years of a Turkish ship sunk by the British during World War I while transporting payment to the Turkish army in Palestine. These rumors now became entwined with the reports on the boat.

I knew that not everyone would be as responsible as Yuvi and Moshele. A Klondike Gold Rush mentality began to develop around the lake. Naive local people, dreaming of treasures of gold, began prospecting the beaches, in search of the "boat of Jesus," which, they were sure, must be full to the caprails with valuable treasure that would make them wealthy beyond their wildest dreams. Otherwise, why would the archaeologists have hidden the hull?

In truth, the boat was a treasure. But that treasure amounted to little more than the old and waterlogged timbers of which it was constructed. A determined farmer, with a shovel-equipped tractor, was all it would have taken at this point utterly to destroy the boat in a matter of minutes.

The history of archaeology is full of horror stories of invaluable and irreplaceable artifacts disappearing or being destroyed by the unenlightened in search of treasure and riches. The archaeologists have arrived too late on the scene, only to find a gaping hole where a valuable artifact had been.

I shivered to think of the possibilities. Perhaps tomorrow's international headlines would read:

JEWS DESTROY "BOAT OF JESUS"
LOOKING FOR GOLD COINS

Fortunately, I consoled myself, we had had the foresight to hide the boat. We hoped that no one would find it, and that the whole ruckus would soon die down by itself.

During the next few days, I was occupied with preparing a report outlining what we had learned about the boat and recommending the steps that should be taken in preparing an excavation of what was already quite clearly an exceptional discovery.

The Lufan brothers kept an eye on the boat. They were careful to avoid visiting the site so as not to attract attention to it; instead, they had been staking out the boat with binoculars from a distance. On Tuesday evening at 10 PM I received a telephone call from Yuvi.

"We saw flashlights in the vicinity of the boat," Yuvi told me. They had also heard voices yelling in the gloom. "Someone is bound to find the boat any time now."

"I'll be right there," I said.

I drove to Ginosar, arriving a little before midnight, and sat with the Lufan brothers and several other members of the kibbutz watching the site through fieldglasses. The whole experience reminded me of scouting prior to an army attack—butterflies in the stomach and all. We dared not even drive out to the boat so as not to attract further attention. The coast was deserted now. Whoever had been there had left—for the time being. At 3 AM we decided to "stand down" for the night.

I stayed at Ginosar for the night—what was left of it. But even as I tossed and turned in bed, one comment Yuvi had made kept coming back to haunt me: "If we don't excavate that boat immediately, there will be no boat to excavate."

I decided intuitively that everything possible must be done to push for an immediate rescue excavation of the boat. I say "intuitively" because "logically" the archaeological, organizational, and logistical problems involved in carrying out such an excavation were truly mind-boggling. A proper shipwreck excavation normally takes months to prepare. There are funds to raise, staff members to bring on board, and a myriad of other details that require attention. Dawn was breaking before I finally drifted off to sleep.

Early that morning, I phoned Avraham "Avi" Eitan, the director of the Israel Department of Antiquities and Museums, and explained the situation to him. We agreed that the next day Avi would come to Ginosar with other Department officials for a meeting to discuss our options. The rest of the day I spent preparing a detailed excavation proposal for Avi. I also called on someone who was to play a key role in the boat's well-being in the days, as well as the years, to come.

Normally, at the culmination of a land excavation, the archaeologist will have a few artifacts—usually made of metal—in need of conservation treatment. If the excavation has taken place at a location that is particularly dry year-round, as in Egypt or in Israel's Judean desert, the ground may also surrender objects made of organic materials: papyrus documents, parchment scrolls, wooden coffins, and the like. These artifacts must be stabilized, restored, and repaired soon after their removal from the ground. Otherwise, the loss of the particular equilibrium that had allowed them to survive through the ages will result in their "aging" rapidly through processes that ultimately will at least distort and may possibly destroy them.

This is where the conservator comes in. A land excavation, even one covering an extensive area, ordinarily results in a limited number of artifacts that require special attention. If we were to excavate a boat, which was built entirely of timber, however, the whole project would become one enormous conservation problem.

Orna Cohen had studied at the Hebrew University's Institute of Archaeology in Jerusalem. During that time she had become fascinated by problems relating to the conservation of antiquities. Orna had also been in the navy during her army service and was a qualified diver. It was therefore only natural that she join Kurt and me on our dives in the Mediterranean. We soon became very good friends.

Fortunately, only a few months prior to the boat's discovery, Orna had returned from an intensive course in archaeological conservation at the Institute of Archaeology at London University. Upon her return to Israel she had been put in charge of the Conservation Laboratory of the Hebrew University's Institute of Archaeology.

I phoned Orna, invited her to the meeting, and requested that she prepare a presentation on the problems that we might expect to encounter during the excavation, as well as a financial estimate of conservation costs for the excavation and ultimate preservation of the boat. Orna agreed to my request. That short telephone conversation was to have an enormous impact on her life.

The next day, under deceptively beautiful indigo-blue winter skies, the group gathered at the conference room at Nof Ginosar. I remember that day well. The atmosphere was tense, yet extremely focused.

Using slides that we had taken during the probe excavation, I explained the history of the boat's discovery and how we had been able to date it, at least approximately. I summarized the results of our probe excavation and illustrated the cooking pot and oil lamp that we had uncovered. I then pointed out the possible historical and archaeological significance of an ancient boat found in the Sea of Galilee. I emphasized the dangers inherent in ignoring the threat to the vessel by treasure hunters and ended with a recommendation that we begin a rescue excavation of the craft immediately.

Next, Orna talked about the conservation problems in excavating a 27-foot-long boat made of waterlogged wood. She proposed a budget of about $300,000 for the vessel's complete conservation.

After a lengthy discussion, during which the pros and cons of excavating the boat were discussed, Avi gave the excavation a green light, conditional on receiving the final approval of the Minister of Education, Yitzchak Navon.

The excavation was scheduled to begin in three days, on Sunday, February 16. I desperately wanted to excavate that boat. And yet, I had informed Avi of one precondition at the meeting that had to be met before we could begin an excavation. To have done otherwise would have been irresponsible on my part.

A competent staff for the excavation that I had proposed could be found in Israel. But one key staff member for a shipwreck excavation would be missing. There was no one in Israel who could make sense of the hull that we would be revealing. We desperately needed an expert ship reconstructor to study and record the boat's timbers in situ. Such a staff member was particularly vital as the likelihood of our safely extracting the boat intact seemed remote.

I strongly recommended that the Department contact Professor J. Richard "Dick" Steffy of the Institute of Nautical Archaeology, located at Texas A&M University. Dick is an internationally known scholar whose knowledge of ship construction is second to none. I had met Dick in the early 1980s when he had come to study another important nautical discovery, one found off Israel's Mediterranean coast: the Athlit Ram, the only known ancient warship's waterline ram (a device at the prow for piercing enemy hulls) ever to have been found.

For such an important hull as this we needed Dick or, at the very least, one of his students. This immediately posed two new problems: Could Dick take time away from his other responsibilities? And, if so, where would we find the funding for his flight on such short notice?

After the meeting, Avi and I crammed into a public telephone booth and called Dick. Dick had already read about the boat in the local Texas papers. Although he was in the midst of a heavy teaching schedule and his son David was getting married at the end of the month, Dick promised to see if he could get away for a short time to visit the excavation.

On the telephone I emphasized to Dick that we would need some time to excavate the boat so that when he arrived the interior of the hull would be cleared of mud and he could begin immediately to record the ship's timbers. I also wanted his advice on how to reference-number the hull's timbers prior to his arrival.

"Do you want us to number the frames with a different numbering system than the planking?"

"No, that won't be necessary," Dick explained. "Tag each timber with a number, and I'll take it from there."

We ended the conversation with the understanding that Dick would call back to let me know if he could come.

When I returned home several hours later, the phone was ringing as I walked in the door. It was Dick. Yes, he could come the next week, arriving at Ginosar on the evening of Wednesday, February 19. He could stay for only five days, however, and would have to leave on Tuesday, February 25. I thanked Dick, asked him to order a plane ticket, and requested that he not pay for it until I could make suitable arrangements for reimbursing him.

Calling Avi, I confirmed that Dick could come. He was kindly donating his time and expertise but we would somehow have to pay for his airfare. Avi was pessimistic that the Ministry of Education could process the request in the time allotted. I understood where he was coming from.

🌊🌊🌊

Let me explain the problem that we were facing. Today, the Israel Antiquities Authority, which is the governmental body responsible for archaeology in Israel, is a dynamic and independent force, well in control of its own budget. I have no doubt that, were the same problem to arise today, it would be solved in the blink of an eye. The creation of the Israel Antiquities Authority as an autonomous body, largely due to the foresight of the present director, Amir Drori, is a significant contribution to the archaeology of Israel.[2]

Such was not the case in 1986. Since the establishment of the State of Israel in 1948, the Israel Department of Antiquities and Museums, from which the Authority was later to develop, was a governmental organization, locked into a straitjacket of Israeli bureaucratic government restrictions. The organization had a long history, having evolved from the British Mandatory Department of Antiquities of Palestine.

As with any bureaucracy, the rules and regulations for our Department were both myriad and stifling. Furthermore, the budget was ridiculously low. Attempting to obtain anything that had not been budgeted for a year in advance was, to put it mildly, an administrative nightmare. Avi even had to secure permission from the main office to make the international telephone call to Dick.

One example from my own experience will suffice. Soon after I had been appointed Inspector of Underwater Antiquities in 1976, I was allotted a significant amount of money to purchase basic diving equipment: tanks, regulators, buoyancy compensators, and the like, as well as an inflatable dive boat. By 1985, much of the dive equipment, having been used intensively for nearly a decade, was beginning to wear out. While it was possible to replace less expensive items—a mask here, a pair of fins there—it was extremely difficult to locate funds to replace more expensive items as the needs arose.

Whenever we dived, Kurt and I would leave trails of tiny bubbles behind us; our buoyancy compensators leaked like sieves. For me the problem came to a head when, during a dive at Caesarea, I looked at my air pressure gauge, which tells the diver how much air is left in the tank, and found the gauge's indicator needle lying at the bottom of the dial.

Realizing that our equipment was fast becoming a diving accident in the making, I notified Avi that we would not dive until the worn equipment had been replaced. Still, we had to wait months to get an allocation for new equipment.

&&&

And now we needed a transatlantic airplane ticket at a moment's notice.

"It is a shame," Avi mused, "that we don't know someone in the United States Embassy. The new American ambassador, Thomas Pickering, is a great lover of archaeology. Perhaps the embassy has funds for cultural exchanges that could be used for Dick's ticket."

Avi's comments lit a 100-watt light bulb over my head. Several American Embassy family members had worked as volunteers with us at a land excavation at Caesarea. They put me in contact with Howard Lane, the officer in charge of the United States Information Service at the embassy. Howard was also skeptical that anything could be done on such short notice but promised to look into the matter and let us know the next day.

Friday, February 14, was a "bite-your-nails-to-the-knuckles" day for me. I came to work yet found myself incapable of doing anything constructive. The minutes became hours as I kept turning over the two possible scenarios. Everything now hinged on whether we could fund Dick's trip. Finally, frustrated and unable to concentrate, I went down to the beach for a walk.

It was one of those icy-cold *sharkia* days. This *sharkia* was a particularly pushy one. It grasped my parka like a sail and shoved me forcefully down the beach. But to which of the two probable futures, I wondered and worried, was it propelling me?

Coming back to the glass factory at 2 PM, I sloughed off the parka, sat down at my desk, took a deep breath, and put in a call to the embassy. It was then that I found out that, after Howard had discussed the matter with Ambassador Pickering, the ticket had been approved. Only fourteen hours had passed since Howard had first received our plea for assistance. To this day I still consider Dick's ticket a bureaucratic miracle.

The day before the excavation was to begin I traveled to Ginosar to make preparations. In the evening Moshele and I walked out to the site to discuss logistics. What we found instead was another, fast-approaching problem.

When we had first visited the site, the water had been some thirty yards to the east of the boat. Now the lake had advanced to within ten yards of the vessel—and the weather forecast was for more rain. We could excavate the boat in a "land dig" or in an underwater "dive." But should the site become inundated with a mere few feet of water, we could do neither. The rising waters for which we had once prayed now threatened the entire expedition. On our way back to the kibbutz, Moshele tried to cheer me up. "Maybe they'll pump enough water out of the lake for the level to go down again," he said. He told me how each summer he would watch as the lake's water level diminished because the huge pumps were lifting the water into the National Water Carrier. This carrier would then transport the water to the rest of the country in arteries of concrete. That gave me an idea.

Avi was going to meet with Minister of Education Navon the next morning to update him on developments with the boat. Upon returning to Ginosar, I called Avi and told him about the rising waters.

"There may be a solution though," I said. "This is going to sound bizarre, but please hear me out."

In order to prevent the lake's waters from inundating the boat until we could complete the excavation, I requested that he pass on a plea to Mr. Navon to contact the Minister of Agriculture, who had ministerial responsibility for the lake, to have water pumped out of the Sea of Galilee into subsidiary reservoirs.

Avi listened and, after a lengthy silence, finally answered, "OK, I'll try."

Keeping the Sea of Galilee at its proper level is a national passion in Israel. Asking to lower its level is tantamount, in the Israeli psyche, to declaring open season on bald eagles in the United States. I doubt that any director of any governmental department in Israel had ever received such a strange request.

Sunday morning—the day the excavation was to begin—brought a new and potentially disastrous problem in its wake: local interest in the boat as a lucrative tourist attraction. A rivalry had existed for years between Moshav Migdal (an agricultural cooperative settlement with individual ownership) and the more prosperous Kibbutz Ginosar (a cooperative settlement with community ownership). Some members of Moshav Migdal decided that the boat was "political gold."

That morning, while I was examining the boat, a group of moshavniks from Migdal approached. The discussion began pleasantly enough. They asked me about the boat, and I related to them what we knew about it. I explained that the boat, like any antiquity found in Israel, was the property of the State of Israel, that this venerable artifact had great historical significance for both Christians and Jews, that the boat was particularly fragile, in a delicate condition, and that all our attention must be concentrated on saving it. I spoke in terms of Zionism and national interest. As I spoke, it was clear my words were having an effect.

Unfortunately, it was not the one I had intended.

The moshavniks smiled. I had dispelled any doubts they might have had, they told me, as to whether they should demand that the boat be exhibited at Migdal. They told me that, should the Department of Antiquities attempt to excavate the boat without first signing an agreement that it would be exhibited at Migdal, they would make sure that the boat would not reach a safe haven. They would rather see the boat destroyed than let it slip out of their grasp.

I could have kicked myself for my naïveté. With a fragile boat to excavate, we could not chance having this potential danger hanging over us. Once the boat had been uncovered, it would take no more than someone walking over it to destroy its ancient timbers.

From Jerusalem, Avi instructed me not to begin the excavation before this matter had been resolved. Time slowed to a crawl as Avi tried unsuccessfully to contact Migdal. Now, with everything in readiness and packed on wagons, people idled around.

In the early afternoon a nursery teacher from Ginosar came back with her kindergarten class from a stroll along the beach and casually asked me, "Who is the man with a loaded Uzi and a walkie-talkie guarding the boat?"

Snatching a pair of binoculars, I scanned the site. She was right. Here we were, ready to begin a critical excavation, with the real possibility of violence clouding the entire project.

The police were called in by Eliezer Janet, head of security at Kibbutz Ginosar. When they arrived, I drove out with them to the site. The two policemen came from Migdal as, of course, did the man with the Uzi. The conversation between the Migdalites went something like this:

"*Chaver!* (Friend!) What in [expletive deleted] are you doing with a loaded Uzi in the middle of Israel? You know that's against the law!"

"I was told to guard the site and report back to Migdal if the archaeologists began to dig."

"Take the [another expletive deleted] magazine out of the Uzi and get into the jeep."

We all drove to Migdal and went to the main office, where others were gathered. The mood was hostile. To this day, I remain convinced that the group believed they needed only to haul the boat out of the mud, plunk it on a platform, and open a falafel stand next to it to cater to the millions of tourists that were sure to come. They had no concept of the precarious condition of the artifact nor the arduous salvage work yet to come.

I asked them to call Avi and talk to him. They refused. I then asked, in that case, if I might use the telephone to report in. They pushed the telephone toward me.

I dialed Avi's number, and when he picked up the phone, I told him, "I'm at Migdal, and there is someone here who wants to talk to you." And then I shoved the receiver into the hand of one of the men. He had no choice but to talk to Avi.

I don't know exactly what Avi said, but from the worried look on this man's face, it seemed clear that Avi was not speaking of high ideals. The man's face went in short order from a grin to a grimace. Every so often he would nod his head sadly.

Finally, he put down the phone and told me with a sigh, "You can excavate."

"You won't make problems for me during the excavation?"

"No."

The excavation was on.

Chapter 2

A Sea of Legends

The celebrated Sea of Galilee is not so large a sea as Lake Tahoe by a good deal—it is just about two-thirds as large. And when we come to speak of beauty, this sea is no more to be compared to Tahoe than a meridian of longitude is to a rainbow.

From *The Innocents Abroad*
MARK TWAIN[1]

As famous lakes go, the Sea of Galilee is relatively small. It is only 21 kilometers—13 miles—at its longest, from north to south, and 12 kilometers—7.5 miles—at its widest.

Many millennia ago, a large body of water, which geologists call the Lisan Lake, covered the entire Jordan Valley. After it receded, the Jordan River system evolved, in which the Sea of Galilee formed the central component, between the Hula Swamp to its north and the Dead Sea to its south.

In modern Hebrew, the lake is called by its ancient name, *Kinneret*, or *Yam Kinneret* (the Sea of Kinneret), keeping alive a tradition that goes back in time at least to the Late Bronze Age and possibly much earlier. Some say that the name *Kinneret* comes from the Hebrew word for a stringed instrument or lyre (*kinor*), for the shape of Kinneret when seen from above is somewhat similar to that of the musical instrument. Another tradition derives the name from the *kinnara*, a sweet and edible fruit produced by the Christ thorn tree (*Ziziphus spina-christi*), which grows in the vicinity. As I was to learn one day, Mendel does not accept either of these interpretations.

He had kindly agreed to take a group of friends on a tour around the lake. One day in spring 1987, we were standing on the low summit of Tel Kinnarot, which is situated on a hilltop at the northwest shore of the Sea of Galilee. It was about a year after the boat had been discovered. The cool afternoon Mediterranean Sea breeze, blowing in from the west, flowed gently over us.

"Throughout recorded history," Mendel said, "the lake was known by the name of the most significant city of the time along her shores. And since the lake saw a number of cities rise and fall, she received different names. The earliest name came from the site on which we are standing, Kinnarot, which flourished during the Early Bronze Age [roughly four to five thousand years ago] and then again during the Late Bronze and Iron Ages [the sixteenth to eighth centuries BC]."

When Kinnarot fell, apparently to the invading Assyrian king Tiglath Pileser III in 732 BC, another lakeside city, named *Ginosar*, rose to prominence. This city bore the same name as the rich region in which it was located: *Biqat Ginosar*, the Valley of Ginosar.

Located at the northwest quarter of the lake, Biqat Ginosar stretches from the ancient site of Migdal, which lies at the foot of Mount Arbel in the south, to Kinnarot in the north. It is in this valley that Kibbutz Ginosar, the home of Yuvi and Moshele, is located, and on this shore their boat had slept her long sleep.

In antiquity Biqat Ginosar was noted for its fertility. Josephus, the first-century AD Jewish historian who knew the valley well, wrote this about it:[2]

> Thanks to the rich soil, there is not a plant that does not flourish there, and the cultivators in fact grow every species; the air is so temperate that it suits the most diverse varieties. The walnut tree, which is the most winter-loving, grows luxuriantly beside the palm tree, which thrives on heat, and side by side with the fig and olive, which require a milder air. One might deem it nature's crowning ambition to force together in a single spot, the most discordant species, and that, by a healthy rivalry, each of the seasons, as it were, wishes to claim the region for her own.

"In the Gospels the lake is sometimes referred to as the *Sea of Gennesaret* after the ancient city of Ginosar or the Valley of Ginosar," Mendel continued, "but it is also called the *Sea of Galilee* after the geographical region of Galilee, in which it is located."

"If the Kinneret is a freshwater inland lake, then why is it called the *Sea of Galilee?*" someone asked.

"In Biblical and Talmudic sources the lake is termed *yam*, Hebrew for 'sea'," Mendel said. "Our ancestors used the same term to describe large and small bodies of water. That's why it is translated 'sea' in European languages."

Mendel pointed to the modern city of Tiberias, visible in the distance to our south, beyond Mount Arbel. "Tiberias was founded in the year AD 20 by Herod Antipas in honor of the Roman emperor Tiberias. It was the largest city ever built on the lake and is the only ancient one that is still in existence, despite the ups and downs of history. That is why the lake has also been called the *Sea of Tiberias*."

Below us lay the lake, lightly sprinkled with fishing boats and tourist ships, which in the distance appeared minute. The view from Tel Kinnarot was magnificent. The Kinneret was alive with activity, while all around her one could see evidence of intensive agriculture. "How different it must have looked not so long ago," I thought to myself.

e e e

Europe's interest in the Holy Land waned following the eviction of the Crusaders. The land reverted to near wilderness after centuries of exploitation, excessive taxation, and neglect had taken their toll.

Only in the nineteenth century, imbued with a new spirit of exploration, did numerous Westerners begin the arduous task of reclaiming the past. These were hardy explorers who were determined to seek out what they had read about in their history books and studied in the Scriptures.

Of these intrepid trailblazers, few were more determined, or more original in their methods, than John MacGregor, who traveled the largely unknown waterways of the Middle East in a custom-built kayak, which he named the *Rob Roy* after an eighteenth-century Scottish Robin-Hood–like hero. The vessel was "built of oak below and covered with cedar" to MacGregor's exacting standards. Shallow of draft and highly maneuverable—the kayak was 14 feet long, 26 inches in breadth, and only a foot in depth (4.27 × 0.66 × 0.3 meters)—the *Rob Roy* allowed MacGregor to explore all but the most overgrown of waterways.

MacGregor praised the beauty and dexterity of the vessel, describing her in loving terms. For him, that boat was very much alive, having a spirit, a character, and a personality of its own:[3]

. . . Are we quite sure that there is no feeling in the "heart of oak," no sentiment under bent birch ribs; that a canoe, in fact, has no character? Let the landsman say so, yet will not I. Like others of her sex, she has her fickle tempers. One day pleasant, and the next out of humour; led like a lamb through this rapid, but cross and pouting under sail on that rough lake. And, like her sex, she may be resisted, coerced, nay, convinced, but in the end, she will always somehow have her own way.

MacGregor began his trip to the Holy Land with the *Rob Roy* in late October 1868 by sailing down the Suez Canal while it was still under construction. From there he went on to explore the Nile Delta. Everywhere his eye caught the beauty of nature, the impression of a sunset.

MacGregor was already middle-aged when he carried out his Middle Eastern trip in the *Rob Roy*. He believed that this was the ideal time of life for a person to travel, for he believed that at that age one is more open to new experiences and more able to appreciate them.

At Ismalia in Egypt, MacGregor rendezvoused with Michael Hany, who was to serve as his dragoman, a combination guide, translator, organizer, butler, and friend. Hany proved invaluable to MacGregor, who repeatedly commended the devotion of his stalwart companion.

Upon his return home MacGregor described his adventures in his book *The Rob Roy on the Jordan, Nile, Red Sea & Gennesareth, & c.* The book saw eight editions and made its author famous in his day. From Port Said, MacGregor sailed to Beirut and from there visited Lebanon and Syria, arriving in the Jordan Valley in January 1869. He was particularly keen to locate the sources of the Jordan River before it entered the Sea of Galilee, a task for which the *Rob Roy* was ideally suited.

The Jordan derives from the joining of three smaller tributaries: the Banias, the Dan, and the Hatzbani rivers. Having become one, the stream, at least until modern times, would wind its way first through the Hula Swamp—the ancient Lake Semachonitis—before entering the Kinneret.

MacGregor explores the mouth of the Jordan.

Following the establishment of the State of Israel in 1948, however, a vast land reclamation project of *yibush ha-bitzot* ("draining the swamps") turned most of this malarial swamp into cultivable land. Now only a small nature reserve preserves a portion of the original wetlands which MacGregor explored.

Undoubtedly, MacGregor's most memorable, as well as most perilous, adventure took place while he was exploring the northern regions of the Hula Swamp. MacGregor entered the Hula Swamp, which was inhabited by Bedouin, who, as MacGregor put it, "had but a poor certificate of character from the tales of travellers."[4] Fully aware of this danger, he sent Hany to make camp at the southwest edge of the swamp while he himself, determined to explore the river's course, paddled into the heart of the swamp.

The serpentine meanderings of the river as it entered the swamp forced MacGregor to "waltz" the *Rob Roy* through them, at times sailing forward, and at others backward. While MacGregor concentrated on his intricate navigation, one of the swamp's inhabitants spotted him. In moments, the banks of the river were covered with hostile screaming natives.

The fast-flowing current sped the *Rob Roy* and her captain out of harm's way. Farther on, however, some other locals spotted the strange-looking intruder in his narrow craft, and the pursuit began in earnest. Several of the rabble removed their scant dress and, jumping into the water, began to swim with swift strokes after the *Rob Roy*. Half swimming and half running over the bends in the river, his pursuers caught up with MacGregor. Turning a sharp bend only to find his path blocked by a row of Bedouin standing across the riverway, MacGregor writes:[5]

> In such times 'tis best to wait for events and not to make them. All were silent and stopped as I quietly floated near one of the swimmers, then suddenly splashed him in the face with my paddle, and instantly escaped through the interval with a few vigorous strokes.

It was to no avail. The Bedouin captured the *Rob Roy*. MacGregor, still sitting in the vessel, found himself lifted out of the

Captured.

water by a dozen of the locals and carried in procession to their village. Only thanks to his icy nerves and Hany's stalwart assistance—and, of course, baksheesh (bribe)—was MacGregor able to extricate himself from this predicament.

For those who wished to see the Holy Land during the nineteenth century in a somewhat more civilized manner, tourism was booming. In June 1867 the good ship *Quaker City* sailed from New York on a pleasure-cruise–pilgrimage to Europe, the Holy Land, and Egypt. On her decks stood a young American writer of humor best known by his pen name, Mark Twain.

MacGregor, still in the *Rob Roy*, is transported to the Bedouin encampment.

During that trip, Twain sent back reports to newspapers in San Francisco and New York and later used these letters-to-the-folks-back-home as the basis for a book entitled *The Innocents Abroad*. Twain's description of the Holy Land, written over 120 years ago, makes fascinating reading not only for his sharp wit, but also for the picture he painted of the land and its inhabitants. When the *Quaker City* anchored in Beirut, the pilgrims split into two groups. Twain opted for the "long trip," which wound its way from Beirut to Baalbec, Damascus, the Sea of Galilee, the Dead Sea, and Jerusalem, finally rendezvousing with the ship in Jaffa. The company set out on horseback. A Jew named Abraham served as the group's dragoman.

From the trip's beginning, Twain had not taken kindly to the American Christian pilgrims with whom he shared the voyage. In Twain's eyes they were overreligious and underconsiderate, either gushing emotionally or lacking in feeling. To him they were the New Philistines, clambering to break off pieces of stone souvenirs from every ancient site that they visited.

As they approached the Sea of Galilee, Twain's pilgrim companions talked excitedly about "taking ship" and sailing on the very waters that had once carried the boats of the Apostles. Sighting a boat—one of only two that they saw on the lake—the pilgrims hailed it. Upon the vessel's approach they ordered Abraham to negotiate a fare.

The Kinneret boatmen demanded two napoleons, the equivalent in value of eight of their American dollars. The pilgrims tried to haggle the price down. Without a word, the sailors turned their boat away and sailed back into the blue, leaving the petulant pilgrims high and dry on the shore—much to their chagrin and Twain's glee.

The Holy Land through which Twain and MacGregor traveled was a land stripped bare of its natural resources following centuries of exploitation and neglect by absentee landowners, vastly different from its modern appearance. Twain rightly took pleasure deriding the guidebooks of his day, which cloaked the parched and desolate hills of the Holy Land with nonexistent greenery. He clearly considered himself above such blather. The

The fare was too high.

descriptions he penned home were of what he saw; he was a totally objective and rational reporter. Or, at least, so he thought.

The Sea of Galilee was a disappointment to Twain, coming in a poor second in any comparison with his beloved Lake Tahoe. And yet, there were times when something touched a chord even in that hardened cynic. One evening on the shores of the Sea of Galilee, as his party slumbered peacefully, Twain penned the following impressions:[6]

> Night is the time to see Galilee . . . when the day is done, even the most unimpressible must yield to the dreamy influences of this tranquil starlight. The old traditions of the place steal upon his memory and haunt his reveries, and then his fancy clothes all sights and sounds with the supernatural. In the lapping of the waves upon the beach, he hears the dip of ghostly oars; in the secret noises of the night he hears spirit

voices; in the soft sweep of the breeze, the rush of invisible
wings.

Twain was on to something. Many legends and fables are
indelibly linked to the Kinneret. There *is* something special—
almost mystical as well as mythical—about that lake which makes
it a "sea of legends." These tales impart to the Kinneret a particular ambience, one that speaks of bygone days and is as much a part
of her as the fish that swim in her waters.

The cast of characters, as found in legends, is a marvelous one
indeed. There are, for example, a satanic bird and a lascivious
river, a murderous goddess and a wandering well with magical
properties, and legions of deaf demons, to name but a few.

えええ

One Jewish legend relates how, before God created the earth,
the Kinneret existed, floating alone in space.[7] On its waters swam
a large bird named Satanel.

"Who are you?" God asked the bird.

"I am God," came the pompous reply.

"But then, if you are God, who am I?" asked the Lord.

"You? Why you are God of all the gods, and Lord of the
Universe!" came the reply.

Then the Lord commanded Satanel to dive down into the
Kinneret and retrieve from it earth and flint. The earth he spread
forth creating land, and striking the flint, he brought forth the
angels.

Satanel took all of this in and wished to mimic the mighty acts
of the Lord, but the Lord was displeased with the bird's ambition
and removed the letters *el*, which means "god," from Satanel's
name, and thus he became the embodiment of evil: Satan.

えええ

From the Hula Swamp, the Jordan River makes its way to the
Kinneret in a fairly straightforward fashion, entering the lake near
the ancient site of Bethsaida-Julias. At the southwestern corner of

the lake, the Jordan makes its exit south of a site called *Tel Beit Yerah*.

From there, the Jordan wends its way in a serpentine manner until it empties into the Dead Sea. The distance as the crow flies is only about 104 kilometers (65 miles), but the river is so convoluted that it takes about 166 kilometers (103 miles) to get there. Legend supplies an explanation for the tortuous path taken by the Jordan.

Long ago, the river did not flow into the Kinneret. But one night the manly Jordan developed an enormous longing for the gentle Kinneret. Unable to quell his desire for that beautiful body of water—a cold shower would have been of little use in this case—Jordan swelled from his cave at Banias and flowed forward, creating a path for his waters through the mountains and the ravines.

When the river reached the lake, his waters mingled with hers, and that night the two became lovers. When the Lord saw the two embrace, he was angered that the Jordan had created the path without his permission. Therefore the Lord commanded the surrounding mountains to create a valley between them. He then washed the Jordan out of the Kinneret.

The river, writhing in anguish, spilled out of the Kinneret, meandering willy-nilly southward, dizzy and drunk with sorrow. As he descended into the lethal grasp of the Dead Sea, his waters turned bitter and lifeless.

And that was the end of the Jordan.

🌊🌊🌊

The earliest recorded reference to the Kinneret was inscribed long ago, and surprisingly far away. It seems somehow fitting that the earliest mention of this particular lake is found in a legend.

One day, 34 centuries ago, a young student scribe named Ilimilku held a tablet of moist clay in his hand and began to record a story, as it was related to him by his master, Attanu-Purlianni.

Attanu-Purlianni was the high priest of the Canaanite god

Baal. As the priest proceeded to tell the legend, Ilimilku finished first one side, and then the other, of the tablet. Putting it down, he took up a second tablet, and then a third.

Ilimilku's tablets were still stored in the house of the high priest over a century and a half later when, around 1185 BC, his city was destroyed by invading barbarians from the sea. Ilimilku's city disappeared into the dusts of time, forgotten through the ages.

In antiquity, the city, which had been named *Ugarit*, had been a major port of trade located approximately due east of Cyprus in what is today Syria. The ancient site was rediscovered only in 1928, when a farmer hit a stone-built tomb while plowing a field at Ras Shamra (Arabic for "Cape Fennel").

Since that day, the archaeologist's spade has revealed impressive remains at Ugarit, including many clay tablets. These were written primarily in two cuneiform scripts: Akkadian, which was the lingua franca of the period, or in Ugaritic, an early alphabetic script that used a limited number of cuneiform symbols to transcribe the West Semitic language that apparently was most commonly spoken in the city. Among the most important documents discovered are those of Ilimilku, which detail the mythological foundations of the Syro-Canaanite religion, insofar as it was practiced at Ugarit in the Late Bronze Age.

The story that Ilimilku wrote down that day related a legend already ancient in his own day. The story begins with a wise and righteous king named Danel, who had no male descendant. To remedy this situation, he offered up sacrifices to the gods of Canaan for seven days. Responding to his pleas, Baal took Danel's plight before El, the elderly head god of the Canaanite pantheon. El granted the request and returned to Danel his missing "passion." Soon his wife was with child.

The heir's name was Aqhat, and the youth's pride and joy was a remarkable bow, made especially for him by the Canaanite god of inventions, Kothar-wa-Khasis. Unfortunately for Aqhat, the bow also caught the attention of the goddess Anat.

Anat proffered gold and silver for the bow. Aqhat politely

declined but offered Anat, in its place, the finest materials required
for the construction of a composite bow like his: wood, tendons,
and the horns of mountain goats.[8]

Anat promised Aqhat immortality in exchange for his bow.
Again Aqhat declined. Rash youth, he called Anat a liar, claiming
that she could not make good on such an offer. Humans were
married to mortality, and even the gods could not change that.
Furthermore, he impiously scolded her, bows were for men, not
women.

This, as it turned out, was not a smart thing to do. Anat
reigned as the goddess of love and war. She proudly wore a grisly
necklace from which dangled the heads of men killed in battle.
Her belt—apparently made by the same couturier—was decorated with the severed hands of men in place of tassels. Clearly,
in her role as goddess of war, Anat was not a lady to be taken
lightly.

Exasperated, Anat decided to carry out the ancient Canaanite
equivalent of a hostile takeover. She would kill Aqhat. Anat en-
listed an assassin, named Yatpan, whom she placed in her pouch
as she soared with the birds of prey above her unsuspecting
victim.

Aqhat was dining in the city of Abiluma when Anat swooped
down, and Yatpan struck. Aqhat died uselessly and needlessly.
Although Ilimilku's text is somewhat broken here, it is clear that
Aqhat's bow—the acquisition of which was the motive for Anat's
dastardly deed—was broken and apparently lost when it fell into
a nearby body of water.

Aqhat's death resulted in the cessation of fertility. Crops with-
ered in the field. When Danel learned of his son's fate, he lamented
mightily. To retrieve the remains of his son for burial, he entreated
Baal to shatter the vultures' wings to permit him to search for the
mangled remains of Aqhat in their gizzards. After decimating
most of the local vulture population, he found Aqhat's fat and
bones in Samal, "mother of all vultures." The grieving Danel then
buried what was left of Aqhat.

Danel cursed three locations which were guilty of having witnessed Aqhat's murder: a "pool of water"; Abiluma, the site of the crime; and another site with an unusually long name, Mararat tagullal-banir.

Danel mourned Aqhat for seven years. Considering Aqhat's male chauvinistic comments to Anat, it was perhaps ironic that it was his sister Pagat who set out on a mission of revenge. She was determined to slay Yatpan for the murder of her brother.

In preparation, Pagat went down to the sea to wash, put on makeup, and dress in a hero's clothes. She armed herself with a knife and a sword, and over all this she slipped the guise of woman's clothing.

It took this archetypal femme fatale a day to walk from where she had bathed in the sea to the encampment of Yatpan. Upon her arrival, Pagat plied Yatpan with wine as he foolishly bragged to her about how he had killed Aqhat.

Unfortunately, Ilimilku's third and last tablet breaks off at this point, with Yatpan in his cups and Pagat—no doubt with a deadly glint in her eye—awaiting her moment to strike.

Ugaritic scholars have long debated where the Aqhat epic takes place. The action has been located plausibly by some scholars in and around the Kinneret region. There are several clues which seem to support this conclusion. First, the site where Danel buries the grisly remains of Aqhat—*bmdgt bknrt*—may be translated "in the fishing-grounds of (the Sea of) Kinneret."[9] If this identification is correct, then it is the earliest reference to the Kinneret.

The second clue given us by Ilimilku concerns Abiluma, the city where Aqhat was murdered. We are told that this is the "city of Prince Moon" (Ugaritic: *ablm qrt zbl yrh*). Now, if the action is taking place near the Kinneret, there is only one site that can claim that title: Beit Yerah, at the southwest shore of the lake where the Jordan parts company with the Kinneret. The name of this site, which was preserved down to the Roman–Byzantine period, means *House (or Temple) of the Moon (God)*.[10]

The idea of burial *in the Kinneret* may seem strange to the

modern ear; however, a more recent medieval Arabic legend identifies the Kinneret as the final resting place of one of Judaism's
most illustrious leaders: King Solomon.[11]

ɹɹɹ

Water, not surprisingly, is a scarce commodity in the Sinai. So
when the children of Israel wandered through the desert for 40
years, they were constantly in need of water. When the multitude
came to Moses and accused him of bringing them to their death by
thirst, the Lord commanded Moses to smite the rock at Horeb, and
water flowed from it.[12] Later in their journeys, the Israelites arrived at a place named *Beer*, which in Hebrew means "well."

"That is the well of which the Lord said to Moses, 'Gather the
people together, and I will give them water,'" the Bible relates.[13]

Now, according to tradition, these biblical references refer to
the *same* well at two different locations. This was said to have been
one of God's last creations before he rested on the sixth day of
Creation. Named after Miriam, the sister of Moses, the well was
indeed a uniquely magical one, for it *traveled* with the children of
Israel. During their wanderings, the well followed them up the
mountains and down the valleys.

When the Israelites needed water, Miriam's well was always
there to refresh and sustain them. The leaders of the camp would
gather around the well and sing its song:[14]

> Spring up, O well!—Sing to it—
> the well that the leaders sank,
> that the nobles of the people dug,
> with the scepter, with the staff.

The well's water would then bubble up and rise in a pillar of
water supplying each of the Twelve Tribes.

Once they crossed the Jordan River and had conquered the
land of Canaan, however, each tribe went its own way and settled
in its own territory. Miriam's well, no longer needed, was abandoned and ignored. No doubt the well felt lonely and unappreci-

ated after all the attention it had received during the years of wandering. According to Jewish tradition, Miriam's well sank into the depths of the Kinneret, where it remains to this day.[15]

Tradition also imparts to the well attributes of both physical healing and spiritual awakening. The tradition of Miriam's well was taken seriously by the Jewish mystics who studied Kabbala—the body of the philosophy of Jewish mysticism—in Safed, a Galilean city perched high up in the mountains overlooking the Kinneret. Rabbi Haim Vital, who was a leading Kabbalist, relates how, in his youth when he had come to study under the preeminent sixteenth-century Kabbalist Rabbi Isaac Luria (better known by his acronym, the Ari, or the Lion), the latter brought him to Tiberias. Taking him onto the lake in a boat, the Ari had his young apprentice drink from the Kinneret's waters and, when he had done so, explained that he would now be able to comprehend the mysteries of Kabbala—for he had sipped from the waters of Miriam's well.[16]

Richard Pococke, an early British explorer who visited the Holy Land in the mid-eighteenth century, records a similar incident:[17]

> A learned Jew, with whom I discoursed at Saphet [Safed], lamented that he could not have an opportunity, when he was at Tiberias, to go in a boat to see the well of Miriam in this lake, which, he said, according to their Talmudical writers, was fixed in this sea, after it had accompanied the children of Israel through the wilderness and that the water of it might be seen continually rising up.

&&&

South of Tiberias are the hot springs which originally were known by the name *Hammat*. One legend explains that these springs are forever hot because, on the way to the earth's surface, the waters flow by the gates of hell. For this reason, in Aramaic the waters were called *Moked de Teverya*, "the Flame of Tiberias."[18]

The Arabs, however, call the hot springs *Hammam Malikna*

Suleiman, "the Baths of Our King Solomon." This name derives from a legend that relates how the hot springs of Tiberias resulted from the direct intervention by the wisest of all men. Solomon was approached one day by a group of sick men who beseeched him to help them relieve the misery of their diseases. Taking pity on the ill and the lame, he called before him a troop of demons and bade them go immediately to the shores of the Kinneret, where a cold freshwater spring flowed into the lake.

"Go down into the bowels of the earth," Solomon commanded, "and heat the spring's waters."

The demons, so the story goes, greatly feared Solomon. They flew to the spring, disappeared underground, and began heating the water.

In the Book of Ecclesiastes, which is traditionally assigned to Solomon's authorship, there is a verse which the New Revised Standard Version of the Bible translates: "I also gathered for myself silver and gold and the treasure of kings and of the provinces; I got singers, both men and women, and the delights of the flesh, *and many concubines.*"[19]

In the Hebrew text, after "the delights of the flesh" come two words *shidah v'shidot.* The meaning of these words is unclear. They may be translated "she-demon and she-demons." Because of this ambiguity in their interpretation, *shidah v'shidot* have received various translations. The King James Bible, for example, renders them *"as* musical instruments, and that of all sorts."

The Midrash Kohelet *Rabbah,* which is an "exposition" or commentary on the Book of Ecclesiastes, interprets this sentence, equating the "delights of the flesh" with the hot baths of Tiberias, while the "she-demon and she-demons" refer to the demonic host which heat the water.

In his wisdom, Solomon knew that, upon hearing of his death, the demons would have no more cause to heat the water. He therefore made them deaf. So when I visit the hot springs in Tiberias—they are now a popular gathering place for both Tiberians and tourists—I try to remember that the heated medicinal waters are courtesy of a band of deaf she-demons who have been toiling there since the Iron Age and are thankfully unaware of Solomon's passing.

🌊🌊🌊

Yam Kinneret, Sea of Gennesaret, Sea of Galilee—this many-named lake inspired legends, provided the backdrop for the teachings of an itinerant carpenter who founded one of the world's three major religions, and served as a battleground for the Jewish people in their struggle against the Roman Empire. Now this small but exceedingly famous body of water had yielded up one of her ancient treasures, and we were about to take possession of it.

Chapter 3

The Excavation from Hell

The sea was wet as wet could be,
　The sands were dry as dry.
You could not see a cloud, because
　No cloud was in the sky:
No birds were flying overhead—
　There were no birds to fly.

The Walrus and the Carpenter
　Were walking close at hand:
They wept like anything to see
　Such quantities of sand:
"If this was only cleared away,"
　They said, "it would be grand!"

"If seven maids with seven mops
　Swept it for half a year,
Do you suppose," the walrus said,
　"That they could get it clear?"
"I doubt it," said the Carpenter,
　And shed a bitter tear.

From *Through the Looking Glass*
Lewis Carroll[1]

*K*adima! *Lazuz! Lazuz!"* ("Forward! Move it! Move it!") With those words, and with an electrical excitement in the air, a ragtag wagon train of kibbutz tractors pulling heavily laden carts moved south from Ginosar along the beach toward the boat.

Rarely had an excavation begun under less propitious circumstances. The Department had not yet completed assembling the excavation equipment and materials. Orna was busy gathering conservation supplies in Jerusalem and Tel Aviv; she would not arrive until the next morning. Other key staff members were still missing. Worse, the rising lake water continued to inch its way toward the site, threatening to inundate the boat within 48 hours, and no sandbags were at hand.

The kibbutz carts were piled high with barricades and barbed wire, hoes, picks and shovels, timber, plastic sheeting, PVC irrigation hose, and anything else in Kibbutz Ginosar that might prove useful until the official supplies arrived.

After passing Nahal Tsalmon, a creek that empties into the Kinneret immediately to the south of the kibbutz, the caravan had to skirt a patch of impassable mud by driving—oddly enough— into the Kinneret's waters where the seabed was firmer. Together with the equipment and supplies came a steady flow of volunteer workers from Ginosar.

Kibbutz Ginosar had "adopted" the boat. It had been found by Moshele and Yuvi, sons and members of the kibbutz, and that clearly made taking care of the boat their responsibility. The kibbutz opened its heart and soul to the excavation. Members of Ginosar gave their time and their skills. They helped in a variety of manners, from excavating, to preparing food, to filling sandbags, to supplying volunteer experts in the field. If there was a problem to point to, it was the kibbutzniks' unflagging zeal. I sometimes had to slow them down.

As Yuvi put it, "Everyone brought something: this one a cake, that one a shovel, and a third some advice."

Behind the scenes, Nitsa organized the kibbutz equipment and personnel. She had a "command center," complete with telephone lines, set up in a nearby boat shed. It looked like an army command post. At first, we had to improvise with what was on hand. We filled a few empty nylon fertilizer bags, scrounged from the kibbutz, with earth and placed them in a semicircle around the boat.

Whereas "normal" archaeological excavation conditions can be brutal—long hours, primitive living arrangements, unbearable heat and dust—there is at least some semblance of order and a schedule to follow. Usually there is time to reflect and to plan. People are assigned tasks, and they know more or less what is expected of them. Throughout our rescue excavation, the only things we came to expect were the problems that arose on a hellishly regular basis. We had to devise makeshift solutions continuously. This stop-gap approach to archaeology proved to be surprisingly effective, however.

The excavation finally began at four in the afternoon on Sunday, February 16. Police barricades were set up as people streamed to the site and waited in anticipation for the archaeologists to uncover the "gold treasure" that they were convinced would be found in the boat. The press of the throng was so great, and our concern about them even greater, that for several hours we purposely dug at some distance from the boat itself, hoping that the onlookers would soon get bored and leave. They obliged us eventually by doing so, but only near dusk. The shadows were lengthening as we at last began to excavate in earnest.

℮℮℮

As for the necessary excavation staff, they seemed to materialize out of nowhere.

I needed a photographer. The night before the excavation Dr. Claire Epstein, who is a noted Department of Antiquities archaeologist, as well as being a veteran member of Kibbutz Ginosar, told me about a young archaeologist and photographer named Danny Friedman (now, Danny Syon) who had worked with her and who wished to volunteer for the excavation. I talked with Danny, and he went home for his cameras, promising to be back the next day.

In order to plot graphically any artifacts that we might find, I had six pipes placed upright into the ground, three on either side of the boat. By taking distances with measuring tapes from any three of the pipes, it was possible to record accurately and quickly the objects' locations.

I needed a registrar, someone whose sole job would be to keep the daily log and to record the artifacts as they were found. Edna Amos, an archaeology student who had dived previously with Kurt and me in the Mediterranean, lived in nearby Tiberias. When she heard on the news about the excavation during that first afternoon, she naturally dropped by to say hello. Edna was standing quietly behind the barricades along with the other visitors when I spotted her.

"I came to see what all the commotion was about," she told me, with a grin.

"Are you doing anything this evening?" I asked.

"No. Why?"

I explained to her our need for a registrar. Could she stay and help us for a while? I asked. Her eyes lit up.

"Sure. No problem."

Edna came around the barricades and on the spot took charge of the recording. She stayed through that first difficult night until six the next morning and returned the next day to become recorder during the excavation and for long afterward. Her skills as an artist and a draftswoman were to prove invaluable to the project.

♪♪♪

By now the sun had disappeared behind the mountains of Galilee, and darkness was descending rapidly. Some kibbutzniks brought to the site gas fishermen's lanterns that cast a gentle, golden, almost magical, radiance over the operation. Thoughtful

The first night of excavation.

of the rising waters and the need to clear the hull before Dick's arrival—now only three days hence—we continued working throughout that first night.

Around midnight, several men appeared at the site. They introduced themselves as representatives from the Kinneret Authority, the governmental organization responsible for administering the Sea of Galilee. Zvi "Orti" Ortenberg, the director of the Authority, explained why they had come.

"I know this sounds ridiculous," Orti began, rather embarrassed, "but we received a message from the Minister of Agriculture actually asking that we lower the level of the lake for you. Of course, there must be some mistake. No one has *ever* asked to *lower* the Kinneret."

Laughing, I explained our predicament. On the spot Orti decided that rather than try to lower the lake—an impossible task

given the amounts of water flowing into it due to the recent rain—
the Authority would build an earthwork and sandbag dike around
the excavation site. He promised to return in the morning with
men, materials, and equipment to commence work.

My primary aim that first night was to remove as much mud
as possible from inside the hull, without exposing the boat's waterlogged timbers to air until Orna arrived to oversee the conservation efforts. However, we also needed an idea of how much of the
hull remained and its general condition. Consequently, a Kibbutz
Ginosar volunteer, Yaron Gofer, and I spent much of the night
lying on our stomachs in the wet mud inside the boat digging a
special section by hand. Slowly, we cleared a narrow path all the
way down the inside of the hull amidships. The vapor of our
breath was visible in the cold, damp air. First the contour of a
frame (rib) and then the planks of the side and bottom of the hull
began to emerge from the muck. Using the groundwater that
welled up in the section, we carefully cleansed the wood. In the
golden glow of the fishermen's lanterns, it seemed as if the frame
and hull planking had been buried only yesterday. This was our
first confirmation that the lower portion of the hull was intact and
well preserved. There was a spontaneous suspension of activity
around the site as everyone came to gaze at the beautiful dark
wood—its features and graining clearly visible—in awed silence.

As we dug, we periodically passed a metal detector back and
forth over the hull to locate small artifacts that might otherwise
have been missed in the dark. In fact, only a few artifacts were
found; these were primarily sherds—small fragments of ceramic
vessels. The boat did not seem to have been carrying a cargo when
she went down. Curious.

Ironically, the only coin excavated from inside the boat was a
1986 United States Lincoln penny that someone had accidentally
dropped. I turned the coin over in my hand.

"In God We Trust," it said to me.

In removing clumps of mud in the semidarkness, it would
have been easy to miss and discard artifacts. For this reason, I
wanted the mud from inside the boat and within a one-meter

The first frame is revealed.

perimeter around it collected in buckets and recorded for later examination.

Soon every available bucket was full. At this point, it seemed that the excavation took on a momentum of its own. Large plastic crates, expropriated from Ginosar's factory, materialized at the site. As each crate was filled, Edna duly labeled and recorded it on our graphic diary. The crates were to be transported and dumped nearby, so that they could be examined for artifacts when we were less pressed for time.

Ever try lifting a large crate filled with wet mud?

Someone brought a tractor with a forklift. The first efforts to lift the crates were unsuccessful, for the prongs of the forklift were

In a short time a method evolved to transport the mud-filled plastic boxes quickly and easily.

too far apart. Boards were quickly lashed across the fork, and with great effort, a few crates were hand-lifted onto it.

I sent Karen Sullivan, an American volunteer, with the tractor to make sure that the crates were properly dumped and that the labels, carefully wrapped in plastic sandwich bags, were securely placed on each mud pile. She recalled later, "That was my first exposure to Israeli improvisation. Returning along that bumpy road a short time later, I was shocked to find that the entire operation had evolved into a smoothly running process. Buckets were being dumped into crates, arranged four to a wooden pallet. The pallets then were loaded easily by the forklift onto a flatbed trailer."

Improvisation is indeed a skill that has been raised to an art form in Israel. What Karen witnessed that night was a "get-it-done-no-matter-what-and-no-matter-how" attitude that was to serve us well in the days to come. In truth, it was the mainstay of the excavation.

The Kinneret, however, was not going to give up her boat so easily. As the night progressed, the water crept toward the site. By morning, it had encroached on our single row of sandbag defenses, which was looking painfully inadequate.

All through the night a moist and cool west wind blew gently. As dawn broke, the trees ominously stopped their rustling; the air stood deathly still for a moment. Then lightly, ever so lightly, a dry east wind began blowing. The *sharkia*.

Yuvi and I shared a knowing glance. We were on the west side of the lake. If the *sharkia* picked up, as it was likely to do, it could swamp the site and tear asunder the parts of the boat that had already been exposed. And there was absolutely nothing any of us could do about it.

As small whitecaps began to drive toward shore, I walked into the lake until I was standing knee-deep in water. In a manner that made perfect sense to me at the time—perhaps because I had not slept in 48 hours—I petitioned the Kinneret in my mind. I realized that we were taking something from the lake which she obviously held dear. And we had not even asked her permission.

The *sharkia* drove the Kinneret's waters toward the boat.

I thanked her for safekeeping the boat for 2,000 years, but now we would take responsibility for it. I assured her that we would treat her boat, this one that had sailed the sea of eternity, with the greatest of loving care.

As I was deep in these musings, heavy motors sounded behind me. Orti had kept his promise. Men from the Kinneret Authority, led by "Shlomkeh" Bahalal, immediately began working on a dike. Within a short time, the boat was surrounded by a rapidly growing barrier of sandbags and earthworks.

Later in the afternoon, the *sharkia* subsided. To this day, I stand personally convinced that the Kinneret gave us her *permission* to excavate that boat. Indeed, from that point on, her waters no longer threatened us, and ultimately, the rising water level turned into a blessing, for it was later vital to *saving* the boat.

As work progressed and the level of the Kinneret continued to rise, the dike was repeatedly strengthened by the men of the Kinneret Authority, who stood on round-the-clock vigil. Even at night we sometimes would see heavy machinery driving in the lake, as the barrier was raised again and again. The rainy weather during those first few days of the excavation created a muddy morass that complicated the use of the heavy mechanical equipment, which repeatedly got mired in the mud. Someone quipped that this was neither a land nor an underwater excavation, but an amphibious one.

Another challenge soon developed. Because the pit we were digging was beneath the water table, water was continually seeping in. Again, the Kinneret Authority saved us by bringing pumps that kept the groundwater at bay.

Often we were cold, wet, and muddy. The mud and the dampness were such that I chose to wear my neoprene diving pants for the first two days of the excavation. *That* was an experience—rather like wearing a tight-fitting thick plastic bag.

That first night of work was intensive, and we had made a sizable dent in the overburden in the hull. Orna arrived the next morning.

"The first thing I remember about the excavation," she once

The marshy lake bed became a morass, presenting problems for the heavy equipment.

reminisced to me, "was a strange man kneeling in the middle of the boat with his arm up to his elbow in water and an incredible grin creasing his face from ear to ear. He called me to him, took my hand, and thrust it into the puddle of water. 'Can you feel it?' he asked. 'Yes,' I told him. I was touching one of the boat's frames. That was my introduction to the boat, as well as to Moshele."

Orna had brought with her small amounts of polyester resin, fiberglass, and polyurethane. Later these materials—in much larger quantities—would prove crucial to the boat's well-being.

There, in the mud, Orna reported on the preparations being made by the Antiquities Department in Jerusalem. We then reviewed the current situation and began to outline our plans.

Good conservators, by training, are methodical and cautious. Like physicians, they are taught first to "do no harm." Orna emphasized that, once it was excavated, we could leave the boat out of water for only a short time before the wood would start to

Bird's-eye view of the boat on the morning of the second day of excavation.

dry and irreversible damage would be done to the hull. Focusing on the conservation difficulties ahead as she saw them, she outlined a number of legitimate problems. Listening to her concerns, however, made saving the boat sound nearly impossible.

Our discussion was illustrative of the innate and unavoidable conflict between excavator and conservator. One extracts artifacts from an environment that has preserved them for centuries; the other strives to protect them under new, possibly adverse, conditions. No matter how delicately the archaeologist may brush away the covering dirt, the very act of exposing an ancient artifact endangers its continued existence and challenges the conservator. Thus the greater my success in rapidly excavating the boat, the greater the number of problems posed to Orna to see that no harm came to it. That "meeting in the mud" was the first in a series of professional debates in which Orna would logically outline the

Orna, Kurt, and I have an impromptu meeting in the mud. At this point, we were stuck in the mud in more ways than one.

problems we faced, often coming to the conclusion that, no matter what we tried, we had little chance of success.

I am an optimist by nature. Some would say hopelessly so. I tried to cheer Orna by saying that we could do only the best we could do. If that meant saving the boat, wonderful. If the boat started falling apart, at least Dick would have had an opportunity to record it.

But what we must do, I said, is not lose the belief that solutions existed to the problems that we were encountering. If we accepted that success was impossible from the start, we would follow those beliefs and might miss solutions if and when they did appear.

"Be realistic, Shelley. You've been seeing too many rainbows," she told me on parting.

🌊🌊🌊

Human dynamics are fascinating in high-pressure situations. By the second day of the excavation, a certain weird euphoria had taken hold of the group. We were fighting an uphill battle against all odds. Whether or not we would succeed was open to question—in a big way. And yet, strangely, it was this particular situation that drew the folks from Migdal back to the excavation. This time, they came not to argue and lay claims to the boat, but to help.

It soon became apparent that a large pit had to be carved around the boat so that we could gain better access to the hull. We first tried to do this with a scraper attached to a kibbutz tractor but found that it could not give the desired results. We needed some special tool: a mechanical backhoe with a small shovel that could dig a deep and narrow passageway. The kibbutz did not own one, and it would take time for the Department to rent one—far more time than we could afford.

"I have one," said a gruff voice behind me.

I turned to face a mountain of a man, his face hidden behind a huge beard.

"I beg your pardon. What did you say?" I asked.

Clearing his throat, the man repeated, "I said, I have one. I have a backhoe."

Shmuel Karasanti, a farmer from Migdal, had been within earshot as we were discussing the problem. "I'll bring it this afternoon. Only please . . . if you could supply the fuel?"

"Sure," I said with a smile. "And thank you."

Shmuel just shrugged his shoulders in response and walked away without saying another word.

A few hours later, a bright yellow mechanical backhoe arrived at the site. And Shmuel was in the driver's seat. Under our supervision, he began to enlarge and deepen the pit around the boat, beginning opposite the starboard bow.

Excavating archaeologically with a backhoe has distinct similarities to waltzing with a hippo: There is a significant danger of

Shmuel Karasanti volunteered his mechanical backhoe to enlarge the pit.

something down there being seriously damaged. And yet, because of Shmuel's expertise, and our guiding him from the pit, we
were able to use the backhoe shovel almost like a scalpel. Soon a
narrow valley separated the boat from its surroundings, while the
craft itself was supported by a mud girdle.

So it was that, by the second afternoon of the excavation,
other members of Migdal, following Shmuel's example, joined the
team. Previous enmities that had seemed so dangerous only a day
earlier vanished like morning fog as everyone pulled together in a
concerted effort to save the boat, which received a new nickname
because of this new-found, and entirely unexpected, harmony.

We called her the "Love Boat."

Ginosar and Migdal were not our only source of volunteers,
however. Others came from all over Israel. Yaron Ostrovski, a tour
guide who had a lull in his schedule, asked to be included and was
taken on board as a full-time volunteer. Others, like Nan Leininger
and Karen Sullivan, were family of employees of the American

We left a mud girdle to support the boat.

embassy. The crew took on more and more diversity as time went by.

e e e

Not smoothly, and certainly not without crises, things began to fall into place. As the day progressed, some semblance of a routine began to emerge.

Some volunteers staked out specific areas of the boat in which they worked. Yaakov Rotem, known simply as "Rotem," soon took charge of the stern area. As the frames began to appear in the stern, still thick with mud, Danny took a photo of Rotem, equally encased in mud and with a delightful "Isn't this wonderful?" grin on his face.

To my mind that photograph captures the feeling of the day. We had embarked on an adventure in a rickety boat. Set sail on an unsure course. And yet, if the truth be told, all of us were enjoying it immensely.

That morning we had a visit from Ambassador Pickering and his wife, Alice. We spoke for only a few moments before I had to get back to the excavation, but I did get the chance to thank him for the embassy's help in bringing Dick over.

By now everyone was getting involved. Kibbutz children, taking time off from school, filled sandbags for the dike. Volunteers from Ginosar continued to flock to the site. Together with them came a steady stream of food.

Yuvi told Aliza Paz that the *hevra*—Hebrew slang for "the gang"—were getting hungry. Aliza relates, "When Yuvi said that they needed food at the boat, I ran home to my pantry and fridge, took out everything I had, and brought it to the beach." Soon the "food connection" was established. Later Nitsa put Aliza in charge of organizing the food. To her credit, we never went hungry during the excavation. Sandwiches and soup, cookies and cakes, hot Turkish coffee, and soft drinks were always available morning, noon, and night.

Two tables, placed inside our police barricades, served as our open-air office. That afternoon, the awaited excavating equipment and materials arrived from the Department of Antiquities. I was

Why is this man smiling?

only too well aware of how difficult it must have been to acquire some of the materials on such short notice. Everything I had asked for was there.

The same van that brought the equipment also carried Michael Feist and Yisrael Vatkin, the Department's surveyors. Yisrael, a recent immigrant to Israel with a thick Russian accent, stayed with us to plot the boat's exact position. He continued working into the night, using a portable lamp to light his surveyor's table.

The second night of excavation, I finally called a halt to work. The Kinneret Authority's dike was safely holding back the rising waters, so the immediate threat was contained, and some of us had been on the go since six the previous morning. Were we to continue at this rate, we would begin to start making stupid mistakes, mistakes that we could not afford.

Yisrael plotted the site at night by lamplight.

For the rest of the excavation, our schedule ran from seven in the morning to about seven or eight at night. The staff would return to our rooms, in the old army barracks at Ginosar, shower, and eat dinner. Then we would gather together again in the lobby of the Nof Ginosar Hotel for staff meetings, consultations, and preparations for the next day's challenges. Ideas flowed at these meetings. Problems we were facing, or anticipated facing, were raised, and everyone had an opportunity to offer his or her solutions. This was invaluable for problem solving, for each person brought a unique viewpoint and background to the situation.

ℯℯℯ

On the morning of the third day of the excavation, Tuesday, February 18, we began to reveal the ship's timbers. First to appear from under the mud was the bow.

For photographic recording, it was necessary to differentiate where one plank began and the other ended. Otherwise, the hull would appear a dark solid mass to the eye—as well as in photographs. With this in mind, I asked Danny, when he wasn't shooting with his cameras, to outline the seams between the strakes. Using white plastic string that we had "borrowed" from Ginosar's banana fields, Danny painstakingly began to lay the string out. As he could not lean on the wood in order to get to the planks and keel in the center of the hull, he and the other volunteers who helped him from time to time were forced to bend over the hull in backbreaking stances for extended periods.

Danny had to be particularly careful that he was not unwittingly falsifying the record by placing the string along cracks in the planking. To prevent this from happening, he searched for the heads of the pegs inside the hull which locked the mortise-and-tenon joints in place. He would then lay the string only in those seams in which he could definitely see the peg heads. Any metal nails protruding into the hull were circled with white string to accentuate them. The resulting planking pattern was unusual for a boat. Some of the planks were exceedingly narrow to be used in the construction of a vessel. "Now why would they do that?" I wondered.

In addition to the white string, Danny attached red tags, cut from plasticized material, on each and every definable timber. These were later numbered consecutively from bow to stern and facilitated considerably the recording of the hull's timbers. The keel was marked with a special sign:

All we had to fasten the string and tags to the hull were metal straight pins, the kind used in sewing. These soon began to rust, and Orna worried out loud that the rust might damage the timbers.

Upon hearing this, Moshele, ever innovative, came up with an original solution to the problem. Kibbutz Ginosar has one of the nicest cactus gardens in Israel. He denuded one of the cacti of its needles and brought them to the site in a paper cup. For a while we used them to pin the string and tags to the timbers. The cactus needles soon became soft and waterlogged from the timbers, however, and Danny had to go back and replace them with straight pins.

Given our situation, it was particularly important that as complete a record as possible of the hull be prepared. Apart from this being normal archaeological methodology, there was another very real and present concern: The boat might fall apart. This scenario, like the sword of Damocles, weighed on us.

It was for these reasons that I assigned to Danny an additional task: the creation of a set of photo mosaics of the interior of the boat's hull, section by section, as it was revealed from the mud. Once he had completed stringing and tagging a section of the boat, Danny would shoot it for a photo mosaic. To do this required a series of black-and-white photographs of the boat's hull, in which each photograph overlapped its neighbor by about 50 percent.

Danny had to keep the camera's lens absolutely stationary while taking each set of photos. Later, when the photos were glued together, we had an accurate map of about 60 percent of the hull's surviving interior.

This method of recording lacked the sophistication of stereo-photogrammetry, a method of photographic documentation which is often used in the recording of underwater shipwrecks. On the other hand, making photomosaics was relatively simple and quick and did not require complicated equipment. The time pressure under which we were working, as well as the continuous press of people working in and around the boat, would have made stereo-photogrammetry impossible, even if the necessary equipment had been available.

Danny also created a deceptively simple notation on the

Danny's photomosaic of the bow section.

black-and-white photographs which gave a considerable amount of information about the subject of the photograph. At the left he defined a letter code: *A* indicates that the photo was taken in the stern, and *B* in the bow; *K* that it is a detail of the keel; and *M* that the photo was part of a mosaic set. *R* means frames (ribs), *S* a specific strake, and *X* additional discoveries at the northeast corner of the excavation pit. *O* stands for "other" and included anything not specifically defined in the previous specific categories.

Danny's second rubric, reading from the left, refers to the side of the boat on which the photo was taken, while the third indicates its location forward and aft. Finally, the last rubric gives the date on which the photograph was taken.

Thus, for example the following notation on a photograph indicates that it depicts a strake on the port side of the bow, and that it was taken on February 17:

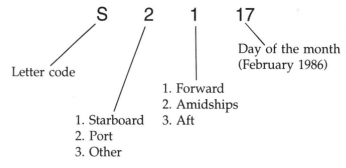

Later, as the excavation progressed, Danny would sometimes supply the specific number of frame or strake. For general photos of the site, or "action shots," Danny gave only the date in year/month/day order. Unlike for most excavations, in which the photographic record usually consists of artifacts and their locations, I instructed Danny to photograph, whenever possible, people and their activities—to capture the human drama.

🌊🌊🌊

The clouds disappeared, and we began having T-shirt weather. During the day, the sun beat down with a vengeance. The boat's exposed timbers began to steam under the sun's relentless attack. Although the wood looked practically modern, it was water-logged. This meant that much of the cellular material had been replaced by water.

Imagine buying a head of lettuce and leaving it uncovered in your refrigerator for a week or so. The leaves go limp because the water that gives structure to the cells has evaporated. Similarly with the boat, if the water were to evaporate from the cells, there would be nothing to support them. The cells would begin to collapse as the wood dried out, and the timbers themselves to warp, twist, and crack as their internal structure changed. Once this has occurred, there is no known method of "pumping up" the cells within the structure.

It was imperative that the hull's timbers retain this water. Therefore the boat had to be reimmersed in water as soon as possible. This was an immediate—first-aid—treatment in order to stabilize our "patient." This critical consideration and Dick's imminent arrival were the reasons for the speed with which the excavation of the hull's interior continued.

Extensive exposure to air had been harmful to the upper edge of the top starboard strake. It was particularly fragmentary, having served its purpose of flagging down Moshele and Yuvi. We carefully covered it with soft spongy rubber which was kept constantly watered.

To prevent—or at least slow down—the evaporation process, we at first placed polyethylene plastic sheeting over the exposed parts of the hull. This solution was soon found to be unsatisfactory, however. Dr. Zvi Goffer of the Soreq Research Center, who dropped by to visit the excavation, pointed out that direct sunlight and the humidity beneath the plastic sheeting would be an ideal breeding ground for destructive microorganisms. As these little beasties posed a direct, although not as immediate, threat to the boat, the sheeting came off. Alternative solutions were needed. We soon had people with garden bottles constantly spraying water on the boat's timbers. Additionally, we experimented with sprinklers, drip-irrigation devices, and perforated hoses. And with all this, it was clear that we were losing the battle. We were slowing the evaporation of the water from the wood cells, but we were not stopping it. The boat had to get back underwater. Fast.

As the day continued, the sun beat down relentlessly under an azure sky. There was not a cloud in sight.

"Well, at least you won't be seeing any rainbows today," Orna said. "Thank goodness for that."

A few minutes later, a hose, connected to one of the pumps used to keep the groundwater from inundating the site, sprung a leak. Almost immediately, men from the Kinneret Authority were taking care of the problem. I walked over and watched as it released a fine mist into the surrounding air.

And in the mist was a miniature rainbow.

"Orna," I called, "Come over here. You have to see something."

"What?" she asked expectantly as she came over, wiping the mud from her hands on her pant legs.

I just pointed to the minirainbow in the mist.

"That doesn't count," she said.

ℓℓℓ

Zvika Malach is another moshavnik from Migdal who joined the excavation. A gentle giant with a long-flowing beard, he later told me that he had never had an interest in archaeology before, but that, after visiting the site on that first day of excavation, he found himself drawn back to it again and again. He would get up before dawn each morning to tend his orchards and then show up at the excavation around noon and work until we stopped for the day. Zvika, who was always willing to do any task asked of him, soon became a welcome member of the team.

That day, in the late afternoon, Zvika and I were supervising Shmuel's work with his mechanical backhoe. We had followed a clockwise pattern around the boat, as we deepened and enlarged the pit. Now, having nearly completed this task, we were enlarging the northeast corner.

Until then, the densely packed clay being brought up by the shovel had been virtually sterile. But in this corner of the pit, just off the boat's port bow, we began to find bits and pieces of ancient wood—loose fragments with old breaks—bearing the scars and markings of mortise-and-tenon joints.

The excavation ground to a crawl as Zvika and I began to examine each of the shovel loads of sediment. Shmuel would scoop up a shallow shovel load and then dump it in front of us in the pit. We then quickly sorted through the mud and removed the wooden fragments, placing them in a plastic milk crate. Once we had sifted through the dirt, Shmuel would delicately scoop up the same shovel load of sediment and carefully deposit it outside the pit, where others would spread it out and go over it with a metal detector to ensure that we had not missed any coins, nails, or other metal fastenings.

Zvika became so preoccupied with this process that he seemed totally oblivious of the backhoe shovel, which often swung perilously close to his head. One of my main concerns at that point was ensuring that he did not accidentally get knocked into the next world as the shovel whirred, bucked, and shook above him.

As we worked, groundwater began to well up and cover the lowest parts of the deepening trench. Therefore, before each scoop of the shovel, we would explore in the water with our hands to make sure the shovel was not destroying anything.

At one point, Zvika, with his hands immersed in the muddy water and the shovel swinging inches from his head, told me excitedly, "I can feel planking, and it is attached to something!"

I signaled to Shmuel to back off with the shovel and had one of the small pumps brought over. As the groundwater receded, we watched in anticipation as not one, but *two* coherent hull fragments came into view.

This area would definitely have to be enlarged by hand. I could not take the chance of the mechanical shovel's damaging the wood. I had Shmuel remove the backhoe.

"Are these only fragments of hulls, or perhaps the uppermost strakes of complete hulls, like the one we were excavating, only

Working with the backhoe.

Zvika's "fleet."

buried more deeply in the sediment?" I wondered. But only for a moment. There was no time to think about that.

We laid down sandbags to protect the hull fragments and began slowly to excavate down from the level of the seabed to enlarge the area. Needless to say, I put Zvika in charge of the fleet that he had discovered. This gave the modern Migdalites an even stronger sense of sharing in the project, which was beautifully illustrated when, that evening on their way back from a wedding, several couples came to visit the excavation. Upon hearing about the discovery of additional boats by one of their own, one man,

still in the dress clothes that he had worn to the wedding, asked
for a pick and began to chip away at the overburden.

ꮛꮛꮛ

There were moments of warmth, smiles, and success, and
other times in which it seemed that all our efforts were only an
exercise in futility. As Zvika was discovering his flotilla, another
drama was unfolding only meters away, at the boat's stern. As I
had already noted in the initial probe excavation, the sternpost
was missing, leaving the ends of the stern planking unsupported.
While this was an interesting archaeological riddle, it also created
a very real and present danger to the hull's integrity.

The boat had come to rest listing on her port side, causing the
starboard stern quarter to curve up and over the interior of the
hull. As the mud which had supported them for millennia was
removed, the planks, detached from the sternpost, dangled, dan-
gerously loose, in the air. While the hull *looked* firm, we knew that
it might not have sufficient strength to support itself.

To counter this problem, Orna had a single flat-sided wooden
stave driven into the mud, hard up against either side of the stern
where the post was missing. When the staves were in place, she
tied them together above the planking. She then lined the interior
of the stern with aluminum foil and created a polyurethane fill.
Once this solidified, she hoped, it would be sufficient to support
the starboard stern quarter.

A short time later, as the sun was setting, gravity got the
better of the boat. We were completing the sandbagging of Zvika's
boats when Rotem shouted a warning. Part of the stern had buck-
led and was about to fall.

In moments, we were all at the stern helping Rotem and
others hold the weakened planking in place. It was obvious, however, that we would not be able to keep it in place for long.
Therefore, using a nearby piece of plywood as an ersatz stretcher,
we gently lifted and placed the detached timbers on the ground.
The collapse left a gaping hole in the stern as well as in my heart. A
more forlorn sight would be hard to imagine.

The stern starboard section curved up and over the interior of the hull.

Orna endeavored to stabilize the stern with a fill of polyurethane.

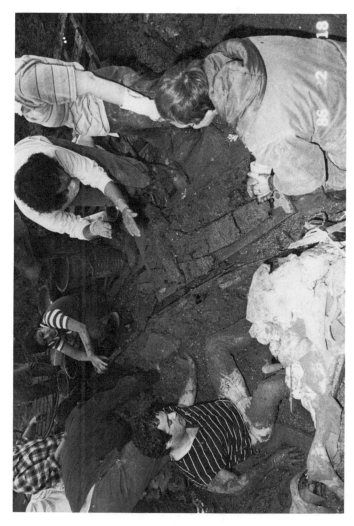

The stern starboard section collapses.

Was this to be the fate of the boat? Would she, piece by piece, collapse around us? Had it been an error, a devastating one, to press so resolutely, as I had done, for the boat's excavation?

Later, as we cleansed the removed timbers of the remaining mud and pebbles that clung to them, Orna and I for the first time discussed at length the scenario of the boat falling apart. Maybe it was time to become, as Orna said, "realistic." Maybe we were just chasing a rainbow in trying to save the boat.

After securing the dismembered segment to the plywood support under a layer of polyethylene sheeting, several of us carried it into the Kinneret to keep it wet. We looked like a group of war-weary pallbearers removing the dead from battle.

It was a horrible feeling. I have known some difficult times in my life, but few of them have come near to eliciting in me the demons of self-doubt that appeared so readily—and weighed upon my shoulders so heavily—that night.

ꝑꝑꝑ

The next day, Wednesday, February 19, was another scorcher. The sun beat down with that kind of morning brightness that makes you squint and your eyes water. By now we had cleared the forward half of the hull of overburden. Upon our arrival at the site, it was clear that the sun was taking a toll on the exposed timbers. Wisps of steam curled up from the hull. And with every puff, more and more wood cells were loosing their aqueous support and, quite literally, giving up the ghost.

Our first agenda for the day, therefore, became preventing the sun's rays from directly striking the wood. Someone hurried back to the kibbutz in search of a truck tarpaulin to stretch over the boat.

To prevent anyone from getting stuck in the mud, wooden pallets had been placed around the boat, forming a walkway. I have to confess that this was done more to protect the boat than to protect the workers. I feared one of us might grab for the fragile hull to steady ourselves if we suddenly slipped.

Another problem. Once the mud from a portion of the hull's interior had been removed, we dared not apply any weight to the area. A person's foot would have gone through the waterlogged hull as if it were made of floral foam. Our situation was reminiscent of a man sitting on a tree branch as he saws it off the tree's trunk.

Now, the boat's bow section was relatively flat, having been preserved only to the turn of the bilge, the imaginary line where the bottom of the hull meets the vessel's sides. As a result, much of the work on this portion of the boat could be carried out by persons standing outside the hull, although with resultant backaches. This would not be possible in the stern, however.

Because of the tree stump on which the bow rested, the boat had settled more deeply into the mud at the stern and was, therefore, better preserved there. The sides rose almost vertically, preventing anyone standing outside the hull from reaching inside it. How were we to continue working inside the hull?

Before the start of the excavation, Moshele had created two bridges by welding together some portions of metal railing. We had used these the first night of the excavation as platforms, placing them over the boat, perpendicular to its hull.

"Why not raise the bridges on supports planted outside the hull and then lower a hanging platform into it from them?" Moshele asked. "They can also support the tarpaulin."

Moshele, together with Gill Klop, who worked in the kibbutz welding shop, went to work and quickly constructed the metal superstructure. Before long, it stood over the boat. It wasn't pretty and certainly would not win any engineering prizes, but it fitted our needs exactly. Once the entire construction was in place and secured by guide wires, Moshele and Gill hung a metal framework from it with nylon ropes. On this they placed pine planks. Soon volunteers were lying prone on the boards for hours as they carefully removed the remaining sediment from inside the hull by hand.

When the tarpaulin arrived, we carefully stretched it over the framework and secured it with guide ropes. The site now took on the semblance of a Bedouin encampment.

Moshele and Gill prepare the hanging platform.

The newly acquired structure was also able to support various garden sprinklers, "borrowed" from the kibbutz landscaper's shop, which were used in a further attempt to keep the boat's exposed timbers wet.

At one point, I stood on the sidelines, taking a breather and drinking a cup of scalding coffee. At all hours of each day, and some of each night, the boat was surrounded by people hurrying about on every side, attending to her every need. Most of the time I was one of them. Now, for a change, I was looking "from the outside in."

What made this involvement so infectious, I wondered? I was an archaeologist. This was my job, my vocation, and my passion. But everyone else seemed to be showing just as much enthusiasm and care. It was as if anyone who came near fell in love with the

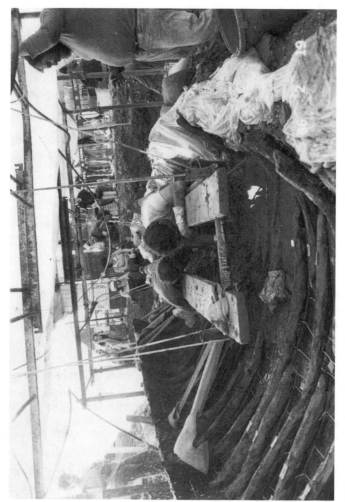

Volunteers spent hours lying on their stomachs on the platform as they completed the excavation of the hull's interior by hand.

boat. I guess all of us realized, each in his or her own unique way, that we were participating in something special. Something out of the ordinary.

The scene reminded me of a queen bee being tended by her workers. It was, I reflected, almost as if the boat was giving off some kind of pheromone to make us all so concerned about her well-being.

I shook my head. What a ridiculous idea, I thought.

But as time went by, I came to view the boat less and less as a "something" and more and more as a "someone" complete with her own personality.

We became an overnight attraction as tourist guides began bringing their charges to the excavation. The crowds were so consistent a presence that one enterprising *gazlan*—Hebrew for "highway robber," used *semi*affectionately for entrepreneurs with concession trucks—set up shop on the beach, to cater to the newfound clientele who were winding their way down the beach in ever-growing droves to see the boat. This would seem to give the boat the unique distinction of being the only archaeological excavation in the world with its own resident ice cream truck.

The visitors, for the most part, were polite. We found, however, that some people felt that the police barricades did not apply to them. Much effort was expended in keeping the curious from approaching the boat. Finally, in exasperation, we brought in bales of razor-sharp concertina barbed wire.

Isaac, Rotem's father, was visibly moved as he watched us with gloved hands string up the concertina wire inside the police barricades. I asked what was wrong.

"You don't know what it does to me," he said, personal memories apparently flooding his thoughts, "to see Jews held back by barbed wire."

On several occasions we had to forcibly evict uninvited guests who approached the boat, after jumping the barriers and walking over loose boards that they had thrown down on the concertina, as if they were attacking an enemy fortress. One persistent man, having hurdled our obstacle course, refused to leave before he could examine the boat.

"I pay my taxes," he shouted at me. "I have the right to be here."

Other visitors, who were still outside the barrier, watched to see how he would fare. That was the only time I remember raising my voice during the entire excavation.

The man did not get near the boat.

♪♪♪

From the outset, the excavation became a media event. The coverage, thanks to the "Jesus boat" label, was overwhelming. Professor Trude Dothan, a prominent Israeli archaeologist, happened to be visiting the Far East at the time of the excavation. Later she told me how surprised she had been, when during an air flight in *Burma*, she had opened her complementary *local* newspaper to find that our boat had made front-page headlines there.

This coverage was not solicited, and in the long run, it did not help the boat. I was saddened to see that, for the most part, the press people writing about the boat really did not take the time to understand the story. Their reports were full of inaccuracies.

I knew what I had told them. When I complained of this to one reporter from an Israeli daily, the man explained to me quite seriously, as if he were talking to a child, "Oh, we never let the truth get in the way of a good story."

All this led me to reflect on how much of the news we receive daily, about which we do not have personal knowledge, is really accurate. I was particularly rankled by the almost universal use in the media, even in Israel, of the term *Jesus boat*. Not only did this imply that the boat had in some way been connected to Jesus—for which we had no evidence—but it also loosened the ties that the boat may have had with the Jewish history on the lake.

I do not mean here to indict all media news reporters. There were some who were outstanding in their accuracy and who gained my respect; Abe Rabinowitz of the *Jerusalem Post*, the late

Dr. Zvi Ilan of the Israeli daily *Davar*, and Jonathan Broder of the *Chicago Tribune* come immediately to mind. And there were others.

Abe, in particular, took the time to visit us often and always made sure that he had his facts straight. As international papers commonly excerpt reports from Israel from the *Jerusalem Post*, Abe's reporting got the real story out. I met him in Jerusalem one day, shortly after the excavation was over. He just stood there staring at me in a weird kind of way for a minute, as if he couldn't quite place me.

"I didn't recognize you," he said. "You're not covered with mud."

We both laughed.

ℯℯℯ

The media related to the boat and the excavation in many ways. The "Jesus boat" nickname had a sure-fire attraction for satirists of various persuasions.

Cartoonists had a field day, particularly after it was reported that parts of two additional boats had been found. One political cartoonist depicted tourists being bused around inside a boat named "Jesus Boat No. 3" mounted on a flatbed truck. A tour guide, hat pulled down over his eyes, blared dollar bill signs at them through a megaphone.

At the time of the excavations, the Israeli shipyards at Haifa port were experiencing financial problems. Under the title "A Third Boat was Discovered on the Shores of the Kinneret," another cartoonist drew a trio of broken hulls on an abandoned shore. The vessels were named respectively "The Boat of Jesus," "The Boat of the Zealots," and "The Israel Shipyards."

Dr. Ronny Reich, a colleague at the Department of Antiquities with an artistic bent, drew a cartoon illustrating a novel idea for preserving the boat entitled, "A Proposal for Conserving the Boat." In the cartoon, he depicted a boat being rowed inside a corked bottle. The boat's name, *Sfinat Ha(ma)shotim*, is a play on words in Hebrew that can be translated either "the oared ship" or "the ship of fools." More than once during the excavation I had cause to reflect that perhaps we all were indeed in a "Ship of Fools." Then again, perhaps we had been blessed with the "wisdom to be foolish." Either way, Ronny's cartoon hit the spot.

After the excavation, I wrote to a veteran cartoonist for *MAD Magazine*, Dave Berg. I had never met Dave, but in 1973, following the cease-fire that ended the Yom Kippur War, my army unit had found itself deployed in the city of Suez after the fighting. While stationed there, I had read one of Dave's books, enjoying its humor and warmth. I had written to him then, introducing myself, and had asked him to draw a cartoon of our experiences for me. I told him that I was in a paratrooper unit, situated *ay-sham* ("somewhere") in Egypt, and that we had spent most of our time filling sandbags.

A few weeks later at mail call, I had received a letter from Dave. In it he had enclosed a cartoon depicting Israeli paratroopers jumping out of a plane. In place of a parachute, however, each soldier is floating down on a sandbag. On the ground are a shovel, a pile of sandbags, and a sign with "101" written on it (the kilometer marker indicating the distance from Cairo to which Israeli forces had advanced before stopping). That cartoon was a very special gift for a "grunt" far from home, and it remains one of my prize possessions.

I now asked Dave to draw a cartoon of the boat.

This time, Dave sent me a cartoon in which I am standing, fishing pole in hand, with the hook caught on a horse-shaped stem ornament of a boat rising from the water with "B.C.E." (for "Before the Common Era") emblazoned on its bow.

"Hey, Shelley, what did you catch?" asks a bearded figure from behind a copse of shrubs.

"Nothing much," I respond. "Just an old boat."

♟♟♟

Almost always there was at least one, and often more, film crew from TV networks around the world capturing our every move. It was a bit like living in a fish bowl. One of the people

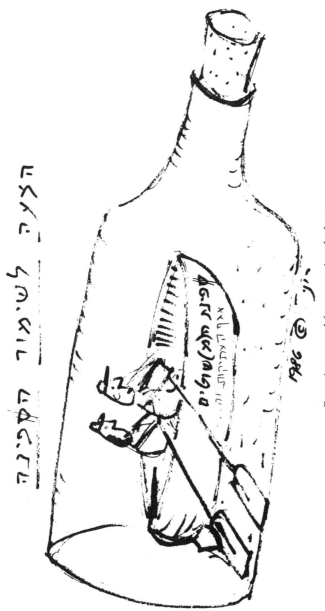

Ronny's proposal for conserving the boat.

Paratroopers with sandbags.

Just an old boat . . .

filming us was a newfound friend of mine who, quite uninten-
tionally, had taught me something of great value.

Moshe Ben Dor was, at the time, a cameraman for a major
American television network. He was also a veteran scuba diver
and had decided to combine his two loves. He, together with a
partner, had purchased a broadcast-quality camera and underwater housing. Shortly before the boat surfaced, he had contacted
me and asked if we had anything of interest to film underwater, so
that he could try out his camera on something other than fish. The
Department didn't have a project going at that time, primarily
because I had called a halt to diving because of our dilapidated
equipment. But although the idea never got off the ground—or in
the water, for that matter—we did become friends, and during my
visits to Jerusalem, I would occasionally look him up.

Several times I accompanied Moshe in his work. It was in this
manner that I got an inside glimpse of how a major television
network operates. I saw how streamlined and electronic the art of
news gathering had become and was impressed—perhaps *shocked*
is a more accurate word—by how easily and quickly things could
be done. Information was sought, located, filmed, and transferred
back to the United States *all in the same day*. This was a different
world from the one I had grown used to.

It was truly a revelation to me. Growing up in a government
bureaucracy for most of my adult life, I had never realized that
needs could be expedited in such a timely manner, outside the
military. I had assumed that things *had* to take time to be accomplished. It was simply a fact of life. Like death and taxes.

This was a particularly valuable lesson for me. Along with
other experiences that I was having at this time, it made me realize
that, *within the realms of physical reality, anything is possible, unless
you believe it to be otherwise.*

That is, if you *really* believe that you can soar like the eagles
and jump off a cliff to demonstrate, reality, in the form of gravity,
will kick in, and you will end up splattered on the canyon floor,
food for the crows. Nor does it mean that if you *really* believe that
you will be the president of the United States—or of Papua New

Guinea, for that matter—you will become the president. Someone else may hold that belief even more strongly than you.

What it does mean, however, is that reality, for each of us, follows our individual belief system. If someone believes that something is impossible, it will be. Period. Even if there is a solution to that particular problem, he will be blind to it. If he is convinced that there is no solution, then even if one is revealed, he will not see it, for he is no longer looking for it. Thus the solution will be invisible to him.

Rather like the story of the Bedouin and the giraffe . . .

e.e.e

There is a story told of a Bedouin guide from southern Sinai who worked, during the years after the Six-Day War when Israel held the Sinai, for the Israel Nature Protection Society. Although illiterate, Mahmud, as we shall call him, was highly intelligent and a keen observer of life.

As a gift for his excellent service, he was given a free, all-expenses-paid trip to Jerusalem. Now, Mahmud had never been out of southern Sinai. He was familiar with jeeps and trucks, knew what an airplane looked like, and had seen buildings as high as two or three stories at his home in Santa Katarina. But that was about the extent of his familiarity with the modern world.

Upon arriving in Jerusalem, Mahmud was taken on a tour of the city by several of the Israelis who had enjoyed his kind hospitality in Sinai. But where do you take someone who has never seen a modern city with all its amenities?

After deliberating on how best to enhance his stay, his Israeli friends took him first to a department store and showed him the escalators. Moving stairs! These clearly made a tremendous impression on Mahmud.

His hosts then took him to the Jerusalem Biblical Zoo. Mahmud studied each of the animals with interest. Some, like the long-horned ibexes, were familiar to him, for they were his neighbors in Sinai. Other animals he had never seen before.

He visited the elephant, and then the hippopotamus and the

tiger. But at the giraffe's cage, he stood transfixed. He gawked in awe at the giraffes, as they majestically strode around their enclosure in long-necked silence, eyeing him from time to time. It was growing dark before his hosts managed to pry him away from the giraffes and out of the zoo.

"What did you think of the animals?" one of them asked as they walked out the gates of the zoo.

"Oh, the elephant was most amazing," he said. Mahmud went on to remark on the hippo, the zebra, and the monkeys. But he didn't say a word about the giraffes.

Finally, unable to hold his curiosity in any longer, one of the Israelis asked, "But what about the giraffes?"

"Oh," said Mahmud, looking into his eyes with absolute assurance, "an animal like that doesn't exist."

𝒆𝒆𝒆

Upon reflection, then, I had recently come to the conclusion that the proper attitude to be taken when addressing any given problem is to see it not as a wall stopping you from moving forward, but as only one side of a coin. *The flip side is the solution.*

Perhaps the French philosopher-mathematician Descartes said it best. When faced with a perplexing problem, he would first imagine that he had already solved it. And then he would sit down and figure out how he had done it.

People live within belief systems. Those sharing like beliefs feel comfortable with each other. When someone within a group shifts his or her beliefs, others in the group feel restless, uneasy, and often even angry at the individual who is seeing the world from a different perspective. From the point of view of the group, the individual is not being realistic. What they mean, of course, is that he or she is not seeing reality in the same manner as the group. Indeed, for that individual, reality has now taken on a new and quite different meaning.

Thus my newfound philosophy was probably behind the differences Orna and I were having. It drove her to distraction that

I refused to admit that what we were attempting was an impossible mission, though I, too, doubted at times that we could pull it off.

ℯℯℯ

By the end of that day, the fourth of the excavation, the majority of the boat's interior had been cleared of overburden. Only a small portion of the hull remained covered. It was none too soon.

Dick arrived that evening.

Chapter 4

Galilean Seafaring
in the Gospels

And when he got into the boat, his disciples followed him. A windstorm arose on the sea, so great that the boat was being swamped by the waves; but he was asleep. And they went and woke him up, saying, "Lord, save us! We are perishing!"

Matthew 8:22–25

I have to confess, I was unprepared for the intense public interest generated by the boat. To some, the immediate connection between an ancient boat found in the Sea of Galilee and Jesus is self-evident. My only prior contact with the Gospels had been while taking an undergraduate course in Jewish history at the Hebrew University in Jerusalem. The possibility that the boat might date to the general historical period covered in the Gospels, as well as the "boat of Jesus" appellation given it by the media, quickly prompted me to learn more.

I was surprised to discover that not a single written word has come down to us from Jesus himself. Our knowledge of Jesus, his actions, and his words derives almost entirely from the accounts of others as recorded in the Gospels of the New Testament. The word *gospel* derives from the Old English word *godspel*, which means "good tale" or "good tidings." After Jesus's death, there must have existed compilations of stories which were kept by the early Judeo-Christian believers. We know that in antiquity there were many gospels recording the life and works and experiences of Jesus.[1] Most of these were considered heretical and were actively suppressed by the emergent church.[2] Only four gospels were accepted and canonized by church authorities. These are the Gospels of Matthew, Mark, Luke, and John. The first three follow a similar narrative and therefore are called the *Synoptic Gospels*. The Gospel of John takes a different viewpoint.

The Gospels are not biographical in the modern sense of the term: Entire periods of Jesus's life are missing from them. Imagine the life of Jesus as described in the Gospels as a play in five acts. Act I deals with the details of his birth and the flight to, and return from, Egypt. Act II, which encompasses his early childhood years, is entirely missing. In Act III, Jesus, already a youth twelve years of age, accompanies his parents on a Passover visit to the Holy Temple in Jerusalem. Act IV, which should cover his teenage years and his young adulthood until his ministry, is also absent.

Act V recounts the entire period of Jesus's ministry. It is primarily this part of the Gospels—in which the message of Jesus is set out—that profoundly influenced human history. With few exceptions, this act unfolded along the shores of the Kinneret and over her waters. And, even though Jesus's ministry is the main focus of all four Gospels, this period is telescoped into relatively few episodes.

When Jesus began his ministry, he left his home at Nazareth and came down to the shores of the Sea of Galilee. The majority of his ministry, at least as recorded in the Gospels, was spent tending to the simple Jewish folk, the *am ha'aretz* (literally, the "people of the land") who lived in the Jewish settlements that ringed the Kinneret, particularly at Capernaum on the northwest shore and at nearby Korazin and Bethsaida.[3]

While Jesus's message is universal, the setting in which it was delivered is most definitely a local one. That setting is the Sea of Galilee. As Twain mused:[4]

> One of the most astonishing things that have yet fallen under our observation is the exceedingly small portion of the earth from which sprang the now flourishing plant of Christianity. . . . Leaving out two or three short journeys of the Saviour, he spent his life, preached his Gospel, and performed his miracles within a compass no longer than an ordinary county in the United States. It is as much as I can do to comprehend this stupefying fact. How it wears a man out to have to read up a hundred pages of history every two or three miles. . . .

Despite its diminutive size, the Kinneret's economic importance was—and still is—considerable. Then, as now, the lake swarmed with a living supply of swimming and swarming protein packaged in silvery scales. Thus the Sea of Galilee was an important source for food that was both tasty and nutritional. Indeed legend has it that the Leviathan, which will feed the righteous in paradise, will have the taste of the fish of the Kinneret.[5]

Until quite recently, fishermen on the lake still employed the same methods and basically the same materials to harvest the same types of fish as those gathered by Jesus's disciples. Only with the advent of modern techniques and materials have these fishing traditions been broken.

In the 1960s, cotton thread in fishing nets was replaced by nylon, which is virtually invisible to fish. Nocturnal fishing techniques could thus be employed during daylight hours. Furthermore, the populations of some types of indigenous fish have declined, while new types of fish have been introduced into the lake.

> As he walked by the Sea of Galilee, he saw two brothers, Simon, who is called Peter, and Andrew his brother, casting a net into the sea—for they were fishermen. . . . As he went from there, he saw two other brothers, James son of Zebedee and his brother John, in the boat with their father Zebedee mending their nets, and he called them. (Matthew 4:18, 21)

The first Apostles were fishermen whom Jesus converted from catchers of fish into "fishers of men."[6] Jesus's parables were suited to their simple lifestyle and were taken from their daily life experiences, thus enabling them to understand and internalize his intended message.

It is not unexpected then, given both the location of Jesus's activity and the vocation of some of his closest disciples, that boats and Galilean seafaring figure prominently in the Gospels. Mendel Nun, who for many years toiled as a kibbutz fisherman on the lake, has used his practical knowledge to understand better the day-to-day reality of many of the references to fishing in the Gospels. He has published extensively on this subject and was a vital source of information for me.

While reviewing the Gospels, I found numerous references to boats. Sometimes they are being used for fishing or for passenger transport. These trips serve as a platform for the expression of beliefs and numinous experiences that are among the most cherished stories in the New Testament. There are also references to less common uses, such as when a boat was used as a podium from which Jesus could address the masses on shore.[7] The following few examples give a feeling for the nautical flavor of the Gospels.

🌊🌊🌊

"Again, the kingdom of heaven is like a net that was thrown into the sea and caught fish of every kind . . ." (Matthew 13:47)

It was only natural for Jesus to compare heaven to a seine net, with which his listeners were well familiar. Some of them had probably been out fishing with a seine net only recently. The seascape of seine nets spread out to dry along the shores of the lake was a view familiar to everyone in his audiences who came from the nearby villages.

Seine nets were still used in this century both on the Sea of Galilee and on the Mediterranean in Israel.[8] In recent times they could be over 400 meters (1300 feet) long, 2 meters (6.6 feet) high at the sides, widening in the center to 5–6 meters (20 feet). To man such nets required a crew of from five to twenty fishermen.

A seine net is used to surround and catch shoals of fish and draw them into shore. In Arabic it is known by the name *jarf*, while in Hebrew the net is called a *cherem*.[9] The Greek name for it is *segena*, from which its English name *seine* derives. In the Parable of the Net, Jesus referred specifically to the *segena*.

In fishing with the seine net, a boat is used for only part of the process, the catch being pulled in by men on shore. Thus the majority of the work with the seine net is on land, and the boat spends much of the time beached or riding at anchor. In the Talmud this is termed *leha'amid et hasefina*, "to stand the boat." The fishermen of Tiberias in particular were known for their use of this type of net and are referred to as *charmei Teveriah*, "the seiners of Tiberias."

> ". . . when it was full, they drew it ashore, sat down, and put the good into baskets but threw out the bad." (Matthew 13:48)

"Good" fish? "Bad" fish?

Jesus was describing a scene familiar to all his listeners in order to illustrate his message about the kingdom of heaven—where angels would separate the evil from the righteous. As Mendel has explained this parable, while Jews were permitted to eat kosher fish (ones with scales and fins), any nonkosher fish (such as scaleless catfish) were cast back into the lake.

ᏋᏋᏋ

> ". . . go to the sea and cast a hook; take the first fish that comes up; and when you open its mouth you will find a coin . . ." (Matthew 17:27)

When the Second Holy Temple stood in Jerusalem, every adult Jewish man of twenty years and over was required to pay a half-shekel, or didrachma, in Temple tax each year.[10] This tax was collected in the month of Adar, roughly equivalent to February–March, and covered general expenses and the cost of the burnt offerings made daily in the name of the people. Each community collected its own taxes and then forwarded them to Jerusalem.

When Simon Peter was approached by the collectors of the Temple tax in Capernaum, Jesus instructed him to go down to the lake and cast a hook into the lake. The first fish that he caught would have in its mouth a *stater*, the equivalent of two *didrachmas*, with which Simon Peter could pay the tax for both of them.

Today, visitors to the Kinneret regularly enjoy eating St. Peter's fish, named in memory of that Apostle's famous catch. This fish's Hebrew name, *amnun*, is a combination of two words, *am* ("nurse") and *nun* ("fish"), and it refers to the fish's curious habit of carrying its fertilized eggs in its mouth until they hatch. The fish's Arabic name, *musht* ("comb"), refers to the fish's comblike dorsal fin.

The "St. Peter's fish" label is so indelibly attached to this fish that I was surprised to learn from Mendel that the fish had bogus credentials.

"The St. Peter's fish is not the type of fish that St. Peter would have caught," he said.

"How can you possibly know that?" I asked.

Mendel smiled. He knew he had me "hooked." "The *musht* is a plankton eater. It can't be caught with a hook and line."

"Then why is it called the St. Peter's fish?"

"The fish St. Peter caught was probably what we call a *binit*. The *binit* prey on small fry and sardines and therefore can be caught with a hook. There are three different species of that fish in the Kinneret. It's a member of the carp family and, when cooked, makes excellent 'gefilte fish.' But it does not fry well."

"So?"

"In the early fourth century, the emperor Constantine the Great adopted Christianity as the new state religion of the Roman Empire. During the following centuries, a brisk tourist trade evolved as Christian pilgrims came to visit the locations that they had read about in the Gospels. The Sea of Galilee became a major tourist attraction to which Christian pilgrims flocked. And where there are tourists, there are innkeepers and restaurateurs.

"The reason that the *musht* was chosen as the fish traditionally identified with St. Peter," Mendel said, "is simply because it fries well and can be prepared quickly and tastily for visitors. Therefore the restaurateurs catering to the many Christian pilgrims who came to visit the holy sites around the Kinneret gave the name to the fish which could be prepared quickly and deliciously for their guests. In other words the best-tasting fish caught the name."

🌊🌊🌊

> One day he got into a boat with his disciples, and he said to them, "Let us go across to the other side of the lake." So they put out . . . (Luke 8:22)

Boats, presumably those belonging to the Apostles or to other disciples, were used for transporting Jesus and his followers around the lake. This was probably a common occurrence along the lake, the Kinneret serving as a transport hub for passengers as well as goods.

The Gospels relate how Jesus sailed with his disciples from Capernaum to the other (eastern) side of the lake. While all three Synoptic Gospels relate this event with minor variations, the locations given by the Gospel writers for where the boat made land are rendered as the "land of the Gadarenes," the "land of the Gerasanes," or the "land of the Gergesenes."[11]

Upon landing on a desolate and for the most part uninhabited shore, the group was accosted by a man possessed by a band of demons, named "Legion." The Gospels relate that Jesus banished the demons to a large herd of pigs that were pasturing on the nearby slopes; the possessed pigs immediately stampeded down into the lake and drowned in its waters. Witnessing this, the pig herders—who must have been more than a little stunned and frightened—ran to notify the local city folks.

Upon arriving at the scene, the citizens saw that the pig herders had not made up the bizarre story. There was the possessed man, clothed now, sitting quite calmly at Jesus's feet, while the lake's shore must have been strewn with dead pigs:

> Then the whole town came out to meet Jesus; and when they saw him, they begged him to leave their neighborhood. And after getting into a boat he crossed the sea . . . (Matthew 8:34; 9:1)

Instead of expressing joy at the miraculous recovery of the demonic, the townspeople urged Jesus to leave their shores and go elsewhere, for they were greatly afraid. This local reaction to the casting out of demons might seem surprising. Why the cold shoulder? Of what were the locals afraid?

Their attitude may have had to do with economic considerations. An estimated 2,000 head of livestock had been lost in exchange for the healing of one demented person.[12] Perhaps the locals felt that they could ill afford such cures, no matter how miraculous.

The herd of pigs is in itself a clue to the location where the event took place. Grazing pigs could have been found only on the southeastern side of the Sea of Galilee, where the lake was flanked by the pagan cities of Hippos (Sussita) and Gadara (Hammat Gader). The rest of the lake was dotted by settlements inhabited primarily by Jews, who considered the pig "unclean."

The site traditionally associated with this story is named Kursi. It lies not far from Mendel's home at Kibbutz Ein Gev. The ancient site came to light as a result of road work. While heavy equipment created a path, Mendel kept an eye open to the changes taking place, watchful that no antiquities might be harmed. During one of his frequent forays to the site, Mendel noticed that the bulldozers had revealed the tops of some stone walls and large quantities of pottery sherds dating to the Byzantine period. He immediately notified the Golan Archaeological Staff Officer.

As is so often the case in Israel, the past took precedence over the present. Work on the road halted abruptly, and Dr. Vasilios Tzaferis was dispatched from the Department of Antiquities to carry out a rescue excavation.[13]

The excavation revealed that had the road been laid down as planned, it would have crossed directly over the courtyard of a monastery, obliterating part of its church. The road was deflected and now skirts the site.

The monastery at Kursi was apparently built to minister to the needs of the many pilgrims who visited the lake during the Byzantine period and wished to visit the location of the "Miracle of the Swine." It was first established at Kursi in the fifth century and continued to be inhabited for the next three centuries.

Vasilios uncovered many beautiful mosaics of flora and fauna which still grace the ruins. Unfortunately, at some time in the past, the heavy hand of the iconoclast destroyed many of the animals represented in the mosaics. Near the gates, gaming boards, consisting of rows of small shallow circles, were cut into the pavement slabs, probably by bored guards attempting to pass the time while on watch. I have seen the same game played in Sinai by Bedouin, who make the gaming board in the sand.

ℰℰℰ

When Jesus had crossed again in the boat to the other side, a great crowd gathered around him; and he was by the sea. (Mark 5:21)

Upon returning from the east side of the lake, Jesus and his boatload of followers went "to his own city" of Capernaum. The boat must have docked in the city's harbor, for Mark relates that Jesus was engulfed immediately by a large crowd of people seeking his assistance while "he was by the sea."

During the first century AD, the Kinneret was ringed by a series of small fishermen's harbors which protected the boats from bad weather.[14] The first harbors were found at Kursi and Migdal in the 1970s by divers from the Underwater Exploration Society of Israel. Subsequently Mendel, who is not a diver, located additional harbor facilities during periods of drought. The most recent discovery is the harbor at Tiberias, which is also the largest on the lake. There are now a total of fourteen known Kinneret harbors that date to the Roman–Byzantine period.

These harbors are not uniform in either shape or size. Each had to take into account the waves that most affected that specific location. They were also, of course, dependent on the financial resources of the constituent communities.

For the most part, the harbors consist of a stone breakwater that protects the enclosed area from the direction of the most dangerous winds on that particular coast. Along the shore opposite the enclosed area, a promenade allowed clear access to the harbor.

The harbor at Capernaum has a unique and strange design, perhaps resulting from its extended period of use: The city was inhabited from the second century BC to the tenth century AD. Apparently it was built in phases over its long history. The harbor's main element was a promenade that extended over 800 meters (0.5 mile) of shorefront property. Along its length were positioned piers which jutted out into the lake. These would have protected boats from the southerly wind. Three of the piers were shaped like triangles pointing into the lake from the promenade.

Apparently during the time of Jesus's ministry, a customs office was located somewhere along this shore. Here new arrivals paid their tolls to Herod Antipas's tax collectors. These officials were reviled by the Jewish inhabitants, who saw them as collaborators in an excessively harsh and corrupt political system. From among these tax collectors came one of the Apostles.[15]

> "When it is evening, you say, 'It will be fair weather, for the sky is red.' And in the morning, 'It will be stormy today, for the sky is red and threatening.' You know how to interpret the appearance of the sky, but you cannot interpret the signs of the times." (Matthew 16:2–3)

Jesus's knowledge of weather lore is another subtle indication of his familiarity with the seafaring life. The warning in Jesus's forecast is of a *storm*, which is the specific fear of the sailor, not the farmer. Sailors have rendered this into rhyme:

> Red sky in the morning,
> Sailors take warning.
> Red sky at night,
> Sailors delight.

There is meteorological wisdom in the rhyme, for in the northern horse latitudes weather flow is generally westerly. A red sunset indicates that the incoming weather is dust-laden and therefore dry, not stormy.

> And leaving the crowd behind, they took him with them in the boat, just as he was. Other boats were with him. A great windstorm arose, and the waves beat into the boat, so that the boat was already being swamped. (Mark 4:36–37)

As is abundantly clear when one reads the Gospels, the Sea of Galilee can be fickle, and the possibility of sudden and dangerous storms exists. In antiquity, sailing on the Mediterranean Sea was seasonal, limited for the most part to the summer months, when storms were rare and the skies were clear. Because of the relatively short distances in the Kinneret, however, seafaring continued throughout the winter months. There is a daily order to the winds during the summer and fall around the Sea of Galilee. In the winter months, the weather system is more chaotic, and the winds have a tendency to shift, blowing first from one direction and then the other. It is also during the winter that the *sharkia* comes howling down the Golan Heights to stir up the Kinneret, raising waves that pound the western side of the lake. *Sharkias* come at a frequency of about once every two weeks and generally last for about three days.

ꞓ ꞓ ꞓ

Is not this the carpenter . . . ? Is not this the carpenter's son?
(Mark 6:3; Matthew 13:55)

The greatest revelation during my study of the Gospels, though, was that—irrespective of the media hype which was distilled into the public outcry of our boat's being "*the* boat of Jesus"—no *one* boat could be connected with Jesus. He never spoke of "my" boat, nor do the Gospel writers refer to "his" boat. Jesus used many boats, it appears.

Of course, there is one other strand that connects Jesus to the wooden boats on the Sea of Galilee: He was a carpenter by trade, as was Joseph before him. Jesus could have appreciated the woodwork and craftsmanship that went into the boats that sailed the Kinneret.

Indeed, as excavation on the boat continued, and more of her timbers came into view, I found myself wondering increasingly about what those timbers might reveal about the boat herself and about the persons who had built—and sailed—her so long ago.

Chapter 5

"Yep, It's an Old Boat"

The fortunate man, in my opinion, is he to whom the gods have granted the power either to do something which is worth recording or to write what is worth reading, and most fortunate of all is the man who can do both.

From a letter to Tacitus
PLINY THE YOUNGER[1]

There was no question in my mind, when forming the expedition's team, that Dick Steffy should study the boat while we were excavating it. I would have settled for one of his students—or "Steffy clones," as we sometimes called them—but I was truly delighted that Dick himself was able to accept Avi's official invitation.

I had first met Dick during a visit he made to Israel in the early 1980s. I was immediately taken by his quiet and good-natured ways. These mask a reservoir of knowledge and an understanding of ancient ship architecture that runs deep and wide and is second to none.

Soon after my first encounter with Dick, he was back in Israel. This time he had come to work on a truly outstanding discovery. The late Yehoshua Ramon, while diving near the ancient harbor of Athlit, had discovered a huge bronze waterline ram, the size of a picnic table, probably dating to the early second century BC. Although ancient history, in the form of sea battles (like the one depicted dramatically but inaccurately in the movie *Ben Hur*), was often written by such rams, the one found at Athlit is the only ram known to date to have come down to us from antiquity.

Yehoshua had found the ram still attached to timbers of the ship to which it had belonged; these held a gold mine of knowledge for learning about ancient ship construction. That is, they held that *potential* if someone could make sense of the wooden jigsaw puzzle. Dr. Elisha Linder of Haifa University, who had taken over research on the Athlit ram, asked Dick to study its timbers.

It was while he was studying the ram that I got to know Dick better. I would find Dick toiling away quietly, trying to make sense of the ram's timbers. What most impressed me was the comfort and amiable curiosity with which he approached his object of inquiry. He was not content simply to define what he was seeing, although this he did admirably. While he was carefully cataloging the minutiae of the interconnecting timbers, Dick was looking much further. I had the distinct impression that he was staring *through* the ship's timbers to the shipwrights who had built her. He wished to understand *how* the builders had originally gone about constructing the bow of that particular ship many centuries ago and encasing it in half a ton of bronze, thus forming a projectile that was the outstanding military naval weapon of its age. But together with this, he was also trying to discover *why* the shipwrights had built it in this particular manner and not in any other.

I came to realize that what Dick was doing—what he was *really* doing—was probing the minds and entering the thoughts of the nameless artisans who had fashioned the ship over 21 centuries earlier. It was uncanny how he seemed to reach right into the thoughts of those distant, yet for him strangely *near*, shipwrights.

Dick had not always been a reconstructor of ships. He had a deep love of ships and the sea, however, and in his spare time he built scale ship models. Over time he became convinced that much information was contained in the timbers of the ancient hulls, which the nascent discipline of nautical archaeology was beginning to excavate. He also felt that research models could be a tool for learning more about how the ships had been put together.

Such models require the modern researcher to replicate the exact actions of the original shipwright, thus explaining the process. In one case, while building one of his first research models in his basement, Dick forced a plank onto the hull. That night he and his wife, Lucille, heard a suspicious noise downstairs. When Dick, flashlight and bat in hand, went to investigate, he found that the noise had been made by the plank popping straight off the model.

"The model was 'telling' me," Dick later explained, "that I had not built it right."

Prior to 1960, "underwater archaeology" usually meant little more than divers, with scant if any archaeological experience,

Professor J. Richard "Dick" Steffy.

plundering shipwrecks for their artifacts. The first excavation of a shipwreck using modern archaeological methodology was undertaken by Dr. George F. Bass in 1960, when he excavated the remains of a Late Bronze Age merchantman that had foundered sometime around 1200 BC off Cape Gelidonya on the southern coast of Turkey.

At Cape Gelidonya, George and his team demonstrated the viability of carrying out the excavation of a shipwreck underwater to the same high standards expected of a land excavation. In doing so, he had initiated a new scientific discipline: nautical archaeology.

Dick met George, then a newly tenured professor in the Classics Department at the University of Pennsylvania, and Dr. Fred van Doorninck. The two young scholars were excavating together the seventh-century AD wreck of a ship that had foundered on a rocky island named Yassiada, off the southwest coast of Turkey.

Then, one evening in the early 1970s, Dick went to a lecture given by another young nautical archaeologist. Professor Michael Katzev reported on a fourth-century BC Greek merchantman that he had excavated near Kyrenia off the northwest coast of Cyprus. Michael had raised the hull in pieces from the seabed, and the timbers were now being conserved in the old Crusader castle at Kyrenia. Later, over cups of coffee and rough sketches drawn on napkins, the two men talked well into the night as to how the hull might be reconstructed.

The outcome of the conversation was that ultimately Michael asked Dick to reconstruct the hull of the Kyrenia ship. Dick put his business on hold and moved to Cyprus while he slowly put together the pieces of the ancient hull and tried to comprehend the logic of its construction.

Eventually, George founded the Institute of Nautical Archaeology, more commonly called by its acronym, INA. Dick threw in his future with George, Michael, and several others to become one of INA's founding staff members. Then in 1976, Texas A&M University invited INA to affiliate with it and to establish a graduate course of studies in a nautical archaeology program. Dick formulated a course of study in ship reconstruction to teach to his students, thus actually creating the new discipline of ancient ship reconstruction. Dick created a ship reconstruction laboratory, shortened to the ship lab, and in it he taught his students how to record ships and with them built research models to understand better the shipwrecks excavated by INA.

As word of Dick's ability spread, he was invited to advise on projects around the world—in Turkey, Israel, Greece, England, Canada, and the United States. In the early 1980s an invitation was extended to Dick to study a particularly intriguing find in Italy, one that dated to the first century AD.

ℓℓℓ

Vespasian was the tenth emperor of the Roman Empire, which he ruled for ten years. During that time he brought order to the chaos of the civil war which had brought him to the throne. History would view him as one of the more capable emperors to have ruled Rome.

Seutonius tells us that Vespasian had a wry sense of humor and that even after he became emperor he never put on airs. He retained this sense of humor even on his deathbed. Mocking the Roman practice of deifying their emperors after death, he was heard to exclaim near the end, "Dear me! I must be turning into a god." Shortly thereafter, Vespasian, muttering that a Roman emperor should die standing on his feet, rose to his and promptly did so on June 24, AD 79.

Titus, Vespasian's son, ruled after him. Titus's short reign was remarkable for the series of natural disasters that occurred during his watch. These included a fire that destroyed much of Rome and one of the most severe plagues in Roman history. For us, living in the twentieth century, however, the most memorable disaster under Titus occurred almost immediately after he took office. Located on the Italian Campanian Coast near Naples, Mount Vesuvius erupted slightly after noon on August 24. Within 20 hours, the Roman cities of Pompeii and Herculaneum had ceased to exist, having been obliterated under meters of volcanic debris.[2]

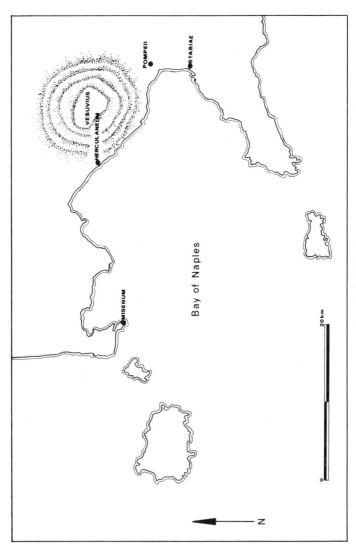

The Bay of Naples.

Archaeologists love a good natural catastrophe. There are few situations in which the past is so suddenly frozen in time, waiting to be revealed. And in the category of ancient natural catastrophes, Pompeii and Herculaneum are hard to beat.

As a boy, I visited Pompeii when the passenger ship on which my parents and I were sailing to Israel docked for a day at Naples. I remember marveling at the antiquity—and the remarkable preservation—of the city's buildings, wall paintings, and monuments. But it was the plaster casts that really held my attention.

In 1771 the discovery in Pompeii of the skeleton of a young girl whose breasts had left their impression in the volcanic ash caused an overnight sensation. Then, in 1864, Giuseppe Fiorelli, the head excavator of Pompeii at that time, realized that the mysterious "hollows" his crews had encountered during digging had been formed by the decomposition of the bodies of the dead buried under the ashen debris. He had his workers inject a type of hard-setting liquid plaster into the cavities, thus capturing the imprint the bodies had left in the hard-packed volcanic ash.

Soon after the eruption had subsided, parties of searchers dug down into Pompeii. Whether they did so as thieves in search of loot or as rescue parties in search of survivors we do not know. Some of these searchers left evocative inscriptions. "Sodom and Gomorrah," wrote one who was, presumably, a Jew or early Christian, while another left the chilling observation, "There were fifty of them, still lying where they had been."[3]

Nothing had prepared me for viewing those plaster casts. They were my first visual encounter with death. Individuals lay, as they had fallen, in every possible pose. Here a woman lay on her stomach, vainly trying to cover her face. There a man crouched, his back pushed up against a wall. In one glass case, a dog lay on its back, as it had died. Despite the many centuries that separated its lifetime from my own, its contorted final agony was still readily apparent to my 12-year-old eyes. I stood transfixed by that dog. I remember thinking, "This is what hell must look like." My parents finally had to drag me away to keep up with the tour.

At the time of the Vesuvius eruption, Pliny the Elder, a close friend of the recently deceased Vespasian, was in charge of the

Roman fleet stationed at Misenum, which is situated nearby at the northern end of the Bay of Naples. His scholarly interest piqued by the unusual cloud rising in the shape of a many-branched pine tree in the distance, Pliny determined to get a closer look. His nephew, Pliny the Younger, who was 17 years old at the time, watched the cataclysm from Misenum and gives us a unique and chilling eye-witness report of the event in which his uncle lost his life.

The elder Pliny had a boat readied and was about to embark when he received a communication.[4]

> As he was leaving the house he was handed a message from Rectina, wife of Tascius whose house was at the foot of the mountain, so that escape was impossible except by boat. She was terrified by the danger threatening her and implored him to rescue her from her fate. He changed his plans, and what he had begun in a spirit of inquiry he completed as a hero. He gave orders for the warships to be launched and went on board himself with the intention of bringing help to many more people besides Rectina, for this lovely stretch of coast was thickly populated.

Pliny never did reach *that* disaster area. Ash, pumice, and black stones rained from the sky as he came closer, and the waters became shallow. He found his path to the coast obstructed by pyroclastic flows from the volcano. Realizing that he could not reach Rectina, Pliny determined to assist another friend named Pomponianus, who lived at Stabiae, to the south. As the wind was blowing in that direction, Pliny brought his ship with ease to Stabiae. Leaving, however, was going to prove more difficult.

At Stabiae he met his terrified friend, who had already loaded his possessions on a ship in the hope that the wind would shift and allow him an escape. The younger Pliny relates how dark night now descended, offset only by the vast sheets of lightning that flashed around the mountain. The elder Pliny, trying to calm his friend, dismissed these as peasant bonfires or houses set afire by the mountain.

Pliny was an obese 56-year-old at the time. Tired by the day's adventures, he retired to sleep, snoring loudly as ash and pumice rained down. So that Pliny would not be caught in the room as the volcanic debris piled up, he was awakened and, together with Pomponianus and his household, escaped the buildings that, because of the accompanying earth tremors, had started to shake and shimmy as if their walls had been constructed of jello.

Making their way down to the coast with pillows tied to their heads to protect them from the ungodly rain of ash and pumice, they reached the shore only to find that the sea was too wild to attempt an escape. Pliny, who was prone to a sore throat, lay down on a sheet and asked repeatedly for cold water to drink. When the approaching flames and the stink of noxious fumes forced the group to move on, they roused him. Supported by two servants, he stood up for a moment but then suddenly collapsed. The others left him behind and retreated. Two days later his body was discovered "intact and uninjured, still fully clothed and looking more like sleep than death."[5]

Herculaneum is somewhat less well known than her larger sister-city. While Pompeii lies somewhat inland, on the southern slopes of Vesuvius, Herculaneum is situated to the west and fronts the sea, on the Bay of Naples. And as it now turns out, it was to the sea that many of the inhabitants of Herculaneum turned in their attempt to escape the mountain's wrath.

As opposed to the hundreds of bodies—or their impressions—found at Pompeii, until fairly recently only a few dozen skeletons had been found at Herculaneum. It had long been thought, therefore, that most of the Herculaneum's inhabitants had succeeded in escaping.

Not so.

Recent excavations at the seawall of Herculaneum revealed a series of chambers. Originally these were probably for storing fishing boats, but for the past 19 centuries they had been storing dozens of skeletons belonging to inhabitants of Herculaneum who had gone down to the sea seeking safety and had met with death instead. These individuals had been felled, suddenly, by hurricane-force avalanches of glowing superhot gases and volcanic debris as they tried to escape.

One chamber by the sea contained what appears to be members of a single household—perhaps like that of Pomponianus—trying to flee the Tophet. The group included seven adults, four children, and a baby, who was found cradled by one of the "adults," apparently a 14-year-old slave girl.

In the chamber next door, Italian archaeologists uncovered about 40 more human skeletons, together with that of a horse, in helter-skelter positions, suggestive of panic and fright. And in the next chamber, 26 skeletons lay as if, one observer pointed out, they were floating down the river of death.

Voices can be added to this tableau. Pliny the Younger, describing to Tacitus his own escape from far-off Misenum on the morning of August 25, writes:[6]

> . . . Darkness fell, not the dark of a moonless or cloudy night, but as if the lamp had been put out in a closed room. You could hear the shrieks of women, the wailing of infants, and the shouting of men; some were calling their parents, others their children or their wives, trying to recognize them by their voices. People bewailed their own fate or that of their relatives, and there were some who prayed for death in their terror of dying. Many besought the aid of the gods, but still more imagined there were no gods left and that the universe was plunged into eternal darkness for evermore. . . . I could boast that not a groan or cry of fear escaped me in these perils, had I not derived some poor consolation in my mortal lot from the belief that the whole world was dying with me and I with it.

In the summer of 1982, Italian archaeologists discovered a boat overturned on the beach at Herculaneum. Apparently it had been tossed over and over, like tumbleweed, by the powerful and hot volcanic winds before coming to rest upside-down on the sand. Perhaps it was one of those in which the Roman refugees had hoped to flee. If so, nothing came of it. The boat is now made of charcoal. It had been burnt, quite literally, to a crisp by the fiery avalanches.

Dick Steffy was invited to study the Herculaneum boat.

"The fact that it was found inverted meant that much of the upper parts of the hull—which are rarely found on Mediterranean shipwrecks—were preserved, although in an extremely fragile state," Dick said.

He was truly excited about studying that boat. She was a beautiful vessel with a graceful sweep to her. Much painstaking labor had gone into preparing the timbers.

Because of the manner in which she had landed, Dick could study only the hull's exterior. Even so, it was clear that the boat was long, narrow, and lightly built. She had an overall length of about 9 meters (29.5 feet), a maximum beam of 2.4 meters (7.9 feet), and an amidships depth of 85 centimeters (2.8 feet). On the hull's exterior Dick discerned an irregular series of bronze nails and treenails; pronounced *trunnels*, these are roughly cylindrical pieces of hardwood which can be driven through joining timbers to connect them. This pattern suggested to Dick that the boat's frames were attached in alternating floor and half-frames, a framing pattern common during the classical period.

Dick thought that some worked timbers found near the boat might indicate that boat- or shipbuilding activity had been going on somewhere along that beach. It was difficult for him to determine how old the boat had been when it was incinerated by the inferno.

"There were no visible wood-eating marine toredo worm holes," Dick said, "so the boat was probably either new or had been kept out of the water when not in use."

"When I first saw the Herculaneum boat," Dick said, "I remember thinking, what a marvelous craftsman must have built it, because there aren't any scarfs [joints] in the planks. The planking chosen for the boat was excellent. Each strake was constructed from a single plank. So I thought, 'Gee, this fellow is great at selecting wood.'"

ᕫᕫᕫ

"What a marvelous find," Dick had thought when he first read a notice in his Texas newspaper concerning the discovery of an ancient boat on the shores of the Sea of Galilee. The vessel in Israel had piqued Dick's curiosity, particularly because of his recent study of the Herculaneum boat. This made him a soft touch when a few days later he received the telephone call from Avi and me inviting him to study our boat.

"The Herculaneum boat was a beautifully crafted little vessel from the center of the Roman Empire, and here was a wonderful opportunity to see what was happening at the same time in the Roman provinces—in the boondocks," Dick told me later.

Dick's plane landed at Ben Gurion airport in the late afternoon of Wednesday, February 19: the fourth day of the excavation. As the plane taxied up to the apron, he was amused to hear his name being called over the speaker system. The United States Embassy in Israel had rolled out the red carpet for him and had arranged for a limousine to meet him on the tarmac.

"It was a very nice way to arrive in Israel," Dick remembers. "We just walked through customs and waved at everybody."

The limousine whisked him off to the embassy, and then Karen drove him to Ginosar, filling him in on the way on the latest developments at the excavation. When we pulled in at Ginosar, we said our hellos over cups of coffee at the kibbutz guest house. Then, forgetting his jet lag, Dick changed into a pair of rubber boots and we drove out to the site, the jeep bumping and sliding over the water-worn stones.

Prior to Dick's arrival, I had explained to the staff and volunteers what it is that a ship reconstructor does. He not only studies the structure of a ship but interprets clues that can provide an entire picture of its birth, its life, and its demise. I had described Dick in glowing terms. He would see where the workers had sharpened their tools and whether their tools were worn or new.

"Dick reads wood the way you or I would read a newspaper," I had explained to them.

The evening was dark and moist. Dick descended into the excavation pit alone and, in the warm, glowing light of the gas fishermen's lamps, began to walk slowly around the hull, stopping to examine it. The planks on the hanging platform had been removed to give him an open view of the parts of the boat that had been cleared of the mud. Every few steps, he would bend over, supporting himself by putting his hands on his knees, to examine this or that detail of the boat. As opposed to the Herculaneum boat, where Dick could view only the exterior of the hull, on our boat he could see only the hull's interior.

Everyone there stood watching and wondering. What was he seeing in the timbers? What would the wood reveal to him? A palpable air of expectancy hung over the site. All eyes followed Dick as he made his rounds. Finally satisfied, he finished, wiped some mud from his hands, and walked back to us. There was absolute silence.

"Well, what do you think?" I asked.

"Yep," he said, "it's an old boat."

🌊🌊🌊

Years later, I asked Dick for his impressions that first evening at Ginosar.

"You had a lot of lights on it, I remember," he told me. "Didn't take but a few seconds to recognize it as a Roman period boat. I had some thoughts, but I don't like to say things unless I can prove them.

"Any boat or ship impresses me. First of all, it was ancient technology. This quaint little boat sitting there on the shores of the Sea of Galilee: It was very impressive. I remember thinking that this boat was maybe the age of the Herculaneum boat, or perhaps a century earlier—but not that much earlier.

"It was obvious that it was an ancient boat. I could tell that by the way the frames were laid and the way the planking was joined edge-to-edge. Obviously it belonged to some period in antiquity, but it was not quite like anything that had been recorded in the Mediterranean. There was a method of putting the planks together that was not familiar to me, one that probably applied only to boats in the Kinneret. And the frames were rather crooked and crude. I'd never seen anything quite like that.

"It was also very complete for a hull in the Mediterranean

area, where normally hulls are not preserved much above the bottom or the turn of the bilge."

What Dick had seen that night was a mortise-and-tenon joining system that was perhaps a little later than the Kyrenia shipwreck. At Kyrenia the keel has rabbets (grooves) cut down either side to take the garboards, the strakes attached directly to the keel at either side. As the garboards go in at about a 70-degree angle to the keel, the pegs locking the tenons are drilled *horizontally* into the *vertical* sides of the keel at the mortise-and-tenon joints.

Dick could see part of the keel. He saw the heads of tenon pegs going down the top of the keel. And the pegs were a little larger than at Kyrenia. He had seen the same pattern at Herculaneum also; indeed it had been recorded for numerous first-century Roman boats and ships.

"On the Kinneret boat," Dick explained, "the garboards' edges butted directly against the side of the keel horizontally, you see, without a rabbet."

One peg of each mortise-and-tenon joint went through the garboard. As the tenon itself was going in horizontally, the other peg—the one that held the tenon to the keel—was driven into a hole drilled *vertically* from the upper surface of the keel: "Now that is something that was not recorded before the second century BC. But mostly it's first-century—either side."

He could also see the alternating framing plan of floor timbers and half frames: "That framing pattern goes with mortise-and-tenon joinery in the Mediterranean and appears already on the Kyrenia ship, although it may have started earlier. It continued at least till the third century AD."

These constructional details put the boat in a period of several centuries, as did other attributes, like planking scarfs and the curved stern: "There were a number of indications to make me go to bed that night thinking that the boat was first-century one way or the other."

Dick had been cautious that night. This was the Sea of Galilee, and everything he had studied had been in the Mediterranean. Perhaps there was a difference in this body of water, perhaps distinct traditions. He couldn't be sure.

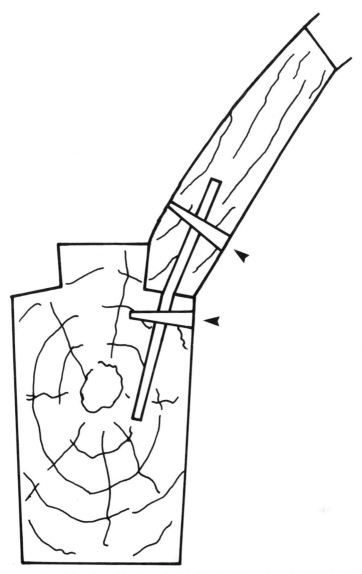

Cross-sectional drawing of the Kyrenia ship's keel and a garboard amidships. The locking pegs were driven *horizontally* into the *vertical* sides of the keel and garboard strakes.

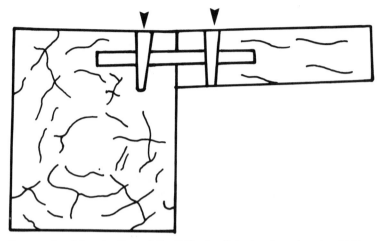

Cross-sectional drawing through the Galilee boat's keel and a garboard amidships. The pegs locking the mortise-and-tenon joints were driven *vertically* into the keel's *horizontal* surface.

The next morning Avi drove down from Jerusalem to Ginosar to greet the visiting scholar. Avi, it turned out, had clearly been harboring some doubts as to whether the boat was indeed ancient. There was no one else in Israel whom he could have asked for a second opinion on ancient ship construction, and obviously, were the boat to be of modern vintage, the Department of Antiquities would have been highly embarrassed.

This must have placed enormous pressure on him. So, as soon as the introductions were over and he had thanked Dick for coming to our aid on such short notice, Avi came to the point. But instead of asking whether the boat was ancient, he asked Dick, "Could this boat be modern?"

Dick contemplated for a minute. He tried to answer *that specific question* as best he could. "Well, I guess it *could* be modern."

Avi's face suddenly turned ashen.

"But that would be *really* interesting. I don't know anywhere on earth that mortise-and-tenon construction has continued down to our times."

An excruciatingly painful expression came over Avi's face. He looked as if he was about to have a heart attack.

"But this boat is ancient," Dick continued quickly.

Avi's sigh of relief was audible.

"I respected Avi for asking that," Dick told me later. "He was being conservative, as one should be. There were enough rumors circulating about that boat."

Indeed, the media hype around the boat amazed Dick. He avoided the media people and photographers like the plague. Even Danny managed to get only a few photographs of him.

I knew that Dick was a Christian and active in his church and wondered out loud how he felt about being involved in this project.

"It went through my mind that this boat might be the type mentioned in the Bible," he explained. "But you see, to me the Bible is sending a message, so that the stories of Galilee don't have to do with the boats or the fishing or anything else. It's the message behind that presentation that is important to the Christian.

"The boat may let us imagine more vividly what went on in that period. I don't look at it as do some of those people around here, as a symbol of worship. To me it's just another piece of ancient technology. I don't connect the two. I consider it a contribution to biblical history, not a holy icon."

Despite the pressure of the excavation, I took every opportunity during Dick's short stay with us to ply him with questions about what he was seeing. These conversations were an education in themselves.

At first, Dick held a poor opinion of the builder who had constructed our boat. It seemed that he could do no right in Dick's eyes.

"To me it looks like slipshod workmanship," he said. "The boatwright was doing a lot of patching. Look how some frames are nailed to the keel, and others are not. And look how narrow the planks are! That is really unusual. Why would any boatwright use strakes that narrow?"

Our boat was almost the same size as the Herculaneum boat. But what a difference! The Kinneret boat seemed to be made up entirely of a crazy-quilt patchwork construction. He pointed out to me frames—some of which still had their bark on them—which sprang from the hull, leaving wide gaps.

"The person who built this boat had no idea of what he was doing. He's using all the wrong materials for the purposes he's putting them to."

Dick seemed to take the whole thing somewhat personally. I had the distinct impression that first day that he felt physically *uncomfortable* with that ancient boatwright—as if there was some kind of guilt through association—and that he was personally responsible for the vessel's embarrassing construction. I would occasionally notice Dick out of the corner of my eye shaking his head, almost in despair, at some unusual detail or other.

It did not take long, however, for Dick to change his mind and gain respect for that long-ago boatwright.

"I was wrong," he told me with a big smile that same afternoon. I had never seen anybody so happy to admit an error. Dick was beaming. He looked positively *relieved*.

"The boatwright who put this boat together knew exactly what he was doing!"

"He did?"

"Yes, *but he was using inferior materials*, you see."

I didn't.

Dick motioned to Danny, who was "stringing" the hull nearby. "If only half the strings that Danny is putting on the hull are actual planking seams, then it still must have been a painful experience for this boatbuilder. Think of all the additional mortise-and-tenon joints he would have had to make. Or are we looking at lots and lots of repairs? Either way, you're looking at something totally different than what I saw at Herculaneum.

"If the Herculaneum boat is a Ferrari," he continued, "then

this boat is a pickup truck." And then, more to himself than to me, he added quietly, "We sure are a long way from Rome."

Dick showed me an already slender plank that narrowed to almost a splinter: "Look here. He's using *recycled timber*. Planks this narrow, with all the joinery they have on their edges and ends, are something you just don't see in normal Mediterranean construction. I think in the planking he was making do with some secondhand materials stripped from older vessels. You see, in order for him to reuse planks from a previous boat, he had to cut away the mortise-and-tenon joint scars. That's probably why the planks are so narrow. I even wonder . . ."

"Wonder what?"

"Hmmm. I wonder. Some of these planks are so slender that he may not have put them on one at a time. Our boatwright may have built up a regular-sized plank by attaching two or three of these narrow-sized planks together with mortise-and-tenon joints before actually attaching the 'reconstituted' full-sized plank to the hull."

And then he added, "But don't quote me on that. It's just a hunch."

I assured him that I would not.

"How could you tell whether narrow planks were placed on the hull one at a time or as a composite plank?" I asked.

One way to determine this, Dick explained to me, would be to see whether the mortise-and-tenon joints at the planking scarfs are perpendicular to the *scarf edges*. He sketched a drawing that looked like the one on page 144.

That would mean that the planks were attached to each other before being placed on the hull.

"On the other hand, if the joints are perpendicular to the *plank edges*, then they were probably attached separately to the hull," Dick said and drew another sketch like that on page 145.

"But that," he said, "will take a considerable amount of study and access to both sides of the hull. That is one question—of many—which will have to be answered by whoever studies the boat after it comes out of conservation."

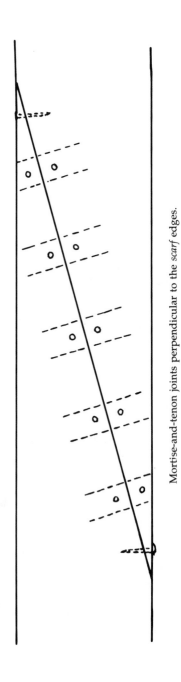

Mortise-and-tenon joints perpendicular to the *scarf* edges.

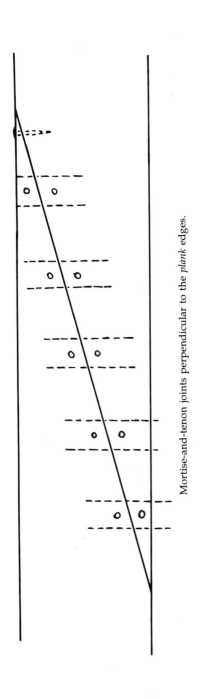

Mortise-and-tenon joints perpendicular to the *plank* edges.

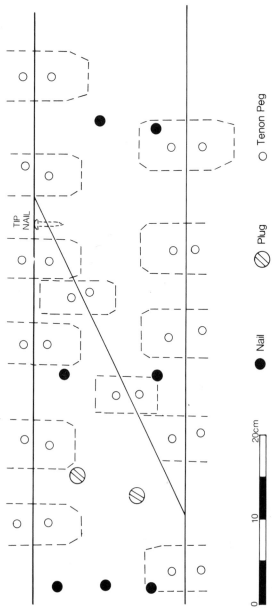

TIP NAIL

● Nail   ◍ Plug   ○ Tenon Peg

0   10   20cm

The only scarf that Dick was able to study extensively was on the collapsed stern starboard section of planking.

As opposed to the use of recycled wood for the planking, the frames were mostly made of "new" timbers—but not quality pieces. In fact, they served only to emphasize the poor selection of available woods. Furthermore, although he would not commit himself to identifying them, Dick thought he saw several different types of timber, particularly in the frames.

"This guy was doing everything he could to frame out his boat with whatever he could get his hands on," Dick said. "He wasn't a poor builder. He just didn't have anything better to frame it with."

Dick took a deep draw on his cigarette. "There is something pathetic about this hull," he concluded.

In ancient Mediterranean ship construction, ships' nails on external fastenings were not simply driven into the timbers. Instead, a pilot hole was drilled through the timbers, and a treenail was hammered into the hole. Then the metal nail was driven down the center of the treenail and "double-clenched" on the inside. The treenail served to distribute the pressure of the nail equally while imparting a watertight fit to the nail. The double clenching—in which the tip of the protruding end of the nail was bent back and then driven back into the timber, leaving a portion of the nail flush with the surface, like a staple—imparted strength to the vessel and prevented the nail from coming loose or being pried out.

"Did you notice that our boatwright didn't clench the nails?" Dick asked. I hadn't.

"I assume that puts him back in the doghouse," I said.

"No. Perhaps the fact that this is a boat, and not a ship, has something to do with it. You don't need the inherent strength. Now," Dick struck his right forefinger against his open left palm, "undoubtedly there are things we have already seen on this boat that were utilized only in the Galilee. But this again would indicate a good, well-trained craftsman. For instance, this method of nailing. You know there aren't any treenails. It's just plain straight nails. Now, you can get away with this on the Sea of Galilee, but I don't think you would want to try it in the storms that you were likely to run into on the Mediterranean. They have much bigger swells."

"But the Sea of Galilee has storms, too," I said.

"I know that she gets a little rough at times, but it's not very far to shore, and you can't get swept out to sea—and these are the things shipbuilders had to think about on the coast."

Dick looked at the boat for a long pensive moment. "I kind of feel sorry for this boatwright because from what I've seen—and we may be talking about several boatwrights, too—there was good boatwrightery there. The joints were put in fine and everything."

After he had "vindicated" the boatwright, Dick seemed to me to feel more comfortable around the boat.

Before Dick's arrival I had been asked repeatedly whether we should have someone draw a picture of the hull as it emerged from the mud.

"Dick can do that when he gets here," I told them.

One of the visitors who stayed on to work at the excavation was Hani Efroni, a talented artist who was studying at the University of Haifa at the time. Kurt, aware of Hani's artistic ability, could not resist having her draw the boat.

As we had no millimeter paper, he gave Hani some stationery that he had brought with him from the guest house of his own kibbutz, Nahsholim. Henceforth, Hani would sit quietly on the sidelines drawing the hull fragments freehand after Danny had finished stringing and numbering them. Hani used the back sides of the stationery, taping pages together as she continued down the hull.

When Dick saw Hani's rendering of the hull, he told me, "I was planning to draw the hull freehand, but to be quite honest, Hani is doing a better job than I can."

Hani drew the boat. Her sketch was the basis for a detailed rendering of all the timbers of the hull that were numbered during the excavation. This drawing proved to be particularly useful in recording the hull at later stages.

No caulking was evident between the seams of the planking. I was mystified. When I asked Dick about it, he explained that in

Hani's drawing of the hull's interior.

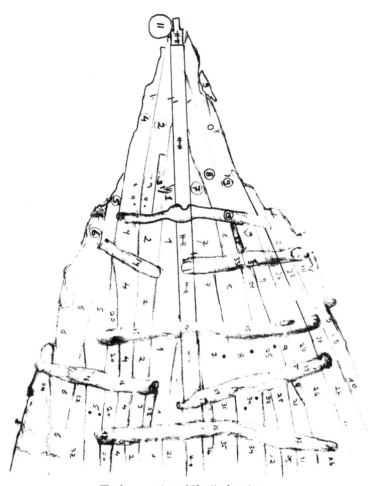

The bow section of Hani's drawing.

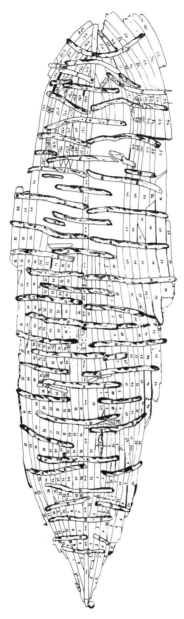

The revised field sketch prepared by Edna on the basis of Hani's sketch.

vessels built with mortise-and-tenon joinery no caulking was used.

"What prevented the planking seams from leaking?" I asked.

"Once the hull was built, it was floated out into the sea or lake. The water would rush in promptly through the inevitable openings in the seams. But soon the water would cause the timbers to swell, closing all of the seams watertight.[7]

"When we built the full-scale replica of the Kyrenia ship—the *Kyrenia* II—we built her with mortise-and-tenon joints and without caulking, because Michael had found no evidence of caulking during the excavation, you see. When we floated her out, she took on so much water that within two hours she had almost sunk," Dick laughed, "The shipwrights who had built the *Kyrenia* II came from a shipbuilding tradition where caulking was the norm. They didn't think that hull would ever be watertight without caulking, and the fact that she almost sank seemed to confirm their suspicions. But a day later, when we pumped the water out of her, that hull was watertight."[8]

Several large staplelike iron fastenings were still in place nailed into the strakes across planking seams; others had been found in the overburden. After Dick studied these, he concluded that they, too, were repairs.

"They were probably used to strengthen the planking where the mortise-and-tenon joints had begun to weaken," he said, "but I've never seen anything like them in the Mediterranean."

"Remember this boatbuilder had another problem that the people in the Mediterranean don't have. His boat was for fresh water. Fresh water is harder on wood than salt water."

"Harder in what way?" I asked.

"Generally, in fresh water, wood doesn't last as long."

"Salt water preserves it?"

"Yes. In saltwater boats, the rotting often occurs from the inside because of sweating, or condensation. In fresh water you can have *external* damage. So, perhaps some of the repairs—the staples, for example—were due to the fresh water."

The *Kyrenia* II takes on water as if she were going to sink.

Staple—or clenched nail—on the hull's exterior.

Another time, Dick showed me a staple on a portion of the *exterior* of the hull that had been cleared of mud.

"So?"

"It's not a staple; it's a clenched nail," he said. Motioning me to look inside the hull, he pointed to the head of the nail protruding from the inner face of Frame 84.

"I don't get it. Why would they clench only one nail?"

"I think it's a repair," he said.

Dick felt the same way about some of the frames. While most of the frames were not attached at all to the keel, eight frames—19, 38, 56, 76, 84, 93, 158, and 153—had nails driven through their upper surface into the top of the keel. Late in his stay Dick noticed little triangular insert pieces in the stern planking. In later ships these are termed *Dutchmen*. These, too, were probably repairs, although again, Dick had never seen anything like them on ancient hulls.

Might the repairs have been made by the same boatwright who had built the boat? I asked Dick if he was able to identify groups of repairs done by different hands at different times.

"No. We don't have enough of the hull exposed."

Determining the different repairs in the life of a boat or ship, I learned that day, requires an extraordinary amount of time. It also requires that the reconstructor have access to the entire hull and also a good planking diagram from both the hull's interior and its exterior. This is best done only after the hull has been treated and the expert can spend hours looking at each individual timber from every possible angle. Only then are such details, like the manner in which the boatwright struck his tools, likely to be revealed.

"What you want to examine," Dick said, "is if plank widths are the same on the outside as they are on the inside. That tells you how much the seams are beveled, and that then tells you a little bit about the assembly technique. This hull was definitely built shell-first, so seam angles are very important."

By looking at the seams from one end of the boat to the other, an expert can determine if the same principles were followed throughout the hull's construction. Sometimes they are not, and it is at such times, Dick explained, that you start thinking about repairs.

"So far I haven't been able even to determine if one or several persons worked on the original construction of the hull," Dick said. "In fact, until someone can study the hull in detail, we won't know how much of the hull is original construction and how much is repairs using, perhaps, secondhand wood.

"She's going to be good little boat to study when she comes out of conservation. And if it's done right, it will require a lot of time. I suspect that the repairs will give a marvelous chronology of the boat. She will probably tell a big story."

Dick was at the site during all daylight hours of every day of his visit. With Karen, whom he had taken on as his recording assistant, Dick quietly recorded the hull as the mayhem of the excavation continued unabated all around them.

At the boat's bow, the stem assembly had been carefully removed in antiquity, leaving only the bow extremity of the keel, which ended in a fixed tenon. One day, while Dick was taking measurements in the bow, I asked him about the missing stem assembly.

"There are two bow shapes, either of which is possible, and again, I am not going to have sufficient time to determine with absolute certainty which is the correct one."

On one hand, Dick explained, the bow might have followed a simple curve upward. The second possibility, which he preferred, however, was that the stem assembly—probably constructed from several timbers—had had the shape of a ramlike forefoot.

"You know, I really wish I had more time to study this bow," Dick said wistfully. "I'm sure the clues are here to figure out the shape of the original bow assembly. One day, after conservation, someone will have to extend these bow planks and figure that out."

"Why do you prefer reconstructing it in a ramlike manner?" I asked.

"See how the keel ends here in a tenon? There is only one example that I know of in which the keel of an ancient Mediterranean ship ends in a tenon rather than a scarf, and that's the Athlit Ram. Had they wished to attach a simple stem, why did they use a tenon to do it rather than a normal scarf? I'm reasonably sure that, because the keel terminates as it does on the Athlit Ram, with a tenon instead of a scarf, we have *that* shape of bow."

The stem construction was only one of a number of missing parts that had been removed in antiquity. What had happened to the stem assembly? Who had removed the two frames in the bow, leaving the nails in place like so many scrawny fingers? Even the sternpost, it turned out later, had been removed.

Where had all the timbers gone?

"If this boat is any indication," Dick said, "it would seem that

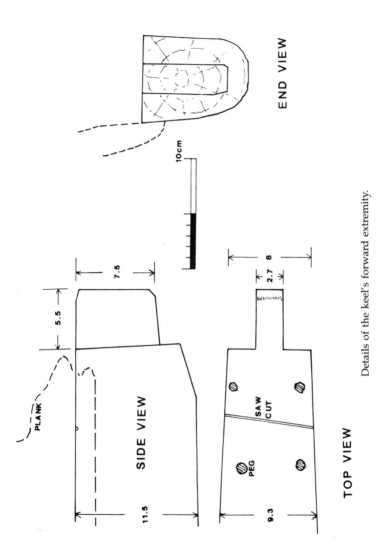

END VIEW

10cm

SIDE VIEW

PLANK

TOP VIEW

PEG

SAW CUT

Details of the keel's forward extremity.

The keel terminated in a tenon at the bow.

timber was scarce. I think that all these pieces were removed for use on another hull. All of the missing timbers would have been valuable to a boatwright. And what they left behind would have been useless to them for boat building."

"What about the rest of the hull? Why didn't they take it, too? Why leave anything? They could have used it at least for fire-wood."

"I don't think so. Notice that these timbers were once covered with pitch. There is still some visible here and there, but in antiquity there would have been much more. That may have made it too foul smelling for use as kindling.

"Along with the repairs," Dick said, "the situation becomes even more complicated because of these pieces that have been removed—carefully removed—in antiquity. There is a story here. A fantastic one."

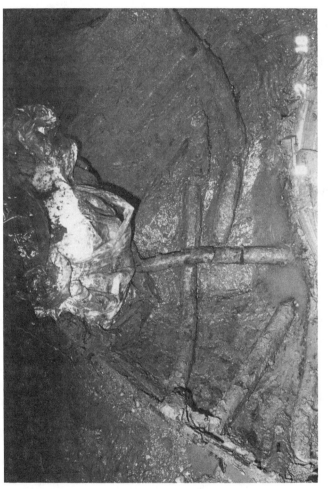

One timber that lay longitudinally over the frames in the stern had probably been removed from the port side (upper right in photo) but was then apparently abandoned.

"There's something I want to show you," I had told Dick on that first day of his visit.

We walked over to where Zvika, on his knees, was carefully uncovering his "fleet." I introduced the two men and, after giving Dick the background of the discovery of the timber assemblies, left him there with his measuring tape and notebook to study them. After he had done so, Dick called me over.

"These are interesting because of their edge joinery," he said, "kind of amusing almost."

In the types of mortise-and-tenon joints and the manner in which they had been applied to the planks, these two assemblies illustrated a chronology that Dick had already studied on Mediterranean shipwrecks. The group of timbers farthest from the boat—let us call them *Assembly 1*—was part of the turn of the bilge. Zvika had revealed several planks and parts of two frames. The frames were similar to those on the boat, gnarly and twisted, and still bore their bark.

"These planks have pegged mortise-and-tenon joints with dimensions similar to those on the boat over there, but here they are spaced farther apart. These timbers are part of a *second* boat," Dick said.

The joints on the assembly were spaced about 22 centimeters (8.7 inches) apart measured from peg to peg, while on the boat the spacing was only 12 centimeters (4.7 inches).

The second group of timbers—*Assembly 2*—of which Zvika had revealed several planks and part of one frame, was even more interesting, Dick assured me.

"This is part of a *third* boat. Look here at the edge of the upper plank," he said.

I looked at it, but I obviously was not seeing everything that Dick saw in that timber.

"There's only one mortise-and-tenon joint along its entire length. It's 51 centimeters [20 inches] from this end of the plank and 12 centimeters [4.7 inches] from the other. What's more, the joint is small and there is no locking peg. This is very much like what we've recorded from the seventh-century AD Yassiada ship-

Assembly Number 1.

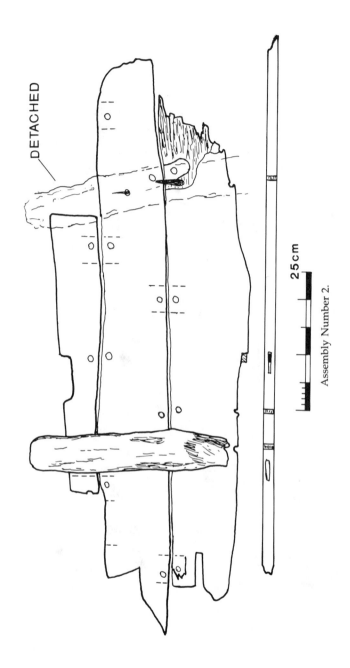

DETACHED

25 cm

Assembly Number 2.

wreck." Although considerably smaller, the assembly had the thin planking and heavier framed construction of ships built during the Byzantine period, when edge joinery had become somewhat vestigial.

"Would that suggest that the evolution on the Kinneret continued more-or-less parallel to that on the Mediterranean?" I asked.

"Not necessarily," Dick said. "It certainly suggests a similar evolution, but whether it chronologically parallels the Mediterranean you can't really tell unless you can date these other finds. It does indicate that mortise-and-tenon joints got smaller and more widely spaced and eventually had no pegs at all here on the Sea of Galilee. That's the same sequence that you find in the Mediterranean. Whether it happened at the same time, though, is another question."

Near sunset one day Dick and I were standing on the dike, at the water's edge. As he motored back to port in Tiberias, a lone fisherman in his little fishing boat made ripples on the lake's otherwise glassy surface. The distance between us softened the sputtering noise of his motor. Dick lit a cigarette with a wooden match, the flame flaring for a moment as he drew it into the tobacco.

The boatman waved to us. We waved back.

"This may have been the only hull form for large boats on the Kinneret." Dick waved the cigarette in his hand in the direction of our boat. "But there were certainly smaller boats. That's a big boat, *but that may be the only hull form*. And that is because it worked very well.

"Nobody writes about small boats because what can you say about them? There must have been smaller boats. Every time you had to do a little something down the coast, even if you wanted to commute you certainly wouldn't take a big guy like that out. What about the single fisherman? You have to have small boats, even if just to work on the big ones."

"How many types of smaller boats might you expect to find on the Kinneret in the first century?" I asked.

"Oh, I think it would have been very limited. You see, that's because your scope of enterprise is limited. You have only so much industry and trade, and what there is of it is mostly agricultural. There is no heavy manufacturing, so you don't need the deep-hulled freighters and big barges. *You can't go to a foreign port.* Throw that out. So you're just talking about small local craft. Craft that have to go 13 miles in one direction maximum. This narrows the field of their requirements down considerably. As they are largely agricultural, everything is seasonal. That again limits the type of craft on a freshwater lake like this. However, you might have been able to go out in winter, a season when sailing was not normally done on the Mediterranean, you see.

"I would guess that the types of crafts are very limited. Maybe only one of these big ones. One type, that is. Many, many big boats, but only one type. All built more or less the same. Because, you see, very quickly whatever works the best would be adopted by others.

"I can't imagine any area not having small boats," he said. "But again they would be limited in type. Look how Venice came up with the gondola. They are all built the same. That is because whatever worked best eventually got to be the accepted design.

"All areas are this way. In England, for example, you have 'this river boat' and 'that river boat.' You know, the Humber River Keels and the Thames Barges. They are all specific types of boats that work well on those rivers. And that's the same here. So you don't usually have many varieties in one spot.

"Now when there is an interchange—as, for example, up and down the Mediterranean—then the variety is expanded."

Dick contemplated the lake as the setting sun changed the color of the Golan Heights on the other side of the lake from a warm magenta to a cool blue.

"How well do you think this particular design of boat would have been suited to the tasks she performed here on the Kinneret?" I asked him.

"I'd say it is a good all-purpose design. Over the generations they adapted the hull form that best suited these waters and the assignments they gave to the boat. It's probably an all-purpose boat. That is, it could be used for freighting and fishing, carrying passengers. I'm sure over the centuries this evolved into something that was ideal. As Mendel pointed out to me, they still had big-sterned vessels in the Kinneret up to recent times. It was something that they really could not improve on."

"Is that normal on other bodies of water?" I asked.

"Oh yes. You see, I think this is the case for all watercraft that you see everywhere. It evolves into what they need based on the technology of that time. This eventually prompts the local boat builders to arrive at the best hull design."

Ahh, the boat builder again. I wondered out loud about our boatwright.

"The boatbuilder was an excellent craftsman. He was—I assume it was 'he'—had been trained or apprenticed under someone who was a very experienced Mediterranean shipwright or boatwright, and as far as mechanical discipline is concerned, he was really good. The material that he had to work with on the boat was not as good as what we usually find in the Mediterranean Sea, and therefore the end result did not have the finesse that we see on some Mediterranean craft. There was no ease of construction, as at Herculaneum; here it was difficult for him.

"There is a Mediterranean tradition in the boat's construction, *but* adapted for the Kinneret. How much they had altered the Mediterranean tradition I can't determine, though, without a thorough study of both sides of the hull. But I think this fellow had techniques that were learned on the Mediterranean. Or I suppose it's possible that a Roman boatwright got into the region and settled down here."

"You think that in each generation boatwrights came over from the Mediterranean coast to build boats on the Kinneret?"

"Not necessarily. You could have just one coming over now and then and training sons and all. Maybe that's what we're looking at, you see."

I asked if our boatwright might have been a normal carpenter who usually worked on land projects but also built boats as a sideline.

"Well, they seem to have been using house nails," Dick said. "That might suggest that he built boats some of the time and houses during the rest. I'm not an authority on land building, though, so I don't know to what degree timber was used in building construction on land at that time in the Galilee. Then again, perhaps some of these reused timbers were brought over from ships that were taken apart on the Mediterranean coast. These are the things that scholars are going to have to look into."

The sun had set by this time. Everything around us was turning one shade of blue or another. Dick continued, "More information about the shipbuilder will come from whoever studies the boat. What has to be done now, when the boat comes out of conservation, is to go over all the things I will highlight in my report, and I will pose a *big* list of questions about the boat-builder. Why were the woods selected as they were? More important, how many different sets of tool marks and working habits can you interpret from this planking? I think you can get this off these planks because they are so well preserved. How many craftsmen may have worked on this boat?"

"You can actually tell all that?"

"Well, not always. But if their tool strokes are quite different, you might have a left-handed and a right-handed worker. Or they may have had totally different working habits. For example, I told you that there were two different applications of frames. Some are nailed to the keel, but most are not. That may represent different generations. It most certainly suggests different boatwrights.

"You see, the problem you get in the Galilee is that you may have had a lot of this repair work done by fishermen. Now, that's both good and bad. You may be looking at things that are not rule-of-thumb technology but something that's done to keep the thing from leaking.

"On the other hand, it might be what the average boat went through. I think, because it appears to be an old boat, that this will be the case. You will get a long look at the life of a Galilee boat."

"What types of tools have you been able to identify so far?"

Dick thought for a minute. "Now, I haven't done a tool study, though, from what I've seen, he used a bow drill, several types of hammers or mallets, chisels to make the mortises, and at least two sizes of drill bits, one for the pilot holes for nails and another for the tenon peg holes. He used adzes of several different sizes and shapes. There were saw marks, so he obviously used a handsaw. Probably brushes or trowels, because there was pitch, and it was applied with some heavy form of application. I assume he used a board to trowel the pitch onto the hull. But I think in general he was very limited in the variety of his tools."

"He couldn't afford the tools?"

"That's one possibility. Or they simply were not available to him."

As darkness descended, I asked Dick what he felt was the boat's importance.

"It's very significant," he said. "For one thing, it gives us a look at parts of boats in the Classical period that we have not been able to study before.

"More important, this boat is on the Sea of Galilee, and therefore it gives us our first look at what water transport was like on the Kinneret. We know less about watercraft on the inland lakes than we do about those on the Mediterranean. At least now we can begin to reconstruct what went on in the Galilee.

"The potential is there. That is what I will try to do in my report. I will point out potentials that will need to be elaborated on when the boat comes out of conservation. I hope not too many will need correcting. I am going to be as conservative as possible.

"The most important thing about this hull, though, is that it is going to suggest things we haven't even discussed here because we don't know enough to ask the questions yet or to think about these possibilities.

"You are going to solve one question and raise five."

Dick was silent for a few moments. Then he chuckled, "And that's the story of my life."

Chapter 6

The First Jewish Naval Battle

Thus pursued, the Jews could neither escape to land, where all were in arms against them, nor sustain a naval battle on equal terms. . . . Disaster overtook them and they were sent to the bottom, boats and all.

From *The Jewish War*
JOSEPHUS FLAVIUS[1]

I heard them before I saw them.

As dusk settled over the excavation one day, two olive-drab Israeli air force Cobra helicopter gunships appeared out of nowhere. They flew low over the lake and sped directly toward the excavation site. Drawing near, they stopped and hovered overhead, like oversized dragonflies, their rotors beating the air. Then they began slowly to circle the site, the pilots observing us from a distance.

As we were immersed in excavating the past, the sudden appearance of the Cobras hovering above us jarred me. For a moment I felt as if I had been caught between time zones separated by millennia. I speculated on how two Jewish gunships might have changed the outcome of a battle that took place over 1,900 years earlier somewhere near the shore on which I stood.

∂∂∂

When Jesus told the people to "render unto Caesar that which is Caesar's," the face on the coin which he held in his hand must have been that of the emperor Tiberias, during whose reign Jesus' ministry took place.[2] When Tiberias died in AD 37, Gaius Caligula became emperor of Rome. Rumor had it that Caligula had murdered the aged Tiberias, who was his grandfather.

The Romans, who despised the grim and morbid Tiberias, were ecstatic when Caligula came to the throne. Caligula's late father, Germanicus, had been deeply loved and respected, and for the first few years of his rule, Caligula confirmed the expectations of his citizens, instituting many popular acts. It appeared to the average Roman that the new emperor would bring a positive

171

change to the empire. Indeed, posterity probably would have recognized Caligula as a very capable emperor, had he had the good grace to die in the first year or two of his reign. Unfortunately, he did not.

Instead, horror replaced delight as the empire slowly realized that Caligula was crazier than a loon and as vicious as a wounded bear. While Caligula's insanity mainly affected those nearest to him in Rome, it also had repercussions farther away in the provinces of the empire.

Roman religion was an extension of state values and devoid of any true spiritual depth. The Romans viewed emperor worship as a statement of faithfulness to the emperor and an expression of loyalty to the empire. Sacrificial offerings in honor of the Roman emperor might be compared to swearing allegiance to a flag today.

As part of this imperial cult, emperors were deified after death. Caligula took the deification principle one step further. Declaring himself a living god, he commanded the attendant trappings, including a temple dedicated to his worship, where sacrifices of rare birds were offered according to the day of the month.

For subservient pagan populations, there was always room in the local pantheon for one more god, even an emperor. The only provincial religion that could not accept another god was monotheistic Judaism.

Caligula's self-proclaimed deification also gave the Hellenized subjects—"Greeks"—of the Roman Empire in the Levant and Egypt an excuse to persecute the Jews living among them. Alexandria in Egypt contained the largest Jewish community outside Judea at that time. Local "Greeks" managed to install statues of the mad emperor in the Alexandrian synagogues.

What to do? The Jews were in a hazardous predicament. They could not countenance imperial cult statues inside their houses of worship. But go explain that to Caligula.

Meanwhile, events were unraveling in Judea as well. At Jamnia (Yavneh), near the Mediterranean coast, Jews destroyed an altar constructed by Greeks in honor of the mad emperor. Caligula then commanded Petronius, the Roman governor of Syria, to place statues of the deified emperor in the very center of Jewish worship, the Holy Temple in Jerusalem. Should the Jews offer resistance, Petronius was ordered to kill the instigators and to enslave the entire population.

Petronius marched with several legions and additional reinforcements from Antioch to Akko-Ptolomais—modern Acco—located north of Haifa, where he was met by a multitude of Jewish men, women, and children who begged him not to desecrate the temple in this manner. Leaving the statues in Ptolomais, Petronius advanced inland to the city of Tiberias and there called a meeting of notables.

The Roman governor tried to reason with the Jews. He emphasized that only the Jews, among all the peoples within the Roman Empire, refused to erect these statues. Warning of the might of Rome, he stressed that such a refusal would be tantamount to rebellion.

The Jewish leaders replied that their beliefs could not tolerate such a desecration; should Petronius persist, he would have to kill the entire Jewish population. The governor was taken aback by their fierce determination and elected to retreat, thus preventing a massacre.

Petronius dispatched a petition to Caligula explaining the situation and asking him to rescind his orders rather than destroy so many innocent people. The emperor responded with a message to Petronius ordering him to commit suicide for disobeying the emperor's commands.

Bad seas slowed down the ship carrying this death sentence. Meanwhile, Caligula was assassinated, and this latter news, sent via a ship that enjoyed fair weather, reached Petronius first. Thus Petronius was saved.

A great and useless tragedy was averted. It was an experience, however, that the Jews would not soon forget, and one that cast an ominous shadow over future relations between Rome and Judea.

Immediately to the south of where the boat had come to rest is the ancient site of Migdal, which is situated at the extreme south-east corner of the Valley of Ginosar, adjoining the Kinneret. It is from this ancient site that the modern agricultural settlement of Migdal—the home of our volunteers Zvika and Shmuel—receives its name.

Migdal means "tower" in Hebrew. In antiquity this city was a major fishing center. Its name in Aramaic, which was the common language of the local populace in the first century AD—was Migdal Nunya, meaning "Tower of the Fishes." Migdal's Greek name, which is the one used by the Jewish historian Josephus, is Tarichaeae, or "salted fish." During the ministry of Jesus, this city was the home of Mary Magdelene, or "Mary of Migdal."

Of all the cities that fronted the Kinneret, Migdal was the strongest in its opposition to Roman rule of the Jewish homeland and was the center for activities against the Romans. During this time, the city was included in the region governed by Marcus Iulius Agrippa. Known to history as Agrippa II, he was the grandson of Herod the Great, the son of Agrippa I, and the last scion of the Herodian dynasty.

Agrippa appears as a minor character in the New Testament. The preachings of Paul caused unrest in Jerusalem, and he was arrested. Paul demanded his right as a Roman citizen to be judged in Rome by the emperor, rather than by a local court, and thus was held in Caesarea awaiting transport. Agrippa, on a royal visit to Caesarea, was invited by Festus, the newly arrived procurator of Judea, to hear Paul's case.[3] After the hearing, during which Paul tried to convert Agrippa to Christianity, Agrippa concluded that Paul was "doing nothing to deserve death or imprisonment" and remarked to Festus, "This man could have been set free if he had not appealed to the emperor."[4]

Agrippa did his best to prevent the revolt from breaking out in AD 66, but when insurrection erupted, he naturally threw in his lot with the Romans. Agrippa's rule over Tiberias and Migdal was nominal at best, and with the onset of the revolt, he lost all control over them.

In the summer of AD 67, following a successful campaign of methodically destroying the Jewish cities of the Galilee, the Roman general Vespasian arrived in Akko-Ptolomais. There he gathered a formidable array of Roman might, nearly 60,000 fighting men. This does not take into account the personal servants, engineers, technicians, carpenters, and other experts and camp followers who traveled with the army. Quartering this massive number of men, when not fighting in the field, must have been a logistical nightmare. Therefore, marching south along the coast, Vespasian stationed two legions at Caesarea, while sending the third to Scythopolis (Beit Shean).

At about this time, Agrippa invited Vespasian to be his guest, hoping to use the Roman general to put an end to the problems in his realm. Vespasian and his son, Titus, left Caesarea on the Mediterranean Sea and journeyed to the other Caesarea: Caesarea Philippi, Agrippa's capital, located at modern Banias, on the southwest foot of Mt. Hermon. For nearly a month that summer, Agrippa wined and dined Vespasian while apprising him of his problems with Migdal, which had openly revolted, and with Tiberias, which was on the brink of revolt. The Roman war-horse decided to repay Agrippa's hospitality by stamping out local sedition against Rome.

Thus it was that the destruction of Migdal began as a social call. Vespasian sent Titus to coastal Caesarea to bring the troops stationed there to Scythopolis. Vespasian met up with the troops in Scythopolis and, with his full force reunited, advanced on Tiberias. Arriving at the Kinneret from the southwest, the army first camped at Sennabris, which was located near Beit Yerah, where the Jordan River exits the Kinneret.

Aware that the majority of the population in Tiberias favored accommodation with Rome, Vespasian sent a cavalry officer named Valerianus with a detachment of fifty horsemen to deliver a peace proposal to the city. So as to appear less threatening upon nearing the city, Valerianus ordered his men to dismount. This, as it turned out, was not a wise move.

While a preponderance of Tiberians clearly wished to avoid a conflict with the Romans, there was a group within the city that wholeheartedly supported insurrection. The leader of these insurgents was a certain Jesus Ben Sapphia, who was also a chief magistrate of the city.

Before Valerianus had a chance to present his offer, a band of armed rebels, led by Ben Sapphia, surprised the Romans. This ragtag group of Jews captured some of the Romans' horses, which they brought back inside the city walls in triumph. The Romans retreated ignominiously on foot. Josephus does not tell us what became of Valerianus, but it is unlikely that he was well received by Vespasian following such a fiasco.

Realizing that Roman retribution would not be long in coming, many of Tiberias's leading citizens rushed to Vespasian's encampment. There they begged the Roman general not to destroy the city for the rash actions of a few.

Not surprisingly, Vespasian was furious. It was no small embarrassment for Roman soldiers to have their horses stolen almost from beneath them. Remembering Agrippa's concern for the city, however, he set terms for Tiberias to capitulate. To save themselves from certain destruction, the elders immediately agreed to the terms. Recognizing that they would no longer be safe in Tiberias, Ben Sapphia and his followers hastily departed for Migdal.

Having been stung by the Tiberian rebels once, Vespasian sent a Roman cavalry unit under Trajan, commander of the Xth Legion (and father of the future emperor of the same name), to reconnoiter Tiberias the following day. Wisely keeping a safe distance this time, Trajan observed the city from a nearby mountain. Only after Vespasian was notified that the city's population was now in compliance with his terms did he march his army to Tiberias.

Tiberias opened her gates and, cheered on by the people, who happily accepted the Roman yoke again, the conquering army marched through them. Vespasian ordered a section of the city's southern wall torn down. Josephus relates that this was done to facilitate passage for the soldiers. More likely, Vespasian was ensuring that Tiberias could not revolt again.

The legions marched past the city and continued north to a location between Tiberias and Migdal, where Vespasian ordered a well-fortified camp to be built. Rebel forces—like those of Ben Sapphia—were pouring into Migdal from the surrounding regions, and it seemed likely to Vespasian that the suppression of Migdal would cost a considerable amount of Roman sweat and blood.

Before the Romans completed their fortifications, Ben Sapphia led an audacious waterborne commando raid against the Roman encampment. Stealthily approaching from the lake, the band of Jewish partisans succeeded in sneaking up on the men working on the fortifications, scattering them and pulling down part of the camp's defense wall. When the legionnaires staged a counterattack, the Jews withdrew to their boats. Pulling out into the lake, Ben Sapphia's waterborne commandos anchored in battle formation—Josephus used the term *phalanx* to describe the maneuver—and engaged the land-locked enemy on the shore in an archery duel.

While this ship-to-shore battle was going on, Vespasian received word that the Jews at Migdal were massing outside the protection of the city's walls. Why they should have chosen to do so remains a mystery. Untrained troops, such as they were, obviously would be easy prey on an open battlefield for the experienced Roman war machine. Perhaps they lacked leadership. Without experienced leaders, men in battle do foolish things. Josephus names no specific military leaders at Migdal apart from Ben Sapphia, who was otherwise disposed for the moment.

Vespasian dispatched Titus with 600 cavalry to Migdal. Upon viewing the number of Jews prepared to fight, he wisely sent a message to his father requesting reinforcements. At this point, wrote Josephus, Titus delivered a speech to his troops. In it Titus shored up the troops' bravery and urged them on to do battle even before the reinforcements got there. By the time he had completed his speech, however, the reinforcements, led by Trajan, had arrived. They included an additional 400 horses and 2,000 archers.

The latter took up a position on the nearby mountainside, with orders to keep the Jews off the walls and to prevent assistance from the city to the Jews in the field.

When the archers were in place, Titus led a horse charge against the irregulars arrayed in the field. Unaccustomed to organized warfare, the Jews fought back bravely for a while but were quickly overwhelmed by the cavalry's momentum. Soon the plain was covered with the dead and the dying, their bodies impaled by cavalry lances. Those that survived the onslaught fled back to the safety of Migdal's walls.

Many never made it. Some were trampled under galloping hooves. The horsemen charged and then charged again, and each time, more and more Jews fell to the Romans. They cut down the stragglers with ease, then raced after the swift of foot. Roman horsemen rode past the fleeing men, wheeled around, and attacked again and again. And again. Finally, some Jews were able to make good their escape and reach the walls—only to find utter chaos reigning inside the city.

Josephus, during the short period that he had served as governor of the Galilee at the behest of the Jerusalem war council in anticipation of the Roman attack, had fortified Migdal on the sides that faced the Valley of Ginosar. Due to a lack of funds, he had left it unfortified on the side facing the lake.

Roman calvary, however, were trained in swimming their horses through water obstacles. The military historian Vegetius, who wrote in the late fourth or early fifth century AD, notes:[5]

> Every recruit without exception should in the summer months learn the art of swimming, for rivers are not always crossed by bridges, and armies both when advancing and retreating are frequently forced to swim. . . . It is highly advantageous to train not just infantry but cavalry and their horses and grooms, whom they call *galearii*, to swim as well, lest they be found incapable when an emergency presses.

There were many times in Roman history when this training paid off. One of them took place that day at Migdal. Titus, aware of the confusion inside the city, used it to press his advantage. Swimming his horse out into the lake and around the end of the city wall, Titus led the Roman cavalry in a flanking maneuver, penetrating the city from its unfortified side. With the Romans inside, all serious resistance ceased. The rout turned into a massacre.

The people of Migdal had previously prepared a large fleet of fishing boats for battle, or for evacuation, in the event that they were vanquished on shore. The boats, noted Josephus, had been "equipped for naval combat, if necessary."[6]

Some Jews managed to make their way down to the lake front with the intention of escaping by boat. There many ran directly into Roman cavalry, who killed some as they climbed into boats and others as they attempted to swim out to those craft already launched. The latter hovered offshore, just out of reach of the Romans.

Inside the city, the slaughter continued as Roman swords devoured all that came in their path. Eventually, Titus called a halt to the carnage. The Jews in the boats that had managed to get away from the killing zone then sadly headed out into the lake, where, for the moment at least, they were safe.

Titus sent a horseman to relay news of his victory to Vespasian, who was pleased by the outcome; Migdal had been a major center of revolt against Roman domination. Soon Vespasian arrived on the scene and ordered that a cordon be set up around the city, to prevent those who had escaped the massacre from now leaving the city. Anyone who attempted to do so was to pay with his or her life.

Still smarting from Ben Sapphia's waterborne raid on the Roman camp, Vespasian knew that he could not allow free rein to those refugees who had escaped onto the lake. The Jewish flotilla was highly mobile and had the ability to move men and supplies with a speed unattainable by the land-bound Romans.

Indeed, during the skirmishing and battles that went on around the Kinneret in the wake of the greater conflict with Rome, boats were used for the rapid transport of troops around the lake. At one point, Josephus fought a battle that took place at Julias

(Bethsaida). In it Josephus led rebel forces against the army of Agrippa II, captained by the latter's military leader, Sylla.[7] During an ambush, Josephus's horse stumbled and fell, wounding its rider. With Josephus incapacitated in this manner, Sylla could easily have won the field. The fact that Sylla retreated upon receiving a report that additional forces had embarked in boats at Migdal illustrates the importance of the rapid transport of troops by boat on the Kinneret.

The boats, Vespasian decided, had to be neutralized. On the day following the capture of Migdal, Vespasian went down to the shore and ordered that makeshift water vessels be quickly constructed so that the Romans could do battle with the Jews on the lake. To describe these vessels Josephus employs the Greek word *sxedia*, a term which is rendered as "rafts" in most translations. These were soon ready for battle, thanks to the availability of large quantities of wood and to the many army carpenters on hand who were set to this task.

When the craft were ready, Vespasian placed troops and *auxilia* archers on board and launched his fleet. From the outset, the Jews were incapable of sustaining a concerted effort against the Roman craft; they were "outgunned," outmanned, and outmaneuvered.

The Roman vessels seem to have advanced in an orderly fashion. The Jews pelted the Romans with stones and sometimes bravely, but rashly, attacked. The Jews were at a disadvantage; Josephus noted that their stones only rattled off the armor worn by the Roman troops. The ineffectiveness of the stones may have been due to the Jews' throwing them by hand, rather than hurling them with slings, for Vegetius writes:[8]

> Often against soldiers armed with helmets, cataphracts and cuirasses [types of body armor], smooth stones shot with a sling or "sling-staff" are more dangerous than any arrows, since while leaving the limbs intact they inflict a wound that is still lethal, and the enemy dies from the stone without the loss of blood.

The Roman auxiliary archers responded with showers of arrows, against which the Jews were defenseless. Some boats tried to break through the Roman line. But the craft were so close that the Romans impaled the Jews on their javelins or actually jumped into the Jewish vessels and slaughtered the occupants by sword. Other boats were captured when they were caught as the Roman watercraft closed in.

Those Jews who tried to reach safety by jumping into the water were dispatched with an arrow when they came up for air. In exhaustion, some tried to grab onto the Roman vessels, only to lose their hands or heads to the snicker-snack of legionary blades.

Jews died in many ways, all of them horrible. Finally, the remaining vessels were corralled by the Romans and forced toward the shore, where, as they grounded, other Roman soldiers who had been stationed there immediately finished off those who had somehow succeeded in surviving till then. The Kinneret's waters turned crimson with the blood of the slain that day; corpses covered her shores, while others floated gently on her waters. Wrecks of their boats littered the coast. The Romans ceased their carnage only when there was no one left to kill.

In the days that followed the battle, a gagging stench hung over the area as the corpses, left unattended, putrefied. Josephus related that, while the Jews who had survived in the city mourned their dead, this overwhelming smell of death even disgusted the Romans. The body count, which included those killed on land, numbered 6,700.

In the aftermath of the battle, Vespasian held a tribunal to determine the future of those still in Migdal. He divided the survivors into those who actually lived in Migdal and those who had arrived at the city just before the battle and had instigated the hostilities.

The newcomers Vespasian decided to deal with in a method that might have been taken directly from a Nazi SS textbook. Vespasian gave them his pledge of amnesty and permitted them to leave through only one route: the one that led to Tiberias. Willing to believe what they wished to be true, the wretches set out carrying their belongings, confident in the Roman general's word of honor.

Vespasian lined the road to Tiberias with Roman soldiers, who prevented anyone from escaping. Arriving at Tiberias, the men were herded into the city's stadium. When he arrived, Vespasian ordered the murder of the weak and the old. His words resulted in the immediate execution of 1,200 men. They had been found guilty of an inexcusable crime: being useless.

From the younger, healthier specimens, an additional 6,000 men were selected for slave labor and sent off to Greece to die digging Nero's canal at Corinth. The majority of the remaining men—who numbered 30,400 according to Josephus—Vespasian sold into slavery, while returning to Agrippa those men who had been his wards, permitting him to deal with them as he wished.

Agrippa promptly sold his own subjects into slavery.

ေေေ

Nineteen centuries after the battle, speculation about the "Jesus connection" to our boat had run rampant in the media and particularly among the foreign visitors, many of whom were Christian pilgrims, who visited the site daily. But for us, the members of the team involved in excavating the boat, and for many local visitors, another question—an important one—was whether the boat might not be one of those washed ashore after the massacre at the Battle of Migdal. Both the place where the boat had come to rest, on the shore near Migdal, and the boat's presumed date made this scenario reasonable, even likely, from an archaeological perspective.

The piles of mud that we had laboriously removed from the boat and its surroundings stood near the shores. It was only much later, after the boat was safely back underwater in her conservation pool, that we could direct our attention to these mounds of sediment. When Moshele examined one of the mud piles that had been removed from *inside* the boat, his metal detector gave off a hum, indicating the presence of a metal object. The source of the sound was an unassuming clump of mud. Carefully breaking away the clay, Moshele found that he was holding in his hand a pyramid-shaped iron arrowhead.

The arrow itself could have been washed into the boat after she arrived on the seabed—perhaps even long afterward. Thus the arrowhead did not necessarily prove that our boat had been involved in the battle. Only further research would provide a probable answer to that question. But could Moshele's arrowhead have come from the battle?

The answer awaited at Gamla, which is situated on the Golan Heights. This ancient city's name derives from the word for "camel." It is a particularly fitting name, for Gamla is located on a razor-backed rocky mountain on the Golan Heights. To anyone viewing the site from the east, it indeed looks like a dromedary's hump. To the north, west, and south, Gamla is set off by steep ravines. Only on the east is it readily accessible by a saddle connecting it to a higher plateau. When Gamla had come under Josephus's jurisdiction during the Revolt, he had built a protective wall—which still stands—along this eastern slope.

Gamla, situated in the territory of Gaulanitis (the northern part of the Golan Heights) was, like Tiberias and Migdal, nominally in the kingdom of Agrippa II, who had been unable to hold it. Nor had he been able to retake it, even though his forces besieged the city for seven months. Another hotbed of revolt against Roman rule, Gamla was the city, immediately after Migdal, which Vespasian chose to destroy. He could not do so, however, without a fight.

Vespasian began a siege of the city, attacking its east wall. This siege lasted over a month, from mid-October to mid-November of AD 67. The Romans used battering rams to break through the walls, and the legionnaires—with a great blowing of trumpets, a yelling of battle cries, and a fierce clashing of arms—attempted to capture the city.

They were repulsed. Many Romans died in the process; Vespasian himself nearly lost his life during the action and counteraction. This Jewish victory was short-lived, however. The next as-

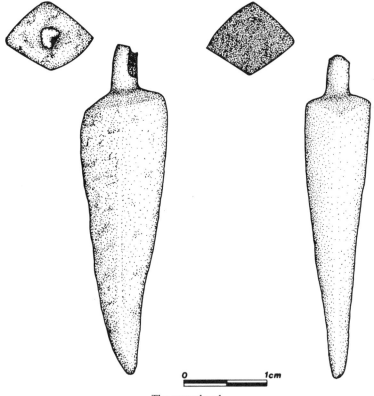

The arrowhead.

sault resulted in the conquest of the city. The remaining Jews retreated to Gamla's citadel, which is located on the far western edge of the mountain.

Vespasian brought up all of his forces to fight the survivors. The Jews fought valiantly against the Romans and, for a time, held their own, killing many of their attackers, while they remained out of reach of the enemy spears and arrows. Then the winds of war shifted against the Jews.

Literally.

Josephus, who considered the wind a portent from heaven, calls it "a miraculous storm." He related that the wind was so forceful that it turned back the arrows of the Jews while blowing the attacker's arrows toward them. Soon the wind had reached such a velocity that it prevented the Jews from standing guard along the ridge, thus allowing the Romans to advance against the last defenders without opposition from above. Josephus does not mention the direction from which this wind blew, but as the Romans were attacking from the east, presumably it was our old acquaintance the *sharkia*, which can spring up suddenly in this area during the winter season and can attain sudden gusts of 36–54 kilometers (22–34 miles) per hour.

As the Romans took the citadel, many Jews plunged into the surrounding deep ravines and died. Of survivors there were few; Josephus related that only two women remained alive after the massacre.

Gamla was never reinhabited. Those with an opportunity to visit the site should climb to the citadel and sit quietly there. The eagles that dwell in this area will visit, silently drifting on the air currents above the visitor's head.

In 1968, shortly after the Six-Day War, when Jews returned to the Golan Heights, Yitzchaki Gal, who is the historian for the Kinneret Authority, identified the site of Gamla. Since 1976 the site has been excavated by the Department of Antiquities under the direction of Shmaryahu Gutman, and more recently by the Institute of Archaeology of Haifa University. These excavations have revealed a vibrant city cut down in its prime. Discoveries include one of the earliest known synagogues, complete with a *mikva* (a ritual bath) and a study room.

Bearing silent witness to the intensity of the fighting, over sixteen hundred arrowheads have been found at Gamla. Many of these lay along a section of the city wall breached by the Romans. Danny, our photographer, was on the staff of the Gamla excava-

Gamla.

tions and knew this material well. I asked him to take a look at the arrowhead that Moshele had found. Danny called me after examining it.

"At Gamla we found 14 examples of the same type of pyramidal arrowhead," he told me. "Most of them were found within 5 meters [16 feet] of the wall along an 80-meter [262-foot] stretch of wall. Presumably they were shot by auxiliary archers attached to the Roman army during the capture of Gamla."

It is an interesting fact of history that some cultures favored the bow as a weapon of war, considering it a "noble weapon": Akkadians, Egyptians, Assyrians, Babylonians, and Parthians, to name but a few. All used the bow in battle and prided themselves in their prowess with it. Other cultures, including the Roman, did not consider the bow a valorous weapon of war. Yet the Romans did realize the practical importance of archery as a long-distance form of warfare and therefore normally had auxiliary contingents of archers attached to their battle groups. These were usually either mercenaries or troops contributed by dependent kings.

Josephus relates that Vespasian's battle group included a total of 6,000 foot archers and 3,000 cavalry contributed by three Asiatic client rulers: Antiochus IV, who was king of Commagene in Asia Minor; Soemus, who ruled in Emessa, which was located north of Syria; and Agrippa II. Malachus, an Arab, sent an additional mixed force of 1,000 horse and 5,000 foot soldiers, most of whom were archers.

The arrowhead that Moshele had found may have belonged originally to one of these auxiliary archers attached to Vespasian's battle group, perhaps one of the same men who later took part in the battle of Gamla. As Josephus specifically mentions that Vespasian had archers on board his vessels, the distinct possibility exists that the arrowhead found its way into the Kinneret during that battle.

ℓℓℓ

As the helicopters continued to hover overhead, I stood in contemplation of those distant times.

Rome and Jerusalem. Jerusalem and Rome.

If history is a highway, the first century AD is most assuredly a major crossroad on it. The more I became involved with the boat, the more the past came alive for me. And with the past came some of its personages, who arrived to haunt my thoughts. This was as close as I probably would ever come to having my very own time machine.

It was as if these persons had walked off the pages of the history books and were standing quietly, unseen yet felt, next to me inside the barrier around the excavation site.

🌊🌊🌊

> I Josephus, son of Matthias, a Hebrew by race and a priest from Jerusalem—having personally fought against the Romans in the early stages of the war, and an unwilling witness of the ensuing events—propose to reveal the facts to the people of the Roman Empire.[9]

Barely a day went by during the excavation without someone mentioning Josephus. I had the impression that he was participating in the excavation.

In a way, he was.

Josephus ben Matthias was born to a venerable priestly family the same year that Caligula took office. Only a year earlier a cruel governor of Judea, Pontius Pilate, had been deposed and recalled to Rome. The attempt by Petronius to carry out Caligula's orders may have been among Josephus's earliest childhood memories—he would still have been in diapers (or the first-century equivalent) at the time—as he grew up in Jerusalem.

As a youth he explored the different streams of Judaism which existed in his day: those of the Pharisees, the Sadducees, and the Essenes. For three years he even became the disciple of a Jewish ascetic named Bannus, who dressed in the bark of trees and frequently partook of cold-water baths to purify himself. When he was 19, Josephus chose the path of the Pharisees.

Then, in AD 64, at the age of twenty-six, Josephus sailed to Rome for the purpose of liberating some priestly friends who had been sent there by Felix, the procurator of Judea, to be judged by the emperor Nero. This trip proved to be an eventful one.

On the way to Rome, the large ship on which Josephus was voyaging sank. After swimming all night, he was eventually rescued by another passing vessel. Upon arriving in Italy, Josephus elicited the aid of Aliturus, a famous Jewish actor and favorite of Nero, who introduced him to Poppaea, Nero's wife. Poppaea, who was attracted to Judaism, achieved the release of Josephus's friends while also showering him with gifts.

The might and power of Rome no doubt made an indelible impression on Josephus during this trip. Upon his return to Judea, he found the entire country up in arms and ready to revolt. Josephus, like many of the priestly and upper classes to which he belonged, felt that accommodation with Rome was an absolute necessity for Jewish survival. The young man worked toward directing the people's passions away from open revolt.

When rebellion did break out, however, Josephus was chosen by the Jerusalem council to govern the Galilee. The extent of Josephus's commission is not clear. Nor is it clear why a young priest, with no prior military experience and with pro-Roman leanings, would be given charge of the Galilee, the area which was to bear the brunt of the Roman attack.

Upon arriving in the Galilee, Josephus tried to prepare the region against the Roman onslaught that was bound to come. In doing so, he raised an army and fortified key cities, including Tiberias, Migdal, and Gamla.[10] His actions were largely ineffectual, in part because of his own ineptitude, but also as a result of the lack of consensus among the Jews themselves. Thus valuable time and resources were frittered away in bitter infighting as the Roman war machine cast its lengthening shadow across the country.

The reasons behind the revolt were complex. Roman cruelty, excessive taxation, and religious and administrative oppression were all undoubtedly major factors. But the revolt also had its roots in a class struggle among the Jews: between the poor, primarily the rural population, who suffered most under Roman rule and therefore had the least to lose, and the wealthy classes, who, to a certain degree, could continue the good life. Among the dispossessed were the Zealots, a breakaway group from the Pharisees, who preached the tenet that it was unlawful to accept any ruler but God and that any foreign rule must be opposed unto death. There also existed in the Roman world during the first century AD a general belief that a person, or persons, coming out of Judea would rule the world. Some Jews believed that this ruler would appear in their hour of need and deliver them from Roman oppression. (Roman historians like Tacitus and Seutonius, on the other hand, took these predictions to refer to Vespasian and Titus, who were campaigning in Judea when Vespasian was hailed as emperor by his troops.[11])

Thus Josephus found himself surfing precariously on a sea of rival factions.

Upon hearing word of revolt in Judea, Nero chose the veteran general Vespasian to take charge of its suppression. This choice was somewhat surprising in that Vespasian had lost favor with Nero for absenting himself or, worse yet, falling asleep during the emperor's musical recitals, a breach of etiquette which could have had fatal results.

Upon taking his command, Vespasian chose to conquer the outlying areas before approaching Jerusalem. He began with the Galilee and, in a grinding campaign, conquered one city after the other. Josephus made his stand in the fortified city of Jotapata in the central Galilee, but when the city fell after a 47-day siege in July AD 67, Josephus managed to deliver himself to the Romans after tricking his own Jewish followers into committing suicide.

Brought before Vespasian, Josephus prophesied that the general would become emperor. Vespasian put him in chains. When Josephus's prediction came to pass, Vespasian removed the chains, and Josephus was freed. Later he was granted Roman citizenship and additional honors.

Josephus ben Matthias of Jerusalem became Josephus Flavius of Rome.

For the remainder of the war, Josephus traveled with the

Roman camp and aided the Romans, particularly during the siege and capture of Jerusalem, where he repeatedly called on the defenders to surrender.

Following the fall of Jerusalem, Josephus accompanied Titus to Rome. There he recorded his impressions of the triumphal parade granted to Titus and Vespasian in honor of the dissolution of Judea. The marvelous floats were the most remarkable aspect of the spectacle, according to Josephus. Some of these contraptions were so high—three and four stories high—that there was concern lest they keel over and injure the onlookers. These floats portrayed stages in the conquest of Judea and the subjugation of its people in all the gory and sadistic detail. Josephus notes:[12]

> Here was to be seen a prospering countryside laid waste, there whole battalions of the enemy put to the sword; here a party of men in flight, and there others led off to captivity; walls of enormous size were demolished by engines, great strongholds overpowered, cities whose battlements were well-manned with defenders utterly overwhelmed and an army streaming within the ramparts, the whole area deluged with blood. Those unable to resist raised their hands in supplication; temples were set on fire and houses torn down over the heads of their occupants; and, after utter desolation and misery, rivers were flowing, not over tilled soil nor supplying drink to men and beasts, but across a countryside still devoured by flames on every side; for such were the agonies to which the Jews had condemned themselves when they plunged into the war. The art and the marvelous workmanship of these constructions now revealed the events to those who had not seen them happen, as clearly as if they had been there. On each of the stages the commander of one of the captured cities was stationed in the attitude in which he was taken.
>
> Many ships also followed. . . .

Josephus did not enlighten us on why ships were being carried in the procession, but it is probable that these vessels commemorated the Battle of Migdal. Indeed, on a sesterius minted by

Titus—one of the coins in the Judaea Capta series, in which Vespasian and Titus celebrated their victory over Judea[13]—Titus stands
with his right foot on the bow of a ship, *perhaps* in honor of the
Roman victory at the Battle of Migdal.[14]

In Rome, Josephus began the second part of a remarkable life.
He lived out the rest of his life as a writer.

Four of his books have come down to us. *The Jewish War* was
completed soon after the fall of Jerusalem. This was to be an
official Roman version of the events. It was largely based on the
author's own experiences as a major player, but Josephus also
informs us that he had access to the Roman military records from
the campaign.

Antiquities of the Jews covers the history of the Jews from
earliest times down to the outbreak of the revolt in AD 66. *The Life
of Josephus* is autobiographical but is limited almost exclusively to
the short period of Josephus's military command in the Galilee in
AD 66–67. The book was written in response to a work by Justus of
Tiberias—which has not survived—in which he attacked Josephus. Finally, *Against Apion*, also known as *On the Antiquity of the
Jewish People*, was written to counter the many and varied slanders
of Greco-Roman writers against Judaism.

For archaeologists working in modern Israel, Josephus's
books are an invaluable source of information about life, events,
and the momentous times of the first century AD. While Josephus's
descriptions may be skewed in his favor and against that of his
political enemies, excavations at Masada, Jerusalem, and Gamla,
to name but a few, have shown his reports to be remarkably
accurate.

Josephus has long been viewed as a traitor by Jews. In a sense
it is almost as if Benedict Arnold had written the only history of
the American Revolution. It was the Christian church that guarded
his writings from the vicissitudes of time, because Josephus was
the only (more-or-less) contemporaneous author outside the New
Testament to refer to Jesus and John the Baptist.

Certainly Josephus was no saint and at times could be described as a self-serving sinner; note particularly the manner in

Titus stands with his foot on a prow: A memory of the Battle of Migdal?

which he escaped death at Jotapata. Nevertheless, we owe him a debt of gratitude for preserving a record of events which might have been lost forever. Without Josephus's accounts, the history of Judea and the Galilee in the first century AD becomes an intricately woven tapestry hung in a room barely penetrated by the light of day.

Josephus's character was complex and contradictory. Recognizing the impossibility of opposing Rome, he had worked to avoid the obvious catastrophe. Swept up in the revolt, he tried the best he could to organize the defenses of this command. After the fall of Jerusalem, Josephus easily could have abjured Judaism. Instead, he dedicated the rest of his life to recording its history and defending its cause against the anti-Jewish slanders of the Greco-Roman world in which he lived.

Josephus—like the builder of our boat—did the best that he could with what he had at hand.

eee

For a short time, the helicopters continued to circle above the boat. Then, as swiftly as they had come, they disappeared into the darkening western sky, leaving behind an audio trail of rapidly fading noise.

Chapter 7

The Impossible We Do Immediately; Miracles Take a Little Longer

"Who are *You*?" said the Caterpillar.

This was not an encouraging opening for a conversation. Alice replied, rather shyly, "I—I hardly know, Sir, just at present—at least I know who I *was* when I got up this morning, but I think I must have been changed several times since then."

"What do you mean by that?" said the Caterpillar, sternly. "Explain yourself!"

"I can't explain *myself*, I'm afraid, Sir," said Alice, "because I'm not myself, you see."

"I don't see," said the Caterpillar.

"I'm afraid I can't put it more clearly," Alice replied very politely, "for I can't understand it myself, to begin with; and being so many different sizes in a day is very confusing."

"It isn't," said the Caterpillar.

"Well, perhaps you haven't found it so yet," said Alice; "but when you have to turn into a chrysalis—you will some day, you know—and then after that into a butterfly, I should think you'll feel it a little queer, won't you?"

"Not a bit," said the Caterpillar.

From *Alice's Adventures in Wonderland*
LEWIS CARROLL[1]

W hile Dick was finishing his preliminary study of the hull, we were rapidly completing the excavation of the boat's interior. Since that terrible night when part of the stern had fallen in, we had successfully protected the hull from further collapse. During this entire period, the remaining hull had been encased in the mud rostrum on which it stood. Now our accomplishments were prompting new questions. Assuming that the hull remained intact, what, then, were we to do with it? We definitely wanted to study the boat further, and under better conditions than those at the crowded, muddy excavation site. And certainly, this venerable artifact was one that merited public display and attention. Avi, concerned about the lengthy time needed for conservation, had from the outset designated the Allon Museum, with its logistical capability and willingness to take charge of the boat's conservation, as the natural location for conserving the boat. The museum, however, was a good third of a mile up the coast.

The manner in which the boat would be conserved dictated how we would have to move it. There were two possibilities. We could take her apart and move her in pieces, or we could try to move the boat all in one piece, as a coherent hull. But which method should we use?

In those cases in which ships still have sufficient structural integrity, they have been raised and moved intact. The *Mary Rose*, for example, which served as Henry VIII's flagship until 1545, when she capsized and sank in the Solent, was raised in one piece. Similarly, the *Vasa*, a seventeenth-century Swedish warship, which sank in Stockholm harbor on its maiden voyage, was also raised in this manner. Both of these vessels, however, are large,

heavy-timbered oceangoing warships with immense and close-set
frames which keep the hulls' integrity intact.

Ancient ships were not built as strongly, however. For these,
the standard manner of excavating and removing a shipwreck for
conservation is by dismantling the hull into individual timbers.
The timbers are removed one by one. (When necessary, longer
timbers may even be intentionally broken—but not cut. After
conservation, a good conservationist can mend a break so that it
becomes invisible, but if the timbers have been sawed, the physical
connection between the pieces has been destroyed.) Once the
conservation process is complete, the ship is reassembled. As
individual timbers are easier to handle and require a smaller
conservation tank—and therefore fewer conservation chemicals—
than an intact hull, this is a more economical method for conserving the hull.

The first shipwreck to be handled in this manner was the
Kyrenia shipwreck. The method proved highly successful. After
undergoing the conservation process, the ship was reconstructed
and now forms a world-class museum display. In fact, for a ship
expert like Dick, who cut his archaeological teeth reconstructing
the Kyrenia shipwreck in the 1970s, taking the hull apart is prefer-
able, for it allows an expert to examine all surfaces of the boat's
timbers.

This conservation technique had been a distinct possibility
for the Galilee boat from the start. In fact, we had also given
serious thought to conserving the separated timbers in the stainless steel tank from an ill-fated milk truck that had been involved
in a recent automobile accident. Prior to the excavation, I had
asked Moshele to prepare wooden trays for storing timbers. However, as Moshele consistently refused to entertain the notion that
his boat would be taken apart for removal, he never did get
around to making the trays.

But then, there was another consideration. Orna calculated
that it would take up to seven years to conserve the boat. During
that time, there would be bills to pay. The process would require
chemicals, equipment, and electricity. The Department of Antiqui-

ties would be hard-pressed to come up with the funding required to initiate and sustain the conservation effort. For at least part of the process the vessel, although submerged, could be visible to the public. Why not take advantage of the public interest generated by the boat to exhibit her *during the conservation process* and then use the funds generated by admission fees to defray the expanses, at least in part. No one would pay to see trays of broken pieces of timber in them, however. Furthermore, Dick soon had to depart, leaving us without a qualified boat reconstructor to record the timbers.

In the end, the boat—as usual—decided the issue for us. She told us very clearly that she had no intention of being taken apart. She was holding onto her physical integrity by her nails.

Quite literally.

While the boat's planks were attached to each other, as well as to the keel, by mortise-and-tenon joints, her frames had been fastened to the planking with iron nails. On ancient Mediterranean shipwrecks, because of the chemical reaction between iron and seawater, iron nails decompose, facilitating the separation of the planking from the frames. All that usually remains are the holes where the nails had been, along with some minor discolorations and concretions. We were in for a surprise, however, when Orna came back from having one of the loose nails sectioned at a laboratory.

There was less than a millimeter of rust on it.

"It looked so brand-new," Orna related, "that the lab technician refused to believe me when I told him that the nail was ancient."

Furthermore, as Dick had pointed out to us, the nails were so deeply imbedded in the wood that they still gave the hull some structural integrity. Additionally, the little corrosion that *had* taken place had permeated the wood, bonding the nails to the surrounding timber. There was no way of taking the boat apart without doing serious, possibly irreparable, harm to her. No, she had to be conserved as an integral hull. But then how does one move a 27-foot-long boat which is built of timbers so weak that they might as

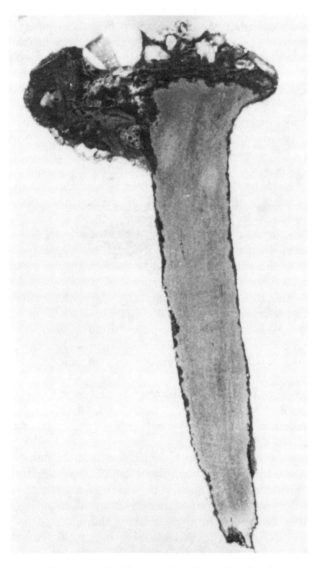

There was virtually no rust on the sectioned nail.

well have been made of yellow cheese or wet cardboard? Again, I solicited Dick's opinion on this problem.

He thought for a moment and then said, "Free advice is one commodity that is never lacking in Israel. Now, that can be used to our advantage. Why don't you call in everyone you can think of who knows anything at all about moving heavy and delicate equipment? And then listen to what they propose."

Dick's suggestion had me burning up the telephone lines for hours. I contacted experts from the Haifa and Ashdod Port Authorities; from the Israeli army, navy, and air force; private contractors; and engineers. Soon a torrent of experts was arriving at the site. Many possible solutions were suggested by the visitors.

"You could build a museum on the site by banging iron pilings into the mud," one expert said.

"What happens when the water eventually returns?" I asked.

He hadn't thought of that.

We had a visit from a special navy rescue unit, which proposed using air cushions to raise the boat. No one could assure us, however, that the air cushions could sustain equal pressure on all sections of the hull at once. Raising the boat unevenly would surely tear her apart.

All the ideas proposed were either too long and complicated to carry out or too expensive. Some experts came up with "Rube Goldberg" methods of scooping up the boat, together with the mud platform on which it rested. The majority, however, once they understood the problems we were facing with the delicate ancient timbers, simply shook their heads and told us that what we wanted to do was impossible.

This common consensus was admirably summed up by one self-assured engineer who pompously told Orna and me, "There is no way that this can be done. It's impossible. If you move this boat successfully to the Allon Museum without its falling apart on you, *az ahni koogelager* [Hebrew slang for 'then I'll be a ball bearing']."

We thanked him and went back, depressed, to the drawing board. There had to be a solution. It was out there.

Somewhere.

In the end, the solution turned out to be close at hand. In fact, it had been incubating inside Orna's mind. The two of us were sitting together on one of the logs that Yuvi and Moshele had scattered about the site during the original probe excavation. We were both bone-weary. Orna puffed on a cigarette.

"There is one possibility," she said quietly.

"Which is?"

"Remember the way I solidified the stern with polyurethane."

I nodded.

"Well, we could do that on a grand scale. Spray the entire boat, inside and out, with polyurethane. It would keep the hull immobilized, like a doctor's cast on a broken bone."

Orna stared off into space. She seemed to have gone for a walk inside herself for a moment. "Of course, the polyurethane alone would not give any structural strength," she continued, flicking the ash off her cigarette, "so we would have to add additional supports to the hull to make sure it doesn't crack the polyurethane coating by its sheer weight."

"OK, how do we do that?" Obviously Orna was on a roll.

She was silent again for a while. "We could girdle the boat with fiberglass and polyester," she said. "Inside, we could add a fiberglass frame between every two original wooden ones."

By the time Orna was done, she had conceived a deceptively simple and yet admirably reasonable method for packaging the boat. One that just might work.

"I told you there was a solution," I said with a grin.

Orna didn't smile.

ᒪᒪᒪ

I immediately conferred with Avi who, quite legitimately, wanted a second opinion before he sprinkled bureaucratic holy water over Orna's proposal.

The next day Avi drove down from Jerusalem together with several other Department of Antiquities officials. With him was Dodo Shenhav, who heads the Conservation Laboratory at the

Israel Museum and is one of the foremost experts on conservation in Israel. Orna presented her ideas to all of them over thick, hot Turkish coffee and burrekas (salty pastries usually filled with potatoes, cheese, or spinach) in the Nof Ginosar cafeteria, where I had first met Yuvi and Moshele.

"Has it really been only two weeks since then?" I mused to myself. It seemed to me as if a chunk of eternity had got itself wedged between then and now.

Smoke from a dozen cigarettes curled about us and clouded the air as Orna began to speak. When she had finished her presentation, Dodo asked several pertinent questions concerning the manner in which she proposed to carry out each step of the process. Orna's answers were specific and concise. Then there was a lull in the conversation, as if everything that needed to be said had been.

I asked Dodo if he felt that the process that Orna proposed had a chance of success. He nodded. Yes, he agreed, it was possible, although no one could assure us that it would work, and, at each step we would face numerous dangers to the boat. But yes, theoretically, it could work.

I looked at Avi. He took a deep draw on his cigarette, stared out the window for a long moment, and then nodded his agreement.

"Let's do it," I said.

ΩΩΩ

Kibbutz Ginosar had a way of constantly surprising us with its resources. Its members rose to each need on every occasion. We now discovered that several of the kibbutzniks were experts in the application of fiberglass and polyester. This time is was David "Davidi" Ronen and Yohai Abbas who came to the rescue.

Ginosar naturally had a large fleet of boats of varying sizes and vintages to take advantage of the pleasures of living adjacent to the Kinneret. At that time Yohai and Davidi were jointly responsible for the kibbutz boats, which were used for recreation as well as for educating the younger generation in the delights of sailing and rowing. As part of this task, they also had to repair the boats, mainly by using fiberglass. In this way the two had become proficient in the use of fiberglass as a material for fixing and constructing boats. Indeed, some of the kibbutz craft were so old that they would have been abandoned had not Davidi and Yohai entirely encased them in fiberglass, using the wooden hull as a core.

It was this expertise which the two men brought to the ancient boat, where, within the hour, they were busily employed turning Orna's theoretical solution into a physical reality. Previously, Yohai and Davidi had discussed between themselves the possibility of packing the boat entirely in fiberglass, but they had realized that fiberglass alone would not give the boat sufficient support.

Together with a third kibbutznik, Yossi Amitai, they first created an external band around the hull at the upper limits to which it was preserved. Once that task was completed, they began working inside the boat.

As overburden was still being removed in the stern, they started amidships and worked their way slowly toward the bow. Amid the noxious fumes given off by the polyester resin that was required to bond the mats of fiberglass, they began to create a new set of frames for an old boat. First, Orna would lay down aluminum foil on the bare wood to prevent it from coming into direct contact with the fiberglass. Then layers of fiberglass matting were laid down and liberally doused with polyester resin.

It was Davidi who came up with a method for strengthening the frames structurally. To each frame they were creating, the two men curved a length of black flexible PVC irrigation hose, which had been "borrowed" from the kibbutz fields, and then bonded it in place with additional layers of fiberglass soaked with polyester resin. When this solidified, the hoses formed an angle in the profile of the frames which made them stronger and better able to resist bending.

Only years later did I discover that this was the second "ancient" boat on which Yohai and Davidi had worked.

Davidi (right) and Yohai create the first fiberglass frame inside the hull.

"There was an air of déjà vu about the whole process for Davidi and me," Yohai recalled. "Some time before the adventure with the Galilee boat, we had been commissioned to build a replica of an ancient boat for use in a movie concerning the life of Jesus on the Sea of Galilee. After looking through some books on ancient vessels, we took an old boat that belonged to the *meshek* ["farm," or "kibbutz"] and added a false stern and bow of fiberglass to it. We even topped it off with a square sail.

"Some of the shots were filmed on the lake. But for a scene of the storm on the lake, the film crew transported our 'ancient' boat into the swimming pool at a nearby kibbutz and created a 'storm' by means of two tractors. These were so successful in creating waves that the boat almost sank in the pool, along with the actors.

"And now, here Davidi and I were, for a second time, using fiberglass to cover an 'ancient' fishing boat. Only this time *she really was ancient*."

It took the better part of three days to complete "fiberglassing" the interior of the hull. Davidi and Yohai worked their way toward the bow, creating a fiberglass frame between every two of the hull's framing stations.

We now had four separate groups working simultaneously on the boat. This gave the whole scene the appearance of an assembly-line construction sequence. Outside the boat, we carefully began to remove the upper part of the mud podium on which she rested. We were concerned that the hull, without this support, might splay outward. To prevent this from happening, Gill molded vertical Styrofoam braces against the hull's exterior at fixed intervals. At the stern, excavators still lay on the hanging platform removing the remaining mud. As soon as they cleared the timbers, Danny was there stringing, tagging, and photographing them, and then Davidi and Yohai would swath the same area with fiberglass frames. Between, over, and among them, Dick was finishing up his recording. And everything was going like clockwork.

While all this was going on, Zvika was diligently enlarging the area around his boat fragments. First, he, together with other volunteers from Migdal using shovels and mattocks, enlarged the area where they had been found, laboriously digging down from seabed level to immediately above the height of the hull fragments. Then Zvika, alone, in what was clearly a labor of love, carefully dug around the timbers. By Sunday, February 23, he had revealed sizable portions of them. Both fragments continued tantalizingly into the mud. They might end a few more inches down, or they might be just the tips of an additional intact hull or two. There was no telling how much of either hull still lay buried out of sight.

I would have given anything to let Zvika continue enlarging the area, but it was now time to clear the way so that we could give our full attention to the boat itself. So, after Dick had completed studying both fragments in situ, and after they had been recorded on film by Danny, and in sketches by Rafi Malka, one of our artists in residence, Zvika and I carefully removed the exposed portions and sandbagged the continuations. While we were in the process of doing so, I made a silent promise to myself to come back one day to retrieve them.

ʔʔʔ

That evening, the last mud was removed from inside the hull at the stern, and the final fiberglass frames were immediately laid. This happened at such speed that Danny did not even have an opportunity to "string" or record on film this portion of the hull. The boat's interior began to take on the surreal appearance of a space-shuttle cargo bay.

The last frames were completed on the evening of Sunday, February 23.

The fiberglass frames, together with the aluminum foil backing and PVC pipes used in their construction, made the hull resemble the cargo bay of a space shuttle.

Rotem, when he wasn't down and dirty with the rest of us in the mud, was in charge of building a new wing of the Nof Ginosar guest house. He arranged for a construction firm that specialized in spraying polyurethane insulation into buildings, which he had recently employed at the guest house, to be on call. They had arrived in the afternoon, their orange truck introducing a bright splash of earth-tone color into an otherwise blue-green landscape.

That evening we placed a thick layer of polyethylene sheeting inside the hull. This was done both to prevent the polyurethane from bonding to the wood and to insulate the boat's timbers from the heat generated by the chemical reaction of the polyurethane as it solidified.

Then a workman from the construction firm climbed onto the

hanging platform. An assistant handed him a spray gun attached to two long black hoses encrusted with rust-colored splashes of old polyurethane; these extended, snakelike, out of the pit to pressurized barrels that had been placed nearby. The workman quietly and methodically cleaned out the spray gun's "barrels" with a rusty nail attached to the gun by an old and knotted string. When he was satisfied that all was as it should be, he began firing short consecutive bursts of two dark orange liquids into the bow. At each pull of the trigger, the gun made a *shfft-shfft* noise— as if a snake with a bad case of the hiccups was trying to hiss— followed immediately by the sound of the liquids hitting the plastic sheetings: *pllt-pllt*.

Beyond straightening out the polyethylene sheeting and making sure that the hoses didn't come into physical contact with the hull, there was not much for us to do at this point. So we all stood around watching, and listening, as the hull filled up.

To the astonishment of those of us unfamiliar with polyurethane spray, upon coming into contact with each other, the liquids boiled and bubbled, frothed and foamed. And then they solidified into a Styrofoam-like material. In the process, the polyurethane changed in color before our eyes from dark orange to bright yellow. As each squirt solidified, it was covered again, and then again, by further bursts from the spray gun.

Into the polyurethane, we put several rigid white PVC pipes, each with its lower end resting firmly on a fiberglass frame. These would allow access to the hull should groundwater seep into the boat from its mud podium.

The hull began to fill slowly with polyurethane. Under the soft glow of the fishermen's lanterns, it looked as if a rapidly expanding living organism was slowly consuming the boat. There was something mesmerizing and unreal, even magical, about the whole experience. This feeling was heightened by the surrounding clammy darkness, barely kept at bay by the lanterns. I had the distinct feeling that somehow we all had fallen into the reels of a Spielberg movie.

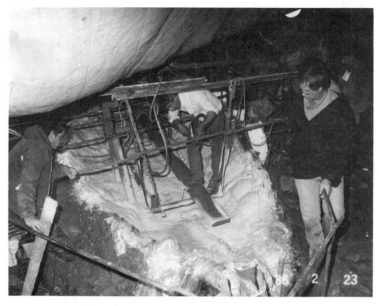

Spraying on the polyurethane.

Spraying the hull took several hours, but by midnight, the entire interior of the hull had been filled with a solid mass of polyurethane.

We called it a day.

ﻩﻩﻩ

Upon arriving at the boat on the next morning, Monday, February 24, we found that the polyurethane fill inside the hull was floating on a pool of groundwater that had infiltrated the boat overnight. Some nervous moments were spent as a flexible pipe was lowered down one of the vertical PVC pipes to pump out the water. Later that day, we had Shmuel come back with his backhoe and deepen the pit to prevent additional groundwater from reaching the hull, as well as to give easier access to the hull during the next stage of the operation. When he had completed the task, the boat stood on a mud podium that rose well above the surrounding pit.

It was vital that the hull be held in a firm grasp by the polyurethane, like a leg in a plaster cast. There must be no room for the hull to slip and slide inside the polyurethane envelope. But now, the fact that the polyurethane had managed to float hinted that it might not have been molded sufficiently snugly to the framing inside the boat, probably because the polyethylene sheeting that we had used was too thick to allow the polyurethane to acquire the hull's curves. Thus, much of the morning was spent cutting away the polyurethane fill in the forward part of the bow, laying down a finer-gauge polyethylene sheeting, and finally re-spraying polyurethane.

With the hull safely insulated from the sun by the polyurethane fill, the hanging bridge and the tarpaulin were no longer needed. When they were removed, the pit appeared to be filled by an immense eclair, while the PVC pipes stuck out of the polyurethane peculiarly, giving the boat the appearance of a miniature steamship.

Now came the tricky part. We had to entirely package the *exterior* of the hull—without moving it. To accomplish this task, we began excavating a series of tunnels under the boat. The width of each tunnel was the absolute minimum necessary for the person digging it to get his or her shoulders through. Meanwhile the mud between the tunnels supported the boat.

Digging these tunnels was an unpleasant affair, rather like working in a narrow, airless mine. The exposed hull was directly above. Diggers would lie on their bellies, as water slowly soaked into their clothing. Inside the tunnels, the diggers were in a dark dank world where the air in the confined space rapidly became stale as they slowly scraped the mud away with their hands. Above their heads, the tunnelers would see vertical rows of the round nail heads which held the frames to the planking.

As each pair of tunnelers—who were working toward each

Digging the tunnels beneath the boat: a particularly exhausting and unpleasant task.

other from port and starboard—met, they were quickly followed by Yohai and Davidi. Using a long strip of polyethylene sheeting as slices of a "fiberglass sandwich," the two would lay swatches of fiberglass matting on half the sheet, douse them with polyester resin, and then cover the whole potion by folding over the other half of the sheet. Gingerly, the "truss" would be passed through the tunnel and quickly molded to the boat's underside by means of ropes wrapped around the hull and supported on makeshift braces made of boards and pieces of Styrofoam. Then, at each of its upper extremities, each truss was attached with fiberglass and polyester. Haste was of the essence in this operation, as the brew solidified in minutes. Soon, Davidi and Yohai had the process down to an exact science.

Once a truss was in place, a fine film of polyethylene sheeting was placed on the floor of the tunnel to prevent the polyurethane from adhering to the mud. Then polyurethane was sprayed into the tunnel, filling the hollow. As the foam has the ability to bond to polyurethane that has already solidified, it was possible to join the external covering to the inside fill by spraying it over the side edges. Soon it solidified, turning the tunnels into external frames, supporting the hull and consolidating the entire mass.

We began the tunnels from the stern and worked toward the bow. It was only during this process of digging beneath the boat that she revealed to us several more clues about herself.

I had naturally assumed that the missing sternpost, which had caused the collapse of the stern starboard quarter, had simply rotted away. I was wrong. In the first tunnel, we found the keel side of the scarf, or wood-locking mechanism, which had originally attached the sternpost into the keel. Someone had clearly

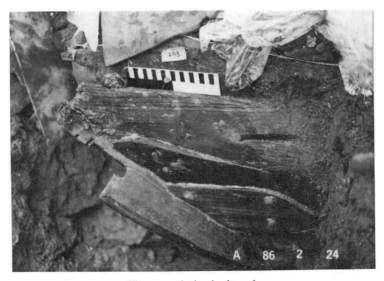

The severed after keel scarf.

disengaged the linchpin and carefully removed the entire stern-post.

Just before he left to return to Texas, Dick showed me some holes in the planking ends. "Look here," he said. "Someone in antiquity pulled out the nails that held the strakes to the sternpost. And he probably used a pair of pliers to do it, to judge from the marks he left."

Hmmm. Curious.

As the tunnels progressed eastward, toward the boat's bow, another odd feature came to light. The day after Dick left, one of the tunnelers working under the boat's starboard bow called me over.

"Take a look in there," he said, pointing to the tunnel out of which he had just reversed, caked in mud.

Crawling into the tunnel underneath the hull, I was surprised to find a row of mortise-and-tenon scars in the portion of the keel that protruded beneath the hull. I could think of no purpose that these joints could have served on our boat. This meant that the keel—at least the forward part of it—had been made of reused wood.

But there was no time to reflect on that now; it would have to be dealt with later. Danny photographed the mortise-and-tenon scars, and soon afterward they disappeared behind a fiberglass truss and billowing polyurethane foam.

In order to package the bow, we had to move the tree stump on which the keel at this extremity rested. After considerable effort, we excavated it and slipped it out from beneath the keel, careful to avoid placing any pressure on the keel.

By the next day, Tuesday, February 25, the first row of tunnels had been completed, packed, and filled. We now started on the second row of tunnels through the remaining mud podium, re-peating the process.

While the fiberglass frames and polyurethane blanket stabi-lized the hull's timbers, we realized that additional structural support would be required when it came time to move the boat. Eitan "Eitani" Shalem, a member of Ginosar and a builder by

Mortise scars on the forward starboard side of the keel beneath the garboards.

profession, designed a wooden base that would give structural
strength to the entire package. As the second row of tunnels was
hollowed out, Eitani supervised the placement of two-by-four
timbers that were held in place by workers when the polyurethane
was sprayed into the tunnels.

We worked throughout that day. The sun crossed the sky in a
hurry and then set in the west. And then it sucked the remaining
light down with it, to be replaced by the lanterns. The first row of
polyurethane frames was now separated by the second row of
tunnels. The extremities of the PVC hoses that had been used to
strengthen the fiberglass frames stuck out at odd angles, like
antennae. The ropes that secured the fiberglass trusses crossed
over the hull. As the night progressed, the boat seemed to me to be
in a state of metamorphosis. She looked like a weird and huge
many-legged caterpillar wearing suspenders.

During the night, somebody—I don't remember who—called
me over to the port side of the boat. There, while digging one of
the tunnels amidships, he had found some timbers *beneath* the
boat that extended outward for a short distance. The night was too
dark, and the timbers were too covered in mud, for us to determine the identity of this assembly. Obviously it was ancient and
must predate our boat, I thought, for it was found stratigraphi-
cally beneath it. Probably these were planks from an additional
vessel. That would make a fourth. Concerned that the assembly's
timbers might be damaged in the dark, I had work on that particular tunnel stopped until the next morning.

The packaging of the boat was nearing completion now. We
continued working late into the night, creeping toward the home
stretch. We were all near exhaustion. I saw one person fall asleep
in the mud, his head leaning forward against one of the polyurethane pillars. He later woke up and continued digging his
tunnel. Eventually, while it was still dark, I called a halt to the
work. We would all need a few hours of rest to prepare for the next
day's work.

In the bright light of early morning, the timbers of the assembly jutting out beneath the boat looked strange. I could make out

the round peg heads of some mortise-and-tenon joints on some of the planking, but the pegs didn't seem to be aligned properly. The assembly had several short planks set edge to edge, aligned more-or-less parallel to the boat. The plank farthest away from the boat had a framelike timber attached to it. On the right side of the assembly, as I crouched facing the boat, there was another roughly dressed log placed over the timber and the planking. A short portion of an additional, similar timber was located parallel to it on the left. Finally, one more timber was placed parallel to the planks, yet over the two side timbers. While the entire assembly seemed to be built of used parts from old boats, the assembly itself was obviously not part of a boat. Strange.

There was no choice but to remove the assembly. The remainder, which continued under the boat, would have to be sacrificed. I had Edna sketch and attach numbered tags to the timbers; Danny

The assembly was made of old boat parts but was not part of a boat.

followed with his cameras. Before the assembly had been re-moved, Eitani had already inserted a set of wire-bound two-by-fours through the tunnel, in anticipation of its being filled with polyurethane.

As the day progressed, first one, then another, and then a third of the remaining tunnels were finished off, trussed up, and sealed with polyurethane. Eitani, assisted by others, finished the structural base by wiring additional two-by-fours along the length of the boat encased on either side.

The boat was packaged and ready for removal; the caterpillar had been entirely encased in its cocoon.

The question of how to move the boat had been occupying our thoughts for several days now. The Israeli air force had offered us the loan of one of its larger classes of helicopters to transport the

At the end of the process, the boat, without having been moved a millimeter, had been encased in a protective cocoon.

boat, but having had the experience of being transported in these more than once during my army service, and having had my insides shaken out in the process, I was wary of what the vibrations might do to the boat. Rightly so, as it turned out, for when we conferred with several pilots who visited us, they agreed that the vibrations from the rotor, which would pass through the lifting cable to the boat, might be sufficiently strong to break the boat into match sticks, even though the stronger polyurethane casing would probably be left unscathed. At the very least, the vibrations were likely to weaken significantly the already weak timbers.

A second possibility that we discussed and turned down was to lift the boat onto the flatbed trailer of an eighteen-wheeler. We could not be sure, however, that such a heavy vehicle might not sink into the mud, so we considered the possibility of laying down a road on the lake bed to the Allon Museum.

It was Shlomkeh who came up with the obvious solution. "Hevra ['Gang'], what's the problem?" he asked. "The lake is here, right next to the boat. The water is high now, and polyurethane floats. All we have to do is to cut a channel to the lake through the dike and sail the boat out. It's that simple."

Now, as the final touches were being put on the boat's packaging, the sounds of heavy machinery filtered down to us in the pit. Looking up, I saw a huge steam shovel lumbering toward us.

Nitsa had arranged for the loan of a steam shovel, which was normally used in removing sediment from the Hula region. The Sachaf Company, which owned it, kindly donated both the use of the steam shovel and its transportation to the site.

As the shovel began carving a tunnel through the dike, we reversed the pumps that had been keeping the groundwater at bay and began pumping water from the lake back into the excavation pit. The water slowly rose in the pit.

Great chunks of mud sheared off from the sides of the pit and cascaded into the pool as they were undercut by the water, reminding me of nature films showing chunks of ice cascading from glaciers into the sea. This was to prove useful. The collapsing mud left almost vertical faces on the sides of the pit, which gave a clear

We reversed the pumps, and they begin spewing water into the pit.

picture of the stratigraphy of the different types of sediment that had covered the boat, and which Danny was quick to record.

Our activities drew many spectators, who ringed the pit waiting for the big moment when the boat would slip her ancient moorings. The inevitable film crews lined the shores. There was a joyous and humorous—almost carnival—atmosphere to the whole experience. Our *gazlan* did a staggering trade in ice cream and soft drinks.

As the water rose in the pit, we would gently rock the boat from time to time, trying to disconnect her from the mud on which she rested. We were concerned that this not be too traumatic a severing. Also, we had taken pains to make the bottom of the polyurethane fill wider than the top, to give the boat better flotation capabilities. Nevertheless, there was no real way of knowing how she would float in the water until she did so. I was concerned that the boat might still be too top-heavy. So was Orna, who climbed up on the boat as human ballast, should the boat need to be stabilized on its journey. As it turned out, when the boat finally came clear from the mud, it sat beautifully in the water and had perfect trim.

The steam shovel operator did not totally breach the dike until the water pumped into the pit had reached the approximately height of the Kinneret's waters, for we wanted to avoid even the slightest wave. At this time my fervent hope was that the steam shovel would not discover any additional boats while cutting through the dike.

As the first waters of the Kinneret mingled with the water inside the pit, a spontaneous shout went up from the onlookers. Now the steam shovel took deep bites out of the dike, creating a channel that connected the pit with the lake. Ofer Sabag, a Kin-

The first waters from the Kinneret flow through the breached dike into the pit.

neret Authority employee who had been in charge of the pumps, now checked the depth of the channel with a stick. When he judged that the channel was sufficiently deep, we had the steam shovel operator desist and, to the cheers of the many onlookers on land, began walking the boat out of the pit. There was an intoxicating feeling of euphoria: of finally reaching the peak.

We immediately ran into a last-minute snag when the boat slid up on a mud bank. We spent several nervous moments maneuvering the boat off and around this bank, and then, she was clear of the final obstacle. She set sail again, for the first time in 2,000 years.

Only *eleven* frenetic days had passed since the beginning of the excavation. To me, it seemed a much shorter time. In my memory, excavating, packaging, and moving the boat all seem to run together. I asked others for their impression of the expedition's "time line." Yohai thought it had been five days; Rotem felt that it had taken two or three. My own estimate was six days.

Many spectators came to witness the launch and to cheer the boat on its way.

And away we go . . .

If I had to choose one moment during the entire excavation which was the most meaningful and packed with emotions, it was when the boat sailed out on the lake. I think that everyone who was involved in the project felt the same way.

Isaac, who had watched from the shore that day, summed it up. "When the boat began to move out was one of the most emotional moments in my life," he told me, with a twinkle in his eyes. "I shivered to watch it sail away. That was really something, a very emotional experience. I remember thinking at the time, those with weak hearts should not watch this. It was truly an historical moment."

We walked the boat through the shallow portion of the lake to the Allon Museum. There we were met by a rowboat crewed by children from the kibbutz's boating school. Our boat was taken in tow by the children, who rowed back to Ginosar's small fisher-

. . . only to get stuck on a mud bank.

men's port. So it was that the boat was *propelled by rowers* to the port. That night, the boat was moored with the modern fishing boats. As Yohai put it, "We wanted her to feel at home again."

Meanwhile, back at the museum, one of the television crews interviewed Orna.

"You were the first person to sail in the boat in two thousand years. How was it?" the interviewer asked her expectantly.

Orna reflected on this for a minute. "Well, quite exciting. I enjoyed it," she said, matter-of-factly.

Later that afternoon, as the sun set, and with the boat safely berthed, we gathered outside the museum to celebrate. Karen had promised a bottle of champagne to the first person to fall face-first in the mud. No one had, although almost everyone had come close at one time or another. So the champagne was used for a party after the excavation.

The boat sailed on the Kinneret once again.

The next day was spent devising a framework platform with which the boat could be raised onto shore, and later into the conservation pool which would be built to her specifications. The platform had to be built in such a manner that it could be removed once the boat had been placed inside the pool. Otherwise, the iron frame would cause problems during the conservation process.

This took some doing, and again several ponderous contraptions were created on paper before someone came up with a simple yet workable solution. He proposed two rails bolted to the upper sides of a pair of three-sided frame pieces.

When the lifting frame was ready, Moshele, Yohai, and I went down to the harbor and attached a cable from a motorboat and slowly towed the boat back to the Allon Museum. We joked about attaching a motor mount directly to the ancient vessel, thus turning it into a speedboat but felt that would have been irreverent, not to mention dangerous. Yohai drove the modern motorboat while

The next morning a motorboat towed the boat opposite the Yigal Allon Centre.

Moshele and I stood on her wooden understructure as the boat cleared the harbor and headed slowly toward the museum.

There a large crane lowered the lifting frame into the water, and the boat was floated over it. Final adjustments were made by Eitani with some two-by-fours to ensure that the boat would sit firmly on the frame. Then I signaled the crane to begin lifting. We watched in silence—I held my breath—as the boat became airborne overhead, rising majestically out of the lake, dripping water. When she had reached sufficient height, the operator slowly rotated the crane, carrying her to shore and gently placing her on land next to a chalk rectangle marked out in the dirt that designated where the conservation pool was to be built. The boat had safely reached shore.

The boat was slowly floated over the frame, and final adjustments were made before . . .

. . . the boat was lifted, finally coming to rest on shore next to the site chosen for its conservation pool.

𐚜𐚜𐚜

Sometimes at night, when I give my imagination full reign, I see the wife of that cocky engineer we consulted who had been so convinced that it was *impossible* to move the boat. In this scene, she is sleeping in bed when she wakes to find that her husband is gone.

And in his place is a large, shiny ball bearing.

Chapter 8

A Pride of Scholars

No one lights a lamp and then covers it with a pot. . .

Luke 8: 16[1]

D uring the excavation everyone had been particularly careful to avoid making unqualified pronouncements about the craft. Under the intense pressures of the rescue mission, we had had no time to study the raw data unearthed. Indeed, there had been barely time to record it. When queried about the boat's historical significance, I stressed that we were at present concerned with saving it. The time for understanding it would come later.

That time had now come. Could she be one of the boats used by Jesus and his Apostles and disciples as related in the Gospels? Or was she perhaps one of the boats that had washed up on the crimson beach after the Battle of Migdal?

These and many other questions had been posed by the media and by visitors, as well as by those of us participating in the excavation. The boat was loaded with a cargo of information; that much was clear. But this information was encrypted in the manner in which she had been built and the ways in which she had been used. It was hidden in the few artifacts which had been found in and around her.

The task ahead was to decode the messages. The answers were there; it was now a matter of asking the right questions and finding a means of answering them.

Between visits to Ginosar to assist Orna in preparing the boat for conservation and my regular inspections and dives along the Mediterranean coast, I began work on a scholarly publication about the boat for the Department of Antiquities. As I conceived it, this report would relate what had transpired since the ancient vessel's discovery and explore new insights gained into life and seafaring on the Kinneret in its day.

In the popular depiction of archaeologists, they seem to be perpetually in the field. In truth, this view owes more to Hollywood than to reality. Immense amounts of time and effort are expended in translating the quantities of raw data from an excavation into meaningful knowledge.

When I was growing up, one of my favorite books, and one of the first books I remember reading, was B. M. Hilleyer's *Child's History of the World*. My old and beat-up copy had a dark green cover. The frontispiece drawing was a delightful black-and-white silhouette of an unshaven caveman in a grass skirt looking up in wonder at two "new-fangled" single-propeller biplanes.

I loved that book. It made the past come alive for me. And although the book, which was published in 1924, related world history up to the end of the Great War (World War I), I rarely read past the chapter on the pyramids of Egypt before beginning anew.

In the book, Hilleyer explained in the simplest and clearest terms I have read to date how it is that archaeologists know about what happened in the past.

The truth is, we don't. *We are only guessing.*

But there are two types of guessing: One is mere chance, the other is *reasoned*. If you find footsteps in the snow the morning after a fresh snowfall, it would be a reasonable assumption that someone has been there, as shoes do not normally walk by themselves. Deductive reasoning, the basis for all good detective work as exemplified in Sir Arthur Conan Doyle's Sherlock Holmes stories, is what archaeology is all about.

The majority of an archaeologist's time is spent—or at least *should* be spent—studying the results of fieldwork in the relative quiet and seclusion of workrooms and libraries. A site's stratigraphy must be studied and interpreted. Artifacts must be divided into like groups, a process called *typology*, and compared with similar objects found at other sites in an attempt to determine how they may be related and what significance, if any, these relationships may have. An artifact is only as valuable as our ability to place it correctly in the context from which it came. And unfortunately, artifacts rarely come with name tags attached.

To illustrate the problems inherent in *interpreting* the past, I am particularly fond of a well-known folktale that relates how an Indian prince once brought an elephant before a group of blind men.

"Touch the beast," the prince commanded the blind men, "and describe its appearance to me."

Each man grasped a different part of the elephant and, from deductions based on his sense of touch, defined the animal.

"Oh," said one who had touched the elephant's trunk, "an elephant is like a snake."

A second, whose lot fell to handling the elephant's ear, corrected him: "No, it is like a sheet of parchment."

"Not true," said the third, who had been feeling one of the elephant's broad legs, "for this animal is quite clearly like a pillar."

"My friends are mistaken," said the fourth, who stood next to the pachyderm's body and rubbed his hands across its wrinkled flanks, "for this beast is most like a wall."

The fifth man, who had grasped the elephant's tail only smiled. He knew that his sightless friends were all wrong—for obviously this animal was like a rope.

It is important to remember that those who study the past are very much like those blind men. *We can touch the past but cannot see it.*

It stands to reason, then, that the more facets of the past which can be studied—the more "parts of the elephant" that can be touched—the more likely is the archaeologist to *approach* an understanding of past realities. As new information becomes available, it is necessary to reconsider previous conclusions, for there always remains the possibility that the archaeologist has attached the trunk to the wrong end of the elephant—in a purely metaphorical sense, of course.

Today no one person can possibly be an expert in all the aspects of research required to study the past. Imagine a chest of drawers. Each of the drawers holds a different treasure, and to open each drawer requires a different key. The "keys" in this case are scholars, each with the expertise that could unlock one of the forms of information encoded in the boat.

The most difficult part of any problem is defining exactly

what the problem is. Once that is accomplished, finding a solution is usually relatively easy. In consideration of this point, I first created a wish list of all the general research questions—"treasure drawers"—that I wished to explore concerning the boat. These questions I then translated into chapter headings. Next to each title I wrote down the name of the scholar (the key) who I considered best qualified to write that specific chapter.

The authors of some chapters were already clear. Obviously, Dick would write a preliminary report on the boat's construction. This was to be the heart of the report. Orna would author the chapters concerning the methods used in packaging, moving, and conserving the hull. I asked Danny to write on Moshele's arrowhead. Together with Edna and Kurt, I would author reports on the discovery and the excavation of the boat.

What now was to unfold was a true detective story, and in many ways, it turned out to be an experience which I personally found to be no less exciting—and enriching—than the boat's discovery and excavation.

The first problem to tackle was the question of the boat's age. When had she lived her life? For a shipwreck found with its cargo intact, dating the hull is normally a fairly easy matter. Date the cargo items, the personal effects of the crew and passengers, and the other articles carried on board, and the ship's date will follow. Our boat, however, contained no cargo, and the few artifacts found in and around her could not be reliably connected to the vessel. The boat chose to be coy and to hide her age. She was going to make me sweat for this one.

Dick, in the hand-written report which he gave to Avi on the day he left the excavation, had noted, "If this were a hull found in the Mediterranean, I would date it between the first century BC and the second century AD.

Careful scholar that Dick is, however, he had also emphasized in his letter that traditions of wooden hull construction may have continued on the Kinneret long after they had gone out of use on the more cosmopolitan Mediterranean Sea. Dating a shipwreck solely by construction techniques is never prudent, even on the

Mediterranean, where the evolution of ship construction has been extensively documented. To do so for a hull found in the Sea of Galilee, when there were no other known shipwrecks, would be doubly unwise.

The pottery found around the boat had already given us a vague estimate for her date, but pottery experts could probably tell us much more. I began by making an appointment to see Varda Sussman and Dr. David Adan-Bayewitz.

Varda, who is now retired, was for many years a curator for the Department of Antiquities. During her time as curator, she took a special interest in the many beautiful and rare lamps among the collections that were in her domain. She began studying lamps and eventually became a recognized authority on the subject of the ancient oil lamps of Israel.

David had recently completed his doctoral dissertation—since then published as a book—which deals with pottery in the Galilee during the Roman–Byzantine period. We could not do better.

On the appointed day, Edna and I brought all the pottery from the excavation. There really wasn't very much of it. The lamp and the cooking pot found during the initial probe excavation were the only complete vessels. The rest amounted to little more than a handful of rather nondescript potsherds that did not look as if they had much to tell us.

Varda's office was in one of the main depots where artifacts belonging to the Department of Antiquities were stored, near the Old City in Jerusalem on Rechov Shlomo Hamelech ("King Solomon Street"). Shlomo Hamelech is a noisy thoroughfare, highly congested during most of each workday with masses of people packaged into cars and trucks and astride mopeds and motorcycles.

Edna and I climbed the steep street and reached the large door with the brass Department of Antiquities plaque. I pressed the well-worn button. Through the din made by the traffic, somewhere within the building I could hear the thin ringing of an antediluvian bell and clapper. Eventually, Varda's elderly assistant opened the door and greeted us with his usual warm smile.

Crossing that threshold was like stepping into another world. The sounds of honking horns and revving motors were muffled by the heavy door. Choking exhaust fumes were left behind. Instead, the air was laden with a scent which, were it to be bottled, might go under the trade name *Old House*. Artifacts from all different periods were stacked systematically from floor to ceiling on the shelves.

Varda greeted us and invited us to some tea. We poured hot water from a tinny electrical samovar. David soon arrived, and we all sat down around Varda's heavy desk. Edna removed the lamp from its box, unfolded the soft tissues that surrounded it, and handed it to Varda. The lamp was not new to her, for she had examined it during the excavation, when the lamp and the cooking pot had been brought to Jerusalem. Now she turned it over in her hands, studying it once again.

"This is a very rare type of lamp," she finally said. "I know of only a few like it."

Fire is one of the greatest discoveries of humankind, but it is not easily controlled. A lamp represents the human harnessing of fire for light.[2]

Lamps evolved through time. Thus their relatively rapid design changes make them a boon to archaeologists, for they provide chronological benchmarks. Because of their peculiar shapes, even a small fragment of an oil lamp is often sufficiently diagnostic to supply a date.

To function, a lamp requires four components: a receptacle (lamp), fuel (oil), a wick, and, of course, fire. It is not clear when humankind first realized that an oil-soaked wick would continue to supply fuel in a manner that would create a level, controllable flame. Telltale soot marks on the sides of otherwise common bowls dating to the Chalcolithic period (ca. 4300–3300 BC) are the earliest evidence of oil lamps in Israel. It took another millennium or two for someone to come up with the idea of pinching or folding the rim of a bowl while the clay was still wet to create a station for the wick, thus inventing what is termed the *open oil lamp.* These first true lamps appear in the Middle Bronze Age I (ca. 2300/2250–2000 BC). One type is simple, with the rim folded in only one location. But someone had the bright idea that more light could be achieved by folding in a round bowl or saucer at four sides, thus creating four positions for the placement of wicks. This "100-watt" lamp gave more light but also required more oil. For some reason, production of the four-wick lamp died out within a few centuries.

The simple open type of lamp, however, began a two-millennium-long unbroken tradition, which ended only in the Hellenistic period. While the concept of a bowl with a fold for the wick remained constant, the open lamp underwent numerous changes. The reasons for these changes are unclear. They may have been matters of taste, or there may have been practical reasons for some of them.

Throughout the Middle Bronze Age II (ca. 2000–1550 BC), the lamp remained a simple bowl with a pinched rim. During the following Late Bronze Age (ca. 1550–1200 BC), however, the lamp received a rim which splayed outward, perhaps in order to allow the user a better grasp.

In the Iron Age (ca. 1200–586 BC), lamps shrank a bit in size. When King Solomon died, the kingdom which Saul had founded and David had extended broke into two different nations, Israel (Samaria) and Judea. This political division was expressed in the lamps. Some Judean lamps had a thick, raised cylindrical base, while the Israelite type, which continued the previous tradition, lacked a base.

Styles of ceramic oil lamps flowed back and forth across the ancient world. During the Late Bronze Age, Mycenaean Greeks in the west were importing open Syro-Canaanite or Cypriot ceramic oil lamps from the east. On the Late Bronze Age Uluburun shipwreck, which was heading west when it sank, the excavators found new, unused oil lamps, packed together with sets of beautiful Cypriot pottery into large ceramic jars called *pithoi*, which served as the ancient equivalent of china barrels.

During the Persian period, lamps in Israel almost lacked a

body. The rim began virtually at the base. By the end of the Persian period, the influence on the form of oil lamps had turned full circle, with styles from the west being imported into the east. The earliest Greek lamps arrived on the shores of what is now modern Israel in the seventh century BC. But this style began to seriously influence local lamp production only in the third century BC, following a visit by Alexander the Great. He had paused briefly in Israel to take over the region on his way to conquering the rest of the known world. While Alexander himself came and went swiftly, the Hellenistic Greek culture which he introduced to Asia was there to stay for a very long time. One archaeological expression of this change may be seen in the lamps.

These Greek lamps—and more particularly lamps of Greek inspiration, for most of the lamps arriving were not from mainland Greece but from places like Ephesus in modern Turkey and Cnidus, off the southwest corner of Turkey—were different from the local open, saucer-shaped oil lamps in that they were made by attaching a separate, closed nozzle to a small open bowl which had been thrown on the wheel. Thus these lamps can be defined as *closed*, having two small openings, one for filling with oil, and the other for placing the wick. They were also generally smaller than the open bowl lamps. Eventually, the hole in the center shrank, and the disk on top of the lamp's body became available for decoration.

The last lamp in the open saucer tradition was a small cup, pinched in the center, which is called a *Hashmonean lamp*. This form was common during the Hellenistic period (fourth to first centuries BC). These "degenerated" lamps are basically an attempt to make an open lamp more like the closed lamps which were now flooding the market. This was achieved by downsizing the body and pinching the rim closed, so that it had two separate openings. The result was a lamp which, to my mind, is unattractive and disproportionate. It looks as if it was designed by a committee.

Each center of pottery production evolved its own style of lamp. This allowed for—indeed encouraged—an explosion of artistic expression. Lamps now became highly decorative.

In Roman period lamps, the hole in the center of the body for pouring in oil shrank to about the size of one made by a modern paper hole punch. Roman lamp makers took full advantage of the space now available to promote their product by covering it with decorative motifs designed to appeal to their pagan customers. These decorations included depictions of emperors, heroes, gladiators, and scenes of daily life, pagan mythology, and erotic acts, to name just a few.

The motifs appearing on the lamps, as well as those motifs *not* depicted, speak volumes about the cultures that produced the lamps and about the individuals who used them. The erotic scenes on some of these "Kama Sutra candles," for example, are remarkably explicit. When Dr. Lawrence E. Stager published photos of several such lamps uncovered in his excavations at Ashkelon in the pages of *Biblical Archaeology Review*, a popular journal dealing with Bible-related archaeology, readers scorched the editor.[3] They complained of being subjected to pornography in a magazine that ostensibly deals with the Bible. Some readers even canceled their subscriptions.

Such erotic lamps are found throughout lands once under Roman suzerainty. They have even been found in Jerusalem, close by the Temple Mount, apparently left there by soldiers of the Xth Legion who were stationed in Jerusalem after the conquest of the city.

Erotic lamps, of course, were forbidden in the homes of Jews and Christians, both groups considering sex a matter of procreation rather than indoor sport. In fact, not only were erotic scenes forbidden, *any* figurative scenes were taboo. Jewish law at that time proscribed the creation of any "graven images"; this stricture limited Jewish art to geometric and floral motifs.

While the pagans were enjoying the titillating scenes on their lamps, the most popular type of lamp among Jews in Israel bore little or no decoration at all. This type of lamp is termed the *Herodian lamp* after Herod the Great, during whose reign it was believed to have first come into general use. Actually, this now seems to be a misnomer, as recent research suggests that its introduction took place only late in that ruler's reign, or possibly even after his death. Nevertheless, the name for the lamp remains. Excavations in the Judean desert indicate that this type of lamp continued in use into the first part of the second century. They are most commonly found in the area of Judea.

In keeping with the stern Jewish regulation, the Herodian lamp is notable for its nearly total lack of decoration, which is limited at most to circles or lines. Strangely enough, it is this stark simplicity and austerity, together with almost perfect proportions, which make the Herodian lamp so aesthetically pleasing to me.

After the destruction of Jerusalem by Titus's forces, many Jews fled south (*Darom* in Hebrew) and settled in the region of Hebron and Beit Guvrin. It was apparently here that a new type of lamp emerged, derived from the Herodian lamp, yet made in a mold. These lamps date from just after the destruction of the Temple to at least the early second century, and possibly later. Unlike their precursors, the *Darom* lamps—as Varda proposed to call them—are profusely decorated.[4] The decorations, however, are limited to types that express the national Jewish aspirations and hopes for the reestablishment of the Temple, which lay in ruins. These included the *lulav* ("palm branch") and the *etrog* ("citron"), which are still used by Jews during Succoth (the Feast of Tabernacles), as well as the menorah.

During the Byzantine period (ca. AD 324–638), lamps characteristically Jewish, Christian, and Samaritan became common. These also often have a seven-branched menorah-like decoration, but on Christian lamps the menorah takes on the shape of a palm leaf. The lamps intended for a specifically Christian clientele appeared relatively late: only in the fourth century.

When the Muslims invaded Israel, they continued to use the elongated forms of lamps common at the end of the Byzantine period, changing only the inscriptions, now written in Arabic, to bless Allah rather than Jesus. In the fourteenth century AD, open bowl lamps with pinched rims made a reappearance.

In addition to the archaeological remains of lamps, ancient writings inform us of the place of the lamp in daily Jewish life. For example, the lamp's wick had to be tended to ensure correct burning. This was the job of the lady of the house, and indeed, in the Bible, one measure of a successful homemaker was that "her lamp does not go out at night."[5]

While virtually any fibrous material can be utilized as a wick, flax was considered ideal. If more light were needed, a more powerful lamp could be created by laying numerous wicks against the side of a bowl, while another bowl placed upside down over it secured the wicks in place. Lamps could also be created with multiple nozzles. One lamp now in the Israel Museum has 21 nozzles. It is made in the Roman mold tradition but contains Jewish motifs.

Since olive trees grew in abundance in Israel, the fuel of choice in lamps was olive oil. Although other oils also could be used, they were not considered suitable for Sabbath lamps. Only the best, ritually pure olive oil was permitted for lighting in the Tabernacle and later in the Holy Temple.[6]

Indeed, a main thread in the modern Jewish observance of Hanukkah, the Feast of Dedication (of the Holy Temple), is traditionally associated with the olive oil used for lighting. In 165 BC, after the Maccabees had succeeded in retaking the Holy Temple from the Seleucid Greeks, who had used the site for the worship of pagan gods, they are said to have found only one small jug of ritually pure olive oil with which to light the menorah. The oil in the jug should have lasted only a day, but instead, is said to have sufficed for eight days, until new ritually pure olive oil could be produced.

Varda continued to turn the lamp over in her hand. She noted that it had a fat discoid-shaped body that had been thrown on a potter's wheel. The body was relatively thin-walled, almost eggshell thin to the touch. A high, bowed rim was situated above the filling hole, presumably to prevent any excess oil from spilling out. The potter had formed the lamp's nozzle separately by hand and had then joined it to the body, smoothing the two pieces together. The tiny handle, which ran from the lamp's "neck" to its "shoul-

der," was almost too small to grasp between one's fingers. The
potter had attached it seemingly as an afterthought. The lamp had
no decorative elements at all. The dark soot that clung to the wick
hole indicated that this lamp had seen use.

"This is one of the types of wheel-made lamps that continued
to be made while the Roman mold-made lamps were so popular,"
Varda said. "It is similar to types of lamps that were common
during Early Roman and Herodian times."

That meant the lamp could date from anywhere during two
centuries.

"The way the neck is formed"—and here Varda ran her finger
against the lamp's neck—"is like those on small cups from a site
called Abu Shusha and from [the late Professor] Avigad's excavations in the Jewish Quarter [in the nearby Old City of Jerusalem].
These date to either the end of the first century BC or the beginning
of the first century AD."

"Where were the other examples of this specific type of lamp
found?" I asked.

"Let's see." Varda reflected for a moment and then began
naming the sites and the archaeologists who had excavated them.
"One was found by Siegelman at Abu Shusha. Another one comes
from Moshe Dothan's excavations at Afula. Oh, and Nurit Feig
recently found a number of them in a tomb that she excavated in
Nazareth."

"Can you be any more accurate as to the date of the lamps and
where they come from?" I asked.

"I would date this lamp anywhere from the middle or later
first century BC to about the early first century AD, that is, from
about 50 BC to AD 50. Judging from the distribution of this type of
lamp, it was probably produced in the Galilee, although do keep
in mind the lamps found in Jerusalem."

Attention now turned to David, as Edna took out of their
boxes the cooking pot and the other sherds found in and around
the boat. David studied them for a while, not saying anything.

If I had sought out Varda's "vertical" knowledge of lamps of
all ages, David had what you might think of as a "horizontal"
expertise. In his dissertation, which he had completed only a year

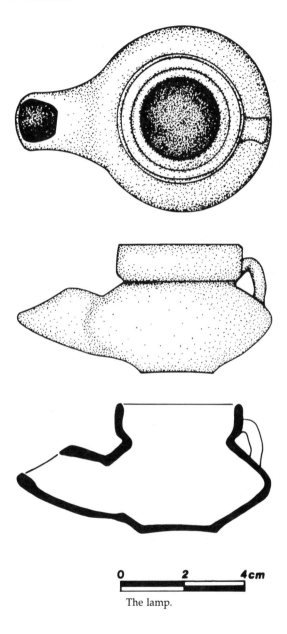

The lamp.

prior to the boat's excavation, he had studied housewares in the Galilee during the Roman and Byzantine periods.[7] In doing so, David had focused on three approaches: textual sources, archaeology, and a type of archaeometry which allows archaeologists virtually to "fingerprint" artifacts. Neutron Activation Analysis (more commonly called NAA) is often used to determine where artifacts—like ceramics or special types of stones—originally came from. A sample of the artifact's fabric is removed with a drill, and from this powder a small pellet is created. The pellet is then irradiated in a nuclear reactor, which turns the various elements in the sample into radioactive isotopes. As they decay, the elements release gamma rays which are identifiable for each element. By determining the amounts of a group of trace elements—those elements available in minute amounts—it is then possible to identify the composition of the clay used in the pottery. By having a reference series of various clays, one can determine which clay source was used in making the pottery.

David had studied Talmudic references referring to a location called Kfar Hananya, which served as a pottery-producing center for the Galilee during the Roman and the Byzantine periods. He was further able to locate the probable location of Kfar Hananya, about 14 kilometers (8.7 miles) northwest of where the boat was found at a site named in Arabic Kafr 'Inan.

The production of the Kfar Hananya pottery had primarily served the Galilee, although such pottery was also used, in smaller quantities, on the Golan Heights. At Gamla, for example, David had found that 13 percent of the material he had studied had come from Kfar Hananya.

Thus there were two questions that David needed to address concerning the cooking pot and the sherds from the boat: First, did the sherds form a cohesive date with the cooking pot and lamp? And second, could they be assigned to the Kfar Hananya ware?

David took the bowl first and carefully studied it. He recognized it as a type of cooking pot which belonged to one of the typological classes he had defined in Kfar Hananya wares.

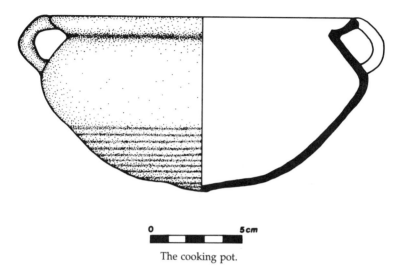

The cooking pot.

"This is what I call a Kfar Hananya Form 3A," he explained to us, pointing to the wide mouth and the rounded shoulders and base. "And this," he said, holding up a small sherd, "is a rim fragment of the same type of cooking pot."

"Date?"

"Mid-first century BCE to about the mid-second century CE."

He then went on to study the rest of the sherds, one by one. Several other sherds belonged to cooking pots. In fact, cooking-pot sherds made up about half of all the pottery found in and around the boat. David separated those that had datable characteristics—some no bigger than a thumbnail—from simple body sherds, which were not chronologically diagnostic.

"All of these identifiable sherds," he said, gesturing toward the former group, "are typical of the period from about 50 BC to about AD 70. Although they continue after that date, I see none of the pottery types that *begin to appear* in the late first and early second centuries."

Five other sherds had originally belonged to storage jars. Two came from vessels that were common during the Hellenistic period, but that continued in use into the first century AD. Two other sherds were derived from jars of a type comparable to bag-shaped jars which range from the first century BC to the mid-first century AD.

Three sherds were derived from small closed vessels. One belonged to a jug, and two others to a type of juglet. All three ranged in date, according to David, from the end of the first century BC to the middle of the second century AD.

Two other sherds—one from a jar, the other a part of a handle, perhaps of a jug—were not sufficiently diagnostic to supply a date, although David pointed out that the material of which they were made was not typical of the Roman era.

Most of the sherds had clean breaks, indicating that they must have been buried in the silt fairly soon after they had been deposited. The only exception to this rule was a single sherd. It was the rim and shoulder of a Persian period jar that showed evidence of being worn by water, its sides smoothed away. This sherd must have tumbled around for some time before coming to rest near the boat.

Pottery found in and around the boat could indicate human activity there. David was able to assign nearly all of it to a specific date range by comparing the pottery from the boat to well-dated groups of ceramics found during excavations from the nearby sites of Capernaum and Migdal, as well as Meiron in the Upper Galilee and Gamla. He noted that, with the single exception of the one worn Persian period sherd, all of the pottery dated from the latter part of the first century BC (ca. 50 BC) to about the First Revolt (ca. AD 66–70).

Although similar wares had been made on the Golan Heights at this time, it is unlikely that the sherds in the boat were made on the Golan. Among 200 samples of these pottery types derived from fourteen Galilean sites, three of which were located near the boat site, David had not found a single Golan sherd.

Before the meeting broke up, Varda and David had agreed to prepare publications on the lamp and the other pottery. Leaving the artifacts with Varda, Edna and I opened the entrance door and stepped out into the street.

Back into the twentieth century.

♪♪♪

Having an entire boat made of wood permitted another method for determining when she had lived her life: carbon 14 dating.

I made an appointment with Dr. Yisrael Carmi of the Department of Isotope Research at Israel's Weitzmann Institute of Science, located south of Tel Aviv in Rehovot. When I had explained the problems concerned with dating the boat to Yisrael and explained that I had no funding to pay for the tests, he kindly offered to do them on a pro bono basis. When I arrived in Rehovot with the samples, Yisrael showed me around the lab and explained to me the nuts and bolts of deriving radiocarbon dates.

This method is the single most important form of archaeometry employed by archaeologists to date their discoveries. Carbon 14 dating, also known as C14, ^{14}C, and radiocarbon dating, is based on a radioactive clock. Carbon atoms normally have six protons and six neutrons in their nuclei, giving them the assignation of ^{12}C. However, the element carbon exists in two other forms. One of these is the result of the tendency of some *nitrogen* atoms to become carbon atoms, when bombarded by solar radiation. These newly formed carbon atoms have an additional two neutrons in their nuclei: ^{14}C. These atoms are unstable and begin to decay back into nitrogen atoms at a known rate. Like all radioactive substances, their rate of decay follows an exponential pattern. In other words, it takes a specific amount of time for half of the ^{14}C to decay. This is known as its half-life. It then takes another, equal span of time, or half-life, for the remaining half of the original amount to decay into one quarter of the original. And so on.

But all radioactive materials decay at fixed rates. What makes ^{14}C so ideal for archaeologists?

Two considerations: availability and timing.

First and foremost, *all* living entities, be they flora or fauna, are continually taking in atmospheric carbon during their lifetime. Plants absorb it from the atmosphere in the form of carbon dioxide, herbivores get it by eating the plants, and carnivores get it from eating the herbivores. Only when a living being dies does it cease to take in atmospheric carbon. The ^{14}C begins to decay, thus starting a radioactive countdown.

This leads to a second quality inherent in ^{14}C. While all radioactive materials decay on a similar curve, they do so at different "speeds." Some of these are too fast and others too slow to be of any use in archaeology. At one end of the scale are radioactive substances which have half-lives that last for less than a second; others last for what is well nigh *forever* in human terms. Uranium with an atomic weight of 235, for example, has a half-life of 4.5 billion years. As opposed to these, ^{14}C has a *reasonable* half-life, which was originally calculated by Dr. Willard Libby (who invented the process of radiocarbon dating in 1949) as 5,568 years. Subsequently, it was found to be 5,730 years. Thus, by determining the remaining amount of ^{14}C in an organic archaeological artifact, it is possible to determine when it ceased to live.

In converting the lab measurements to chronology, scientists initially give the years in BP, which stands for "before present." To prevent confusion, given the consideration that the present marches ceaselessly onward each year, the year 1950 has been accepted for this purpose as the "present," or permanent baseline.

Of course, ^{14}C dating comes with its own ingrained problems. There is always the danger of contamination of the samples. Then there is the given statistical error in measuring the amounts of surviving ^{14}C. This is called the *standard deviation* and is expressed by a plus-or-minus number indicating that there is a two-in-three chance (67 percent) of the artifact's death dating to within a single standard deviation. To be 95 percent sure that the ^{14}C date falls within the time range, we must go two standard deviations before and after a given date. Thus, for example, if a fragment of wood gives a laboratory date of 2,000 ± 100 BP, there is a 67 percent likelihood that the tree had been felled between 2,100 and 1,900 years before the year 1950 and a 95 percent probability that it dates from between 2,200 and 1,800 years before 1950.

Furthermore, Libby had assumed that the proportion of ^{14}C had not changed through time. More recent studies on the individual yearly tree rings of long-lived bristlecone pines in the American Southwest have revealed that levels of the isotope have fluctuated through time. For this reason, radiocarbon dates must be *calibrated* before they are assigned a calendrical BC–AD date.

It is also important to conduct a *series* of datings, as a single test can be contaminated or otherwise incorrect. Yisrael was ultimately to do ten ^{14}C datings on timbers from the Kinneret boat. The results of these samples varied, after calibration, from 130 BC to AD 80.

"The average date," Yisrael told me when all the tests had been completed, "is 40 BC ± 80."

Coins can be the most valuable method of dating in archaeology, during the historical periods when they were minted. Usually they can be assigned to a specific date, or to within a limited number of years. The latest coin on a shipwreck which comes from an archaeologically secure context indicates that the ship could not have sunk prior to that year.

Unfortunately, the coins found during the discovery and excavation of the boat were found without any archaeological context. Even so, I thought, they might be able to supply information on periods of human activity in the area.

To interpret the coins I met with Dr. Yaakov "Yankele" Meshorer, who is a curator at the Israel Museum in Jerusalem and one of the foremost authorities on the coins of ancient Israel. Yankele assigned the coins from the excavation to Dr. Haim Gitler, his apprentice, for study and publication.

A total of 57 coins were found prior to and during the excavation. Of these, Haim was able to identify 43. The rest were so worn that they were unrecognizable. The earliest coins in the group dated to the third century BC, and the latest one—not counting the United States penny found in the boat—dated to 1808. The mint at Ptolomais, the ancient site of Akko, produced some of the coins; others come from mints as far away as Constantinople (modern Istanbul).

"The most interesting coins from your excavation are those which were minted by Ptolemy Lathyrus," Haim told me later.

Ptolemy Lathyrus (116/115–80 BC) was a Hellenistic Egyptian king who, after being deposed in Egypt by his own mother, ruled in Cyprus. When the Jewish Hashmonean king Alexander Yannai (103–76 BC) laid siege to the pagan city of Akko-Ptolomais, it turned to Ptolemy with a plea for help.

Ptolemy raised a large fleet and sailed for Akko-Ptolomais, but by the time he arrived, the fickle people of that city had changed their minds, having concluded that the cure might be worse than the illness. Ptolemy, after all, was an absolute monarch who would require the city's absolute subjugation. Furthermore, his mother, Cleopatra (not the famous one), still wished to remove him from Cyprus. She would never have allowed him to attain a toehold for himself along the Levantine coast.

Then Alexander Yannai proposed to Ptolemy an alliance, which he offered to sweeten with the promise of a large sum of silver. Ptolemy agreed. Alexander, however, was playing a game of intrigue. While wooing Ptolemy, he also secretly sent word to Cleopatra asking that she attack her son.

Actually, it wasn't all that secret. Ptolemy soon learned of the subterfuge, which must have made him a very unhappy camper. Leaving some of his forces to besiege Akko-Ptolomais, he led the rest of his troops inland, with the intention of conquering Alexander's kingdom of Judea. He began by attacking the Galilee.

The inevitable clash between the armies of Ptolemy and Alexander occurred along the Jordan River near Asophon, perhaps near Tell es-Saidiyeh, which is located about halfway between the Kinneret and the Dead Sea. Alexander made the tactical error of allowing his opponent's forces to cross the Jordan. Ptolemy's troops managed to use this mistake to their advantage and won the upper hand. This victory allowed Ptolemy to overrun parts of Judea until he was eventually forced to retreat by Cleopatra.

"Coins minted by Ptolemy Lathyrus are rare in Israel," Haim told me. "The appearance of four coins minted by him, along with three others which may be assigned to either Ptolemy Lathyrus or Ptolemy XIII, almost certainly indicate a connection with Ptolemy's expeditionary force into the Galilee in 102 BC."

There must be a story behind how they found their way into the lake; one that we will probably never know.

ееe

The materials from which the boat was constructed—literally, the "nuts and bolts" of which she was made—also had a story to tell. Considering the seemingly bizarre use of recycled timbers in the hull that Dick noted, what might the *types* of wood used in the hull reveal? What types of resin had the boatwright used to protect the boat from dry rot? What kind of iron was used in the nails? Every additional bit of information might supply another clue to our understanding of the boat and her milieu.

In ancient ships, it was customary to limit the timber used to one or two types. You might say that our boat was a nonconformist.

Dr. Ella Werker, of the Department of Botany at the Hebrew University in Jerusalem, agreed to identify samples of wood from the boat and to prepare a report on her identifications. Ella is widely known for her ability to identify wood types from the slender samples under her microscope. For this purpose, Orna removed small chips of a representative sampling of the boat's timbers. She took one sample from both of the timbers that made up the keel, as well as from 18 strakes, 17 frames, three tenons, and one peg, for a total of 41 samples.

Ella shaved off thin slices from each of the specimens, staining some of them with chemicals to emphasize various features, then mounted them on slides which she examined under a light microscope. She was able to make the identification by examining the anatomical details of each sample.

Ella's conclusions supported Dick's impression in the field. While our boat was built primarily of two types of wood, Ella's study revealed that the craft contained a total of at least *seven* different types of timber. Whoever built this boat had indeed scraped the bottom of the barrel for timber.

The aft part of the keel was made of a timber from a jujube, also known as *sidder tree* (*Ziziphus*). Two types of *Ziziphus* grow in Israel. One is a shrub, however, and could not have produced the sizable timber used in the keel. The other type, *Ziziphus spina-christi*, or Christ thorn, is one of the plants which are traditionally identified as being the source for Jesus's crown of thorns.[8] These trees can grow quite large and could have produced a timber of the size used in the boat's hull.

Other than for minor items like tenons, this is the only recorded occurrence of jujube used on an ancient hull in the Mediterranean region. *Ziziphus spina-christi* has been identified with the bramble (*atad* in Hebrew) in the Parable of the Trees:[9]

> So all the trees said to the bramble (*atad*),
> "You come and reign over us."
> And the bramble said to the trees,
> "If in good faith you are anointing me king over you,
> then come and take refuge in my shade;
> but if not, let fire come out of the bramble
> and devour the cedars of Lebanon."

As to whether or not Jesus's crown of thorns was indeed derived from *Ziziphus spina-christi*, the noted Israeli botanist Michael Zohary writes:[10]

> There are at least a dozen different spiny plant species in Jerusalem. Of these, the thorny burnet (*Sarcopoterium spinosum*), a dwarf shrub, is extremely common, and might therefore with much more reason be regarded as the plant in question. . . . Christian tradition, however, looks upon the *Ziziphus* as the "crown of thorns," and for those who insist upon having a Christ thorn growing in Jerusalem, there are still a few Christ thorn trees on the eastern slopes of Mt. Moriah (the Temple Mount).

The forward part of the keel—the one in which we had discovered mortise-and-tenon scars—was made of cedar, as were 17 of the 18 strakes that Ella examined. Two types of cedar fit the specific anatomical details which Ella noted in these timbers. One type, however, grows only in North Africa, in the area of the Atlas Mountains, and therefore can reasonably be dropped as a possibility. The other is Lebanese cedar (*Cedrus libani*), which grows in Lebanon, Turkey, Cyprus, and North Africa.

The majestic cedars of Lebanon have been valued throughout antiquity as an ideal wood for the construction of ships and monumental buildings. The earliest documented evidence of the use of cedar imported into Israel was found in a Middle Bronze Age (early second millennium BC) palace at Lachish.[11] Lebanese cedar continued to be imported during most subsequent archaeological-historical periods. Lebanese cedar was obviously being imported into Israel around the time that the boat was plying the lake. From around the time the boat lived her life, cedar was commonly used in the construction projects of Herod the Great. Remains of cedar wood have been identified at the Herodian fortress/palaces of Masada, Herodian, and Cypros.

At great expense and considerable effort, Agrippa II had imported large quantities of timbers from Lebanon to be used in strengthening the Holy Temple. Josephus relates that these timbers were "for size and straightness worthy to see."[12] Although Josephus did not mention what specific type of timber Agrippa imported from Lebanon, the description fits cedar. The timbers were used to make engines of war during the internecine warfare among the various Jewish factions inside Jerusalem prior to the arrival of Titus and his legions.

However, at least one of the boat's planks (Number 97, which is situated in the stern port section of the boat) was not made of cedar. Instead, it was made of Aleppo pine (*Pinus halepensis*).

Pines of various types were a popular wood for ship construction on the Mediterranean Sea. The fourth-century BC Kyrenia shipwreck was made almost entirely of Aleppo pine. This wood is ideal for shipbuilding and grows locally. This being the case, one wonders how our particular boat came to have planking of imported Lebanese cedar, rather than locally available Aleppo pine.

The majority of frames examined by Ella were made of oak (*Quercus*), as were all three of the tenons and the peg. Oak was particularly popular for shipbuilding. Dick has noted that oak has possibly been the most popular wood overall for ship construction throughout history.

Two types of oak are possible. One grows only on Mt. Hermon, while the other, the Tabor oak (*Quercus ithaburensis*), grows extensively in the Galilee and its surrounding areas.

The Hebrew name for oak is *allon*. And it is from this noble tree that the late Yigal Allon, for whom the Allon Museum is named—and where the boat is located—derived his family name.

Although most of the frames examined were made of oak, three frames were made of other types of wood. Frame 19 is made from a branch of willow (*Salix*). There are two types of this tree that grow in the vicinity in areas that are well watered. The willow is one of the "four species" (*arba'at haminim*) which Jews are required to take together at Succoth, the Feast of Tabernacles.[13] Frame 15 is made of hawthorn (*Crataegus*), while Frame 38 is of redbud (*Cercis siliquastrum* L.), which grows in Israel in the Galilee, Mt. Carmel, Samaria, and the Judean Hills. None of these last three types of wood are known to have been commonly used in antiquity in ship construction.

The 41 specimens account for a reasonable sampling of the total timbers of the hull. The general picture to come out of Ella's research is that, for a timber large enough to serve as the keel, the boatwright had to resort to joining two timbers, one of which is made of a wood rarely if ever utilized in shipbuilding elsewhere, while the other had been reused from a previous construction. The hull consisted primarily of Lebanese cedar planking and oak frames but—at least, in the final phase of its life—contained examples of a *minimum* of four other types of wood, some of which are not ordinarily considered good timber for boat building.

This patchwork use of multiple woods is abnormal in the building of watercraft. Any boat builder would prefer not to use such a plethora of timber types. In other words, extenuating circumstances must have required the boat builder to use these timbers to construct a watercraft. With the exception of the Lebanese cedar, all the types of wood which Ella identified in the boat could be obtained locally. Ella and Dick both felt it likely that the timbers other than those of cedar or oak, used in the planking and framing of the boat, were probably repair pieces.

During the excavation, splotches of red coloration were observed on some of the planking, particularly on the external side of the starboard, where the late afternoon sun would hit it at an angle that emphasized this feature. Dick had pointed out that it was probably the residue of resin applied by the boatwright to prevent rot, which he noted is more of a problem in a freshwater environment than in the briny sea.

To learn more about this material, I contacted Dr. Raymond White of the Scientific Department at the National Gallery in London. He graciously agreed to investigate samples which Orna removed from the hull.

Using a method known as *chromatography*, by means of which the constituent parts of amino and fatty acids can be identified, he found that the material was probably a pine resin. One of the five samples from the boat appears to be Aleppo pine resin.

Orna was particularly intrigued by the quality of the nails and carried out a joint study with Dr. Itzhak Roman from the School of Applied Science and Technology of the Hebrew University, Jerusalem, to learn more about them. They sectioned one of the nails and found it to be of a high quality of manufacture. The nail had undergone hammering, presumably in the process of its production. It was made of relatively clean 0.4 percent carbon steel. This type of steel is still used today.

෴෴෴

Hours were spent turning Danny's sets of photos of the interior of the boat's hull into composite mosaics. When these were completed, I was pleasantly surprised to see how much of the hull's interior Danny had succeeded in recording. Two parts were missing: the centerline of the hull and its stern. And there was good reason for this. The center of the hull had almost always been obscured during the excavation, first by the mud and then by the hanging platform. The stern, which had been the last part of the hull to be excavated, had been plastered with fiberglass by Yohai and Davidi almost as fast as it came out of the mud. Given the urgency and the constant press of people around the boat during the various phases of the excavation, it is a tribute to Danny's dedication that he had amazingly succeeded to string, tag, and record so much of the boat's hull.

Once the photo mosaics were ready, I chose 14 of them and had Edna draw a plan of the boat locating the photo mosaics on the hull.

ℯℯℯ

One of the first items on my list of many questions pertained not to the boat's life, but to her burial and survival once she had been deposited in the lake. For her to have survived at all, the hull must have been buried fairly swiftly, in archaeological terms, under the wood-saving blanket of Kinneret sediments. Had she been left exposed to the water for any considerable amount of time, she would have disappeared long ago into the maws of voracious microorganisms.

On the other hand, the average rate of sedimentation for the lake overall is calculated at about 1.0–1.6 millimeters (0.039–0.063 inches) per year. Thus, assuming a situation in which the sedimentation was constant throughout the lake, an artifact deposited about 2,000 years ago should theoretically be buried under 2.0–3.2 meters (6.6–10.5 feet) of sediment. Had the deposition of sediment been equal through time at the site, the boat should have been buried so deeply that Moshele and Yuvi would never have found her.

What had happened?

I wondered if anything could be learned from how the boat had subsided into the sediment. I put together a folder containing information we had recorded about sedimentation at the boat site.

On Dick's line drawings of the boat's sheer, or profile view, he had included a dashed line (X–X'), which represented the approx-

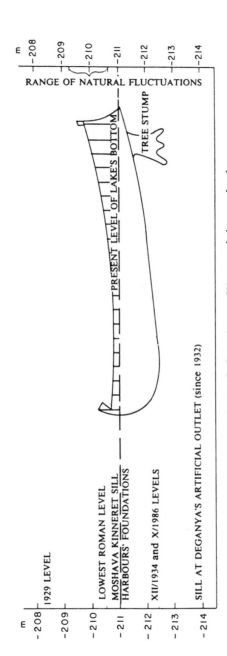

The level of the seabed at the boat site was 211 meters below sea level.

m
-208
-209
-210
-211
-212
-213
-214

RANGE OF NATURAL FLUCTUATIONS

PRESENT LEVEL OF LAKE'S BOTTOM

TREE STUMP

m
-208 — 1929 LEVEL
-209
-210 — LOWEST ROMAN LEVEL
        MOSHAVA KINNERET SILL
-211 — HARBOURS' FOUNDATIONS
-212 — XII/1934 and X/1986 LEVELS
-213
-214 — SILL AT DEGANYA'S ARTIFICIAL OUTLET (since 1932)

imate height of preservation on the boat's starboard side. As the boat was preserved up to the surface of the mud, this line also represents how the boat had come to rest. I drew on a page of paper a horizontal line to represent the height of the lake bed where the boat had been found. Then, cutting out a copy of Dick's sheer view, I turned it so that the line of preservation was aligned with the horizontal line. This gave an approximation of the boat's alignment, from bow to stern, in the sediment.

Although I remembered the slope from bow to stern, I was surprised at how steep it looked on paper. Beneath the boat's bow, I sketched in a rough approximation of the loose tree trunk on which the bow had been supported. To this I added the two absolute levels which the Department of Antiquities surveyors had established vis-à-vis the boat during the excavation. They had determined that the level of the lake bed at the boat site was 211 meters (692.3 feet) below mean sea level, while the lowest part of the stern, measured from inside the hull at the stern, was 1 meter (3.281 feet) deeper, at 212 meters (695.6 feet).

Armed with some photos that Danny had carefully made of details in the sediment and the cutout drawing, I drove over to talk to Dr. Yaakov "Yankele" Nir. Yankele is a geologist-sedimentologist who works for the Geological Survey of Israel and specializes in coastal geology. I presented him with the dossier and asked him to give me a "sedimentological" viewpoint of the boat.

We sat in Yankele's tiny office, its walls covered with shelves groaning under the weight of books, reports, and files of old aerial photographs.

"The area that the Kinneret drains," Yankele said, "is about two-fifths basaltic in nature, two-fifths limestone, and one-fifth alluvial deposits. All of these affect sedimentation in the lake."

He explained to me that the majority of sediment is fine and reaches the Kinneret via the Jordan River. Upon arriving in the lake, the particles suspended in the water gradually settle out, more or less evenly, throughout the lake. The larger pieces—stones, pebbles, and gravel—are flushed into the lake with the winter rains through a network of wadis (dry river beds) that empty into the Kinneret.

When water poured into the excavation pit, its west face sheered away revealing a picture of interbedded layers of fine clay and clastic sediments.

Yankele studied the boat diagram I had prepared and then looked at the pictures.

"Modern changes have affected the rate of sedimentation," he said. "For one, the Hula Swamp used to act as a natural filter for the Jordan, but since the swamp has been reclaimed, much more of the sediment is reaching the lake. Then there's the artificial dam at Degania—at the outlet of the Jordan—which slows down, or stops altogether, the flow of the Jordan, allowing more time for the sediments to settle out on the bottom of the Kinneret. And there are other causes of sedimentation in the lake, like the shells of mollusks as well as the precipitation of calcium carbonate from the supersaturated water."

Changes in water level also have an influence on the sedimentation rate. Mendel, in his research on land sites, has concluded, based on strictly archaeological evidence, that the average height of the lake in Roman times was about 210 meters (689 feet) below sea level, give or take about half a meter.

Most of the sediments that surrounded the boat were fine and silty, with some intrusions of coarser material, apparently washed down from nearby Nahal Tsalmon. Thus this sediment in which the boat was found is a curious mixture of layers of coarser sediment combined with layers of fine silt, which are more typical of deeper parts of the Kinneret.

"It seems that there is a unique and isolated environment in this particular location that permitted the rapid burial of the boat," Yankele said.

The burial of the lower part of the boat must have occurred very quickly to a level of at least 211 meters below sea level, that is, the highest point to which the boat's timbers had been preserved. Under normal conditions, the boat would have been exposed far too long for the hull to have survived. Following its arrival on the lake bed, layers of coarser material were deposited during times of high-energy action in storms, while layers of finer silt settled during periods of relative calm on the lake.

The boat's burial may have been facilitated by the liquidlike state of the mud at this location when the boat was deposited. Presumably, fairly quickly after this, the boat was covered with additional sediments. It was this rapid burial in the sediment that saved the lower part of the boat for posterity. Perhaps the burial process spanned several years.

What happened after this at the boat site above the −211 meter mark is not clear. There are two possibilities. Either no additional sediments were deposited, or if they were, these sediments were deposited and removed by the Kinneret's currents and waves in what can be described as a winnowing effect.

🙙🙙🙙

And so it continued. Each scholar approached added his or her piece to the puzzle, until the puzzle began to evolve into a picture.

Chapter 9

Good Night, Sleeping Beauty

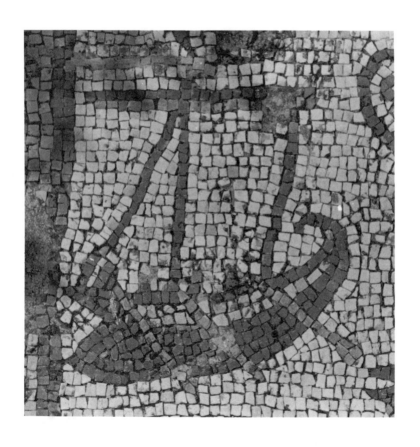

They are like trees
  planted by streams of water,
Which yield their fruit in its season,
  and their leaves do not wither.

Psalms 1:3

The boat rested safely on land, having made the journey—presumably without mishap. At least the polyurethane casing had remained intact during the move, which seemed a good sign. We speculated as to how well the boat inside had survived the trip. There was no way of determining this until the entire package was physically in the conservation pool and we could remove the casing. I remember having an irrational fear that, when we opened up the polyurethane, the boat would have vanished.

While the polyurethane would probably protect the wood from further dehydration, to be on the safe side Orna cut a row of small holes in the casing along the line of the uppermost strakes of the hull, into which she inserted a garden-variety drip hose. Another, complementary row of holes was cut beneath the boat. The hose was turned on several times every day, giving the timbers a refreshing shower of water, which flowed freely through the polyurethane cocoon before dripping out through the holes at the bottom.

When the crane had lowered the boat onto land, the pool in which it was to be conserved existed as little more than a rectangle, marked out on the ground with chalk. So uncertain was the outcome of moving the boat from the excavation site that no one had been willing to start building the pool until the vessel arrived safely on terra firma. From the moment the boat had "landed" at the Yigal Allon Centre, however, all attention turned to the special conservation pool that was to be built under Isaac Rotem's guidance with funding from the Department of Antiquities.

Isaac had been there to greet the boat, his tape measure in hand, verifying the dimensions of the craft and its casing. As the cost of the conservation materials in which the boat was to be

immersed was expected to be considerable, Isaac carefully designed the pool to allow for the boat, its cocoon, and her lifting
pallet, but for precious little else.

The site where the boat rested and where the pool was laid
out was a landfill. To gain extra space, the Allon Museum had
filled in an area along the shores of the lake with boulders and
earth. For this reason, rather than the foundations of the pool
being dug into the ground, the pool was built with its base at
ground level.

While Isaac was building the pool, the rest of us had an
opportunity to relax for a bit. Meanwhile, the outer surface of the
polyurethane casing weathered to a dark honey color. The boat sat
quietly by, like an immense golden whale stranded on the beach,
seeming to observe all this silently.

Under Isaac's expert management, the pool was completed in
an amazing eight days. It was constructed of reinforced concrete,
specially insulated at Orna's request, and then finished off in
shiny-white ceramic tiles that glinted so brightly in the sunlight
that they made me squint.

With the pool's completion begins the story of the boat's
conservation—still going on as I write these lines. It did not begin
smoothly.

Nitsa arranged for a crane to come to hoist the boat, still
resting on her iron pallet, into the pool. The day was sparkling
bright, and a small, cheerful crowd gathered to watch what we
naively thought of as the boat's being finally put to bed.

The huge crane lumbered up, and the operator jumped down
and began to lower the hydraulic legs onto wooden blocks to
stabilize the machine. I walked over to him, wishing to explain
what exactly it was that he would be lifting that day. For the few
moments it took to move the boat into the pool, he would have
complete control over it. I wanted to explain to him the responsibility this entailed.

No sooner had I started talking than he waved me off with his
hand. "*Al tidag habibi, ahni yodeah b'diuk mah ahni oseh poh!* [Don't
worry my friend, I know exactly what I'm doing!]," he said.

Al tidag habibi. Preparing the boat for lifting into the pool.

My lesson for that day was that, when someone tells you *not* to worry, it's a sure sign that you should do just that.

Isaac, who was going to direct the operation, had two kibbutzniks posted inside the pool to receive the boat and position it properly in the center of the pool as it was being lowered. Lifting wires were attached to the pallet, and these were duly connected to the crane's hook. The boat slowly rose, suspended below the crane. While the boat was hanging in midair, the operator pressed another lever, and the boat began to swing slowly toward the pool.

Everything went smoothly—until he began to lower the boat into the pool. Several times the boat hovered over the pool, like a spaceship trying to dock at a space station, and several times the kibbutzniks inside the pool had hold of the pallet, trying to guide it into the confined space. The boat was now far off to the side of the main body of the crane, shifting the center of gravity away from the truck. The operator had parked the crane on a slight

Two kibbutzniks were inside the pool ready to receive the boat. Isaac (with his back to the camera) eased her into place.

incline, and recent rains had made the ground slippery. Suddenly the huge machine lurched, as one of its hydraulic legs slipped off the wooden blocks on which it rested.

The next moments unwound for me, dreamlike, in slow motion. The boat began free-falling. One side of the iron pallet hit the side of the pool, causing the boat to careen sideways. Danny, Edna, and Karen, who were taking photos and observing the scene from their perch on a nearby wall, told me later that their hearts almost stopped as they watched in horror. It seemed that any second the boat would crash down on the men inside the pool. The operator—I never did learn his name—pulled another lever, sinking the hydraulic leg deep into the soft mud. The boat teetered and then stabilized. Momentarily.

"Get that boat back on land," I yelled to the operator.

The boat was soon safely back on land. I sent the crane operator packing. On his way out of the kibbutz, he got stuck in the mud. The next day another crane, with a more experienced operator, was brought in, and shortly the boat was resting safely inside the pool.

To remove the metal pallet upon which the boat rested, we filled the pool partially with water, so that she floated free of it. Then, with Rotem, I unbolted the frame from the runners and slipped the separate pieces out from beneath the boat. We then pumped the water out of the pool, carefully making sure that the boat came to rest in the middle of the receptacle.

Now we could finally begin the task of removing the polyurethane cocoon. It was only at this stage that we realized that, in our rush to get the polyurethane onto the boat, we had not given sufficient consideration to how to remove it.

Oops.

If anyone uses this method in the future, I highly recommend taping cut wires to the outer surface of the fiberglass frames. When the vessel is ready to be unpacked, rings can be attached to the ends of the wires, which then can be used to cut through the polyurethane. Not having had the foresight to do this, we had no choice but to "reexcavate" the boat. A timber framework went up

Suddenly a corner of the boat's supporting frame hit the side of the pool.

The next day, with another crane and a more experienced operator, the boat was safely berthed in the pool.

over the pool, and upon it we stretched the tarpaulin. Under its shade we set to work again.

To the sounds of modern Israeli hit songs, emanating from a ghetto blaster that Moshele had wired to the wooden staging overhead, we began to chip away at the polyurethane. Each person brought the cutting device of his or her choosing. One volunteer showed up with an electric turkey carver, but we deemed it too dangerous. Polyurethane contains cyanide, which might have been given off as a gas if heated by the friction of an electrical knife. I preferred my stiletto dive knife. Edna attached a pruning hook at right angles to a staff for use on those "hard-to-reach" corners. She looked like the Grim Reaper in blue jeans and a sweatshirt.

Excavating inside the pool, it turned out, was far more difficult than excavating in the field. Isaac had left only minimal space, with a view to saving the volume of conservation materials in the future. This resulted in our barely being able to maneuver around the boat and her casing. The original excitement and publicity over the boat's discovery had died down somewhat. Thinking that the boat had been "saved," many of our volunteers had gone back to their regular work, leaving us with fewer helpers. The process of removing the polyurethane progressed excruciatingly slowly.

There were occasional moments of humor to lighten the burden of working in those hot, cramped quarters. We kept referring to the removal process as the second excavation of the boat. We thus made a big fuss over the first "artifact" we discovered: a sharp-ended excavation hammer. Someone using it to remove mud from inside the hull had left it there, and it had become incorporated into the polyurethane during the spraying process.

As we chipped away at the polyurethane, it rapidly clogged up the spaces on either side of the boat. Several of the women in the excavation took charge of this problem. They would walk around the "excavators" collecting all the loose pieces of polyurethane in large plastic garbage bags. We lovingly called them our "bag ladies."

The boat had been packaged the same way she lay in the sediment, listing to port. As we operated on the polyurethane, we had at the same time to create supports under the boat to maintain this position. This was done by Davidi—Yohai had had to go back to his university classes—who set up a table at one corner of the pool. There he mixed brews of polyester and fiberglass and attached them to heavy-gauge PVC irrigation hose to create rudimentary support legs.

I returned one evening from my daily round of telephone calls to find Orna wheezing her lungs out under a lamp. Someone had added a little too much catalyst to the polyester, and one of the paintbrushes had ignited spontaneously, billowing smoke.

We were careful to cut away the polyurethane beneath the boat in the same manner that we had removed the mud. We dug tunnels, while leaving blocks of polyurethane that supported the boat. Danny, who is slim, was particularly good at channeling beneath the boat.

Before he left, Dick had instructed me how to collect the additional information he would need. A series of horizontal measurements had to be taken from the outside of the boat to the sides of the pool walls. With these data, Dick would be able to generate the boat's "lines," that is, an architectural drawing of the basic structure. I assigned this task to Edna, who recruited Karen to help her. They crawled under, over, and around fellow workers and groveled in the mixture of mud and polyurethane chippings on the floor taking these measurements.

While this was going on, someone made another interesting discovery, which had gone unnoticed during the excavation. Slightly astern of where we had noticed the mortise-and-tenon joints in the keel, one of the tunnelers found part of a scarf, a type of connecting joint between wood timbers. It was then that we learned that the keel was constructed of two separate parts.

As we removed the protective casing, the boat continued to dehydrate at an alarming rate. Until all of the polyurethane had been removed, however, we could not fill the pool with water.

A Davidi original.

Edna records offsets for the boat's lines drawing.

Had we done this, the boat would have been torn apart by unbalanced buoyancy. Our schedule reverted to punishing hours, from early in the morning until late into each night. The guard who had been hired to watch over the boat during the long, dark nights was never alone. He was busy primarily in keeping a small fire going nearby.

To keep the timbers wet, people were constantly watering the boat with spray cans. Nothing we did, though, could arrest the inevitable drying of the wood. While most of the hull at least looked moist, there now began to appear patches which, try as we might to dampen them with water, remained dry and parched-looking.

Then, one day a hairline crack appeared down the center of the hull.

On the removal the polyurethane, the forward half of the central keel scarf comes to light.

"By the time we get water into this pool," someone commented, "the boat will be so dry she will probably float."

No one laughed. It was too near the truth. Waterlogged wood doesn't float—unless it has begun to dry out. The previous day Orna had placed a bucket of water in a corner of the pool. In it we placed the small wood chips that occasionally came loose from the boat, primarily from the edges of the uppermost strakes, which were badly fragmented from having been in contact with the air. I had picked up one of these wood fragments and put it in the bucket. It floated. I weighed it down with a stone and did not tell anyone else.

Photographs that Danny took during those difficult days show all of us, without exception, with looks of utter exhaustion on our faces. We have haggard faces, bleary eyes, and sagging spirits. It was obvious that we were losing the battle to keep the boat from drying out. I felt like a surgeon who, after hours of effort, was about to lose his patient on the operating table. Time was running out.

ᏱᏱᏱ

Although nowhere near the number which had appeared each day at the excavation, visitors still continued to show up at the pool, brought by their tourist guides. One day an elderly lady politely asked me if she might be permitted to touch the boat.

"I'm sorry," I explained to her, "but the boat is very fragile. We can't let people handle it."

"Have you touched the boat?" she asked me.

"Yes, I have."

"Well, then, can I touch you?"

I cannot begin to describe how uncomfortable that request made me feel.

ᏱᏱᏱ

Our response to the imminent danger the boat faced was to double our efforts. Working around the clock, we reached the saturation point of exhaustion. Each day more and more of the casing was removed. More and more of the boat was revealed. Polyurethane was in our hair and stuck to our clothes. Finally, after what seemed an eternity but was a total of eleven days, the last of the polyurethane had been removed and the final PVC-pipe "legs" had been attached to the cradle. There was no longer any more polyurethane to remove.

Orna has a beautiful smile, and when we began to fill the pool with water, we saw it for the first time in many days. I doubt anyone can imagine the enormous stress she had been under and the crushing responsibility she had so capably borne as the conservator for this unique artifact. That evening, as the water level in the pool rose slowly, Nitsa brought out some cake and wine, and we raised our Dixie cups in a toast of *L'chaim* ("To life!"), celebrating the successful return of the boat to the water.

And no, she didn't float.

🌊🌊🌊

The next day we took down the wooden staging. The tarpaulin was stretched tight over the pool to keep the curious from touching the boat until we could erect a structure over the pool.

Moshele borrowed some large black PVC fish tanks from the nearby hatcheries, where fish are raised to ensure that the Kinneret will remain well stocked at all times. We used these to store the loose fragments of wood, in preparation for placing them in the pool. Karen, Edna, and I had spent the better part of the day preparing and tagging these loose timbers: Here was the part of the stern that had collapsed; there were the fragments of Zvika's boats which we had removed; and over there were timbers from the assembly found beneath the boat.

Toward dusk I went outside to stretch and take a breather. When I had entered the basement, I had left a blue sky behind. Now, when I came out again, the weather had changed dramatically. Clouds, dark blue yet strangely translucent, covered the sky above the Kinneret.

Lightning, the kind that flashes from one cloud to the other without hitting the ground, back-lit the clouds in an incredible

Edna and Orna—weariness etched on their faces—stand by the boat moments before the pool began to fill with water.

pyrotechnical exhibit of lights. It occurred to me then that this might be the Kinneret's manner of putting on a fireworks display in honor of the boat's safe return to water. Certainly it was a massive release of pent-up energy.

The lightning shot out in utter silence. It made not a sound. Nor was there a whisper of wind in the air. I called Karen and Edna to see what was happening. Then suddenly the wind was swirling all around, seemingly blowing in all directions at once. Edna, who had grown up along the Kinneret, said she'd never seen such a display.

One of the corners of the tarpaulin came loose and began to flap up and down in the wind, like a sail loosened from its rigging. Concerned that it might harm the boat, I ran over to the pool, caught the flapping tarp, and lashed it down.

Soon, the wind ceased, as did the lightning. And a night as dark as pitch descended upon us. The whole event was rather strange.

🌊🌊🌊

Soon after the boat was placed in the pool, the Department of Antiquities funded the construction of a metal shed to cover it. First, Isaac had the entire area filled in with earth, so that most of the pool was now located underground. The structure was designed with an air-conditioned visitors' corridor along its eastern wall, separated from the boat by a wall of plate glass.

During a visit to the boat while the building was under construction, I fell into a conversation with an Arab who was working there.

"*B'emet zeh olam muzar* [Truly this is a strange world]," he said to me in strongly accented Hebrew, shaking his head. "Here I am, a Muslim, building this structure to protect a boat, saved by Jews, but of great meaning to Christians."

Since that day I have thought about that comment often. Clearly he was onto something.

On another day, while in the shed working on the boat, I was accosted by an excited tourist.

"Could you please explain something to me?" she asked.

"If I can."

"How did you get the boat through the doors?"

So it goes.

eee

Submerging the boat in water was only a first-aid treatment; rather like giving CPR to a crash victim before the doctor arrives. It prevented the boat's timbers from drying out, but it was a temporary measure until the actual conservation treatment could be initiated. Water is loaded with bacteria, which feed on organic materials such as wood. Orna reminded us that it was the portion of the boat that had been buried in mud that had been preserved, while the parts exposed to air and to water had disintegrated with time.

In waterlogged wood, the cells are deteriorated, and most of the cellulose and hemicellulose (the internal material of the cells) have been replaced by water. Conservation treatment replaces the water in the wood cells with a substitute material, which then supports them, removing the danger of the cells' collapsing. In this way the weakened wood is strengthened and the dimensions of the timbers are stabilized.

The boat, though fragile, was intact and provided a unique opportunity for future study and exhibition. It was imperative that the technique chosen for conservation be safe and tested. The process had to avoid damaging the boat and also preserve its surface qualities and marks. Furthermore, it had to be affordable.

There are a variety of methods for conserving waterlogged wood. Some are very good, some less so. Orna had weighed each one in turn. There are methods calling for freeze-drying or the impregnation of resins. One new method calls for impregnating the wood with sugar. Each of these has its advantages and disadvantages.

Freeze-drying, the same process used in producing instant coffee, requires preimpregnation with a synthetic wax, followed by extraction of the water in the wood through vacuum freezing.

artifact the size of the boat were not available in Israel, not to mention the potentially astronomical costs. Of course, the thought of dismantling the boat and transferring the pieces into smaller tanks or freezers had been ruled out.

Orna studied reports on the use of sugar impregnation in the conservation of waterlogged wood. This is a fairly new method, however, and its long-term results were as yet unproved. It had never been used on an entire hull. The Kinneret boat could not be the test case for its validity. Orna chose a more conservative technique.

There has been more experience in conserving shipwrecks by using polyethylene glycol, more often called by its acronym: PEG. This is a water-soluble synthetic wax and has the tendency to replace the water in the wood cells through a process of osmosis. PEG, a waxy solid, is added to heated water to form a solution. The heat and the concentration of PEG are increased until, over time, the water in the wood cells has been replaced with the PEG.

PEG can be impregnated by spraying, as was the case with the large warships: the Swedish *Vasa* and the British *Mary Rose*. However, the Kinneret boat is a small vessel and lent itself to immersion rather than spraying. Treatment time—and thus costs—would also be reduced.

Let us reexamine the boat. She is 8.27 meters (27 feet) long and 2.3 meters (7.5 feet) wide and has a maximum preserved height of 1.3 meters (4.3 feet). Her timbers are of modest dimensions, with the average thickness of planks being 3.1 centimeters (1.2 inches). The two-part keel, which is the largest surviving component of the boat, is only 9.5 centimeters (3.7 inches) at its widest and 11.5 centimeters (4.5 inches) at its highest.

In further refining the conservation treatment best suited to the hull, Orna made a thorough study of its components. When the boat was discovered, its timbers were soft, fragile, and cracked and showed signs of penetration by plant roots, presumably during times of drought when the lake had receded and plants had grown over the site. The upper portion of the hull, which was closer to the surface of the mud, was more damaged than the lower. The iron nails were in excellent condition, having some surface corrosion, which had penetrated into the surrounding wood. Each of the seven wood types that Ella Werker had identified had a different internal cellular structure and would react differently to any given type of conservation. In addition, a wide variation in the degree of degradation of the wood was evident. Thus the conservation process would have to take into consideration not only the wide range of wood types, but also the different levels of deterioration among and within them.

Orna contemplated using various molecular weights of PEG. In general, lower-molecular-weight PEG is used with less degraded woods and hard woods, and higher-molecular-weight PEG is more successful with more degraded woods and softwoods. To treat the variations of degradation found in the Kinneret boat, Orna, after careful study, chose a two-phase treatment. She decided to use low-molecular-weight PEG 600 in the first phase to penetrate deeply into the better preserved and more compact woods. This PEG would be gradually introduced into the heated water, so that its concentration would be brought up to 50 percent weight/volume over time. Orna rejected the even lower-molecular-weight PEG 200 because of its hygroscopicity (tendency to absorb humidity from the air after treatment).

Once the first impregnation step was completed, the solution would be changed with a solution of PEG 4000 (the average molecular weight of which is 3400). This brew was to be slowly brought up to a concentration of 80–90 percent weight/volume and kept at a maximum temperature of 60 degrees centigrade (140 degrees Fahrenheit). This impregnation would fill the inner structure of the cells, giving the cell walls support, and would be particularly important for the softer and more degraded timbers. PEG 4000 also has the advantage of low hygroscopicity upon drying. The wood would have to be monitored constantly and adjustments made to achieve the best results. At the end of each of the two phases, a large percentage of the PEG would be recoverable for future use. Orna estimated that it would require up to seven years to fully impregnate the wood. The boat would then be removed from its bath, air-dried, cleaned of excess PEG on the surface, and finally prepared for study and display.

I had chosen Orna to be in charge of the boat's conservation because I felt that she was the person best suited to the task. From the day I called her, after my first visit to the boat, there was no question in my mind that she was the *right* person. She had supported my efforts by caring for and protecting the boat throughout its excavation and transport. For the conservation part of the project, my role was not to lead but to support Orna in her decisions. This role led to some interesting experiences.

$$\text{eee}$$

Soon after we had got the boat underwater, I received an invitation from U.S. Ambassador Pickering asking if I would be willing to give a slide presentation about the excavation at his residence in the Tel Aviv suburb of Herzlia Pituach for the embassy staff and their families. I was delighted to do so. I considered it a small way to thank the Ambassador and the embassy for assisting us with Dick's flight at such short notice. I immediately accepted the invitation.

This was to be the first public presentation ever given on the boat. The room was packed. After the Ambassador's introduction, Avi Eitan was called upon to say a few words. In gracious and modest terms, Avi expressed the appreciation of the Israel Department of Antiquities and the Museum for the immediate assistance that the embassy had given us. He also emphasized the problems that lay ahead.

Then it was my turn. I truly enjoyed giving that lecture. I felt a very strong desire to tell the story of what had taken place. I remember becoming engrossed in the slides, almost slipping back inside them during the lecture. At the conclusion of the presentation, I was exhausted, as if I had physically relived the experiences we had undergone in the past few weeks.

I concluded the lecture by explaining Orna's plans for conserving the boat. As financing the PEG had been heavily on my mind, I mentioned our predicament in passing. After the lecture, I found myself talking with Ambassador Pickering.

"I can't believe," he said, "that it would be *that* difficult to get the synthetic wax you need *donated* to the project."

Were my ears hearing right? This was too good to be true.

"Bud, would you come over here for a minute, please?" The Ambassador called over a man, about my age, who was standing nearby. I was introduced to Bud Rock, the embassy's Science Attaché.

"I'm sure that one of the chemical companies would be willing to supply the material these folks need for the boat as an in-kind donation," he said to Bud.

Bud concurred.

"Try getting on the phone to major producers, and see what we can do to help them."

Several days later, I received a call from Bud.

"I've made contact with the Israeli distributors of Dow Chemical, a company named Jacobsen and Sons, and they are willing to supply the PEG."

₰₰₰

Under Orna's guidance, we slowly began preparing the craft for the conservation process. Once or twice a week, we would meet at Ginosar to work. The water would be pumped out of the pool, till only the bottom of the hull—from the turn of the bilge—was still submerged. Then we would begin to work on the boat. When we were done for the day, the pool would be topped off with water again, totally covering the boat.

The straight pins that we had used to attach the identification tags to the timbers were now rusting away. Furthermore, the excavation and move had not been kind to the edges of the upper strakes, which had already been in poor condition when Yuvi and Moshele found the boat. A method of securing these fragments to the hull and of replacing the written tags with new plastic Dymo tags was needed.

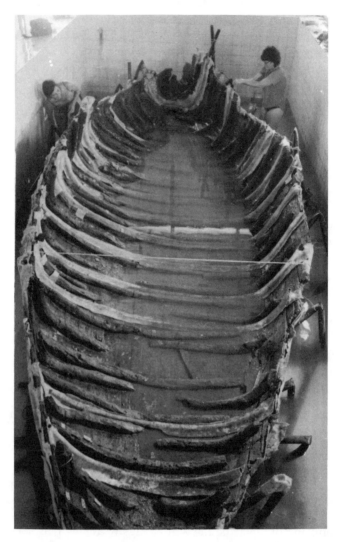

Orna and Karen prepare the boat for the first phase of conservation.

The PEG itself set limitations on what materials we could use, for PEG is very corrosive to most metals. We needed some type of sturdy wire which would not rust during the conservation process and yet could be bent.

We searched for an alternate material. Kibbutz Ein Harod has a factory which builds stainless steel equipment. When Nitsa called her friend who ran the factory, he told her that one of the spools of stainless steel wire used in the construction process had become entangled and was useless for their purposes. He donated the spool to the project.

The stainless steel wire turned out to be ideal for our needs. With a pair of pliers, it could be cut into any length and bent into any shape. From this wire, we prepared staples of various lengths to hold together the tiny fragments of wood which had become loosened and would surely have fallen off had we left them to their own devices. I spent an entire day locking together one small fragmented portion—about the size of two or three playing cards—on the highest strake located amidships on the starboard side.

The downside of this metal wire was that, no matter how much we tried to avoid it, the sharp ends were always puncturing our fingers, and we finished work each day with our hands looking and feeling like pincushions.

To allow the PEG maximum surface area in which to penetrate the boat, each of the fiberglass frames covering the inside of the hull had to be removed, cut down, and reattached with wire. Aluminum foil had been laid down in the field to prevent the fiberglass–polyester frames from sticking to the timbers. Instead, they stuck to the foil. As the foil would decompose under the attack of PEG, we now spent much time removing it. This was easier said than done. The foil had been glued tight to the polyester, so that in most cases the only way to remove it was to sand it off.

In removing the fiberglass frames, we had to cut through them with a small pneumatic saw. Particular care had to be taken when cutting through the fiberglass, so as not to harm the boat's timbers that lay immediately beneath it.

One day I overheard two tourists discussing the operation. "You see," said one, pointing to the saw, "they are using a special saw that stops as soon as it touches the wood. That way no harm can come to the wood. Isn't that right, young man?"

"Yes ma'am, that's right."

I didn't have the heart to tell her the truth.

While we prepared the boat for conservation, the water became infested with little red wormlike larvae. Orna, concerned that they might damage the boat, had them examined in a laboratory. They turned out to be a type of mosquito larvae, not threatening to wood or people, but extremely unpleasant companions with whom to share a pool. Orna considered adding an insecticide to the water but feared harming those of us working in the pool. With no apparent solution to the problem, we moved about in the shallow water tending to the boat, while surreptitiously batting at the water around our legs.

One morning we arrived to find three large goldfish swimming about in the pool. Moshele, having observed our discomfiture, had come up with the *ecologically* correct answer. He had stocked the pool with fish, which merrily went about gobbling up every last little crawly creature. Within days the water was clear, and the goldfish, who seemed highly contented, swam idly around the pool. We became quite fond of our new companions.

🌊🌊🌊

Orna and I were sitting in her small conservation laboratory in the basement of the Hebrew University's Institute of Archaeology, which is located on Mount Scopus overlooking the Old City of Jerusalem. She had just finished preparing a steaming hot *finjan* (a small metal vessel, with handle and spout) of Turkish coffee on her Bunsen burner and was pouring it into two small handleless cups on a small brass tray decorated with Arabic calligraphy.

"I need to go to England," Orna had told me a week earlier.

She had a tremendous responsibility in conserving the boat. One of her main problems was the number of different types of wood that had been used in the boat's construction. Each wood had a different density and variety of characteristics. Orna had come up with the theoretical solution that would provide a viable answer to dealing with all of the different types of timbers. Before committing the boat to years of conservation that would ultimately require a great deal in funding, work hours, equipment, and electricity, she wanted to be absolutely sure that all bases were covered, all contingencies considered, and that this was the best possible method of conserving the boat. Orna was hesitant to begin the process before she had had the opportunity to discuss her ideas with other conservation experts.

"No conservator in Israel has ever before tried to do anything on this scale," she had explained. "I need to go to England to confer with experts at the Greenwich Maritime Museum. They have considerable experience in the use of PEG. I would like to discuss the effectiveness of various molecular weights of PEG, the amount of time required for maximum treatment, the best temperatures to achieve, and the type of heating systems I could use. I need some feedback."

I had broached the subject with Avi, hoping that the Department might foot the bill, but I was not surprised to find that a trip for Orna to England was not high on the list of the Department of Antiquities' allocations. The Department would not pay for the trip.

Funding for Orna's stay in England, I knew, would be available though friends at the Anglo-Israel Archaeological Society, an English organization that promotes archaeology in Israel. But where could I find the money for her plane ticket? I drew a blank.

"I promise that I will get you to England," I told Orna.

"In your dreams," she said and continued to sip her coffee.

Maybe so. I honestly had no idea how I was going to keep my promise. I just knew that I would keep it.

Several days later, Providence came calling in the form of my ringing telephone. Have you ever noticed how sometimes you meet someone who drifts in and out of your life, making no perceptible mark on it? And then months—or years—later he or she suddenly reappears and in some way helps you move along your chosen path. It is almost as if your "chance" meeting in the past was the result of a future need that the person would come to fill.

My caller was Ami Eshel, a veteran diver and a member of Kibbutz Ma'agan Michael, on Israel's Mediterranean coast. In the summer of 1985, a full half-year prior to the discovery of the Kinneret boat, he had brought to my attention another exciting discovery. While instructing a dive certification course at his kibbutz, Ami had noticed something interesting on the seabed.

"Between the island and the shore," he told me, "I saw some unusual stones—definitely not local—and some rotten wood."

Ami's words had lit up all sorts of red lights in my head. It sounded as if he had come across a shipwreck buried under her own stone ballast. If so, she might be well preserved.

Ami agreed to show me the location, but he could find time only in the late afternoon, when, because of the sea breeze, beach waves made diving difficult. Each day, we would meet on the beach in the late afternoon, and each day, the sea would be so rough that we couldn't dive. We finally agreed to meet on the shore at 6 AM one weekend morning.

The sea was quiet as I finned after Ami. He brought me over the site, which lay near shore in less than a dozen feet of water. Within moments I had located the hull planking—Ami's "rotten wood"—and there, cut into the edge of the uppermost plank, I could clearly see mortise-and-tenon scars. The dark-red broken tenons stuck out starkly against the yellow-brown planking. The hunch had been right; it was a shipwreck, and she was definitely ancient.

Caramba!

But how ancient was she? Carefully moving some of the stone ballast which covered the hull, I came across a ceramic oil lamp and some pottery loop handles buried *under* the rock ballast. They had obviously gone down with the ship, and dating them would give us the age of the ship. Still underwater, I showed Ami the oil lamp in my hand. It was a type dating either to the end of the Iron Age or to the Persian period. Similarly, the handles belonged to a type of amphora (called a *basket-handle jar*) which is unique to that same time frame. The ship must have sunk, therefore, roughly 2½ millennia earlier, sometime between the sixth and fourth centuries BC. I speculated to myself later as I swam back to shore: Perhaps she was a Phoenician ship, the first one ever found!

Double caramba!

The Ma'agan Michael shipwreck, as that vessel has come to be known today, was subsequently excavated by the Center of Maritime Studies of Haifa University by Dr. Elisha Linder and a student of Dick Steffy's, Jay Rosloff. She probably is *not* Phoenician. However, that is another story.

Since our mutual adventure in the sea, Ami and I had not been in contact. Meanwhile, he had gone to work for a public relations firm. In the course of his work, he had met Orna Fraser, the editor of *IsraEl Al*, the in-flight magazine for the national air carrier. When she heard that Ami was a diver, Orna told him how much she would like to have an article for her publication dealing with that "Jesus boat" that had been so prominent in the media.

"You wouldn't happen to know someone who could write a piece on that boat, do you?" she asked Ami.

"*Ain ba'ayot* [No problem]," Ami told her. "I know the guy who excavated it."

That evening, over the telephone, he gave me Orna Fraser's number. Calling her the next day, I agreed to write the article for her. But only on one condition. In place of the normal writer's fee, she had to provide me with a round-trip ticket to England for Orna Cohen. Orna Fraser agreed.

"OK, now when do you need the article?" I asked.

"Yesterday."

I sat down that afternoon and wrote the article out longhand. It was the first manuscript I wrote about the boat. I titled it—forgive me, but I couldn't resist it—"Raiders of the Lost Boat." The piece appeared in the next edition of *IsraEl Al*, accompanied by a beautiful cover photo by Danny showing the boat about to be floated onto the lifting pallet opposite the Allon Museum.

Orna Cohen read it on her way to England.

≈≈≈

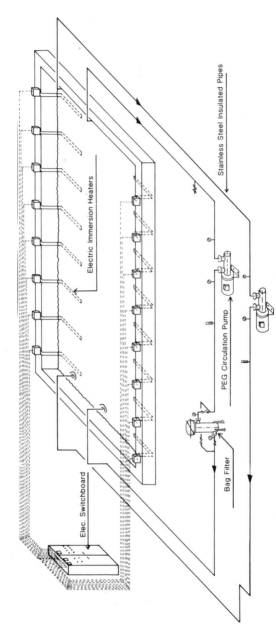

The heating and circulation system.

Orna's plans solidified after her consultations in England. The pool would be surrounded by a series of electrical immersion elements, which could be removed and replaced should a problem arise. As PEG is denser than water, a circulation system would be required to keep the solution uniform and to gain maximum penetration. Orna envisioned two stainless-steel screw pumps; two parallel systems of pumps and heating elements would ensure continuity in case of the temporary failure of one. The PEG solution would pass through a filter that would keep it as free as possible from small particles of wood, mud, bacteria, and other microorganisms. Because the vibrations of the pumps resonating through the solution might endanger the fragile hull, Orna designed the system so that the pumps would be located outside the building.

Energy to run the heating and circulation system would be a major expense to the project, so Orna and Nitsa researched various sources. They examined the possible use of solar-powered heating, but because of the amounts of energy required, it would have proved unreliable and expensive. Fossil fuels were prohibited on the site for ecological reasons. Orna and Nitsa concluded that the heating elements would have to work on electricity. A special electrical line would need to be installed to provide the necessary amperage. Fortunately, the museum electrician, Shalom Kinarti, was able to assist greatly with the installation of the system.

As it would be impossible to remove the PEG from the pool in order to fix anything once the process began, everything had to be built in such a manner that, should it break, it could be fixed from outside the pool.

As the concentration of PEG in solution was to be increased gradually by adding more chemical, the water level would be kept constant by evaporation. Heat loss and evaporation were to be controlled by a removable thermal insulation cover for the pool. Normal tap water would be used in the solution at the beginning of the process. However, since the local water contains much calcium, and a great deal of evaporation would occur over the years, distilled water would be added later after passing through an ion-extracting filter.

There are cases in which ships' timbers have been left unattended in tanks after excavation. I had heard of a situation where a museum guard, who had been put in charge, forgot to keep the conservation tanks topped off. Consequently, the water evaporated and the wood crumbled away. This could pose a real threat to our boat. Similarly, an extended breakdown in the heating system, if the PEG concentration had reached a critical level, could result in the entire pool's hardening into solid wax.

Orna intended to visit the boat at least two or three times a week, and Nitsa would assign one of her museum people to check the systems daily, add chemicals, and assist Orna during her visits. As a further safeguard, the whole system would be controlled automatically to maintain the heating, circulation, and water levels. If any troubles occurred, an alarm would sound. In case of a power failure, an emergency generator would be ready.

The loose pieces of wood that had fallen off, or that had been removed from the boat and around it, would be protected by plastic netting and placed in plastic trays. These trays were to be submerged in the pool so that all woods received uniform treatment. Orna also anticipated that insecticides and antifungal agents might be needed from time to time to protect the wood from attack, especially after the treatment was completed.

ℓℓℓ

As Karen had noted during the excavation, Israelis are phenomenal at handling emergencies, improvising with whatever is at hand. Well-thought out plans for long-term projects, however, seem to take forever to get under way. Thus it came to be for installing Orna's heating system and beginning the conservation treatment. Occasionally we would become discouraged, but always something would occur to lift our spirits.

One day the phone rang for Karen.
"Hello?"
"Karen, this is Orna. I just had to tell someone."
"Orna, are you all right?"

"Yes, I'm fine. Karen, you won't believe what I saw."

"What was it?"

"Early this morning I was driving from Safed [in the mountains overlooking the Kinneret on the northwest where Orna's parents live] down to the Kinneret to work. It was still dark outside and it was pouring rain. I looked down at the Kinneret, and *I saw a rainbow over the lake*. It was night out. And it was raining. And there was a rainbow. I almost ran off the road. I had to stop the car to get out and look at it. I got soaked standing there in the pouring rain just staring at it."

"I guess Shelley isn't the only one who sees rainbows," Karen chuckled.

"I guess not. I was so shocked I'm still shaking. I don't know if I should tell Shelley about it. I've never seen a rainbow at night. Have you ever seen one?"

Orna never did bring herself to tell me about *her* rainbow. She let Karen do it.

ee e

It seems that when you have something valuable, everybody wants it. Several museums vied for the opportunity to exhibit the boat. One enterprising museum director even called me up to clarify something.

"I have just one question," he said. "How wide is the boat?"

"Why on earth do you want to know that?" I asked.

"I just want to make sure that we can get the boat through my museum's door."

"Oh."

I gave him the measurement, said good-bye politely, and hung up.

ee e

Finally. In 1988—nearly two years after the excavation—the heating and circulation system had been installed and was up and running. The first batch of PEG had arrived. All was in readiness to begin the conservation process. Orna introduced a 5 percent solution of the PEG 600 into the pool and gave final instructions to Nitsa and Yaron Gofer, who would be in charge of the day-to-day running of the facility.

Everything was under control at last. Orna decided to treat herself to a well-deserved vacation. She left for Greece.

It seems that no sooner had she departed than the water in the pool began to ferment. It then turned green and began to stink like a cesspool.

After a few days in Greece, Orna called Nitsa to find out how things were going. After their conversation, Orna returned to Israel on the next available flight.

Upon returning, Orna discovered that the introduction of the PEG had caused bacteria to multiply wildly. The boat was being eaten away. The "fermentation" was the process of the bacteria turning the cellulose in the wood into glucose (sugar)—on which they were feasting. The stinking miasma was nothing less than the boat dissolving into pieces. It was, quite literally, the attack of the killer bacteria.

The first task, the immediate one, was to find an experienced bacteriologist who could help Orna determine which biocide would best control the outbreak of bacteria without causing any undue problems in continuing the conservation effort. After numerous telephone calls, Orna reached Dr. Ayala Barak, an authority on bacteria.

The next day Orna and Ayala drove to Ginosar. After they took samples from the contaminated solution, it was pumped out of the pool and replaced with fresh water. Then the pool was flushed repeatedly.

After many experiments, Ayala succeeded in finding the appropriate biocide. The chemical was introduced, the bacteria were brought under control, and the first phase of the conservation process was begun again.

ᥱᥱᥱ

When a *sharkia* comes howling down from the Golan and whips up a storm on the Kinneret, it is the west coast of the lake—

the side on which the Yigal Allon Museum is located—which
receives the brunt of the attack. And this attack can be so strong
that entire portions of land fronting the lake are liable to be eroded
into the sea during the space of the storm. This is such a graphic
occurrence that legends have been created about it.

About a mile and a half south of where Yuvi and Moshele had
found the boat, beneath the imposing flanks of the mountain of
Arbel, a large solitary rock is visible just offshore in the water. This
is known in Hebrew as *Selah hanemelah* ("the Rock of the Ant").
Legend has it that the boulder derives its name from a colony of
industrious ants which once had its nest there. At that time, the
rock was attached by a strip of earth to the shore. Each day, the
hardworking ants would go about their work, busily collecting
food for their sustenance.[1]

Then, one day, a mighty storm hit this western side of the
lake. The storm, in its ragings, tore away the land bridge, and the
ants' home became an island. The ants, who could not swim, were
left stranded without food.

In their distress the humble ants prayed to the Lord, so the
legend goes, for divine intervention. It came to pass that the reeds,
which grew thickly along the lake, heard the ants' prayers and,
after conferring among themselves, bent down their heads and
made of themselves living bridges, by means of which the ants
happily scurried to the safety of land.

The pool, as I have already noted, is located on a portion of
land (between the museum and the lake) which has been reclaimed from the Kinneret. This landfill is composed of huge
boulders, covered with a layer of earth. After the first phase of
conservation was well under way, a *sharkia* attacked the coast and
washed away much of the earth on the lake side of the pool.

Nitsa reported that the pool was intact and the systems
undamaged—this time. However, were a second *sharkia* to hit
before the area could be rebuilt and strengthened, the pool could
crack. The ramifications of such an occurrence for the boat's well-
being were unthinkable. We had adopted "Never a Dull Moment!" as our motto in response to the constant tensions of safely

excavating and moving the boat; and it seemed that the excitement was not over yet. Nitsa and Isaac, with Antiquities Authority emergency funding, rushed to secure the frontier by adding additional boulders and recovering the enlarged area with earth. Providentially, good weather held long enough for them to complete the job.

♪♪♪

At the end of 1991, nearly six years after the boat's excavation, Orna finished the first of her two-phase PEG treatment. I was out of the country at the time, but she gave me a detailed report of developments.

Jacobsen and Son had supplied thirty-eight tons of PEG 4000, the heavier-density type needed for the second phase. The PEG was shipped in the form of a white waxy powder, rather like old-style soap flakes.

"You missed much hard work," Orna related. The PEG had arrived in two large shipping containers. It was the Lufans—Moshele, Yuvi, and their brother, Israel—who came to help, along with tractors from the kibbutz. Isaac was also there, despite a bad back. The small group used a tractor to remove the pallets, which were stacked high with the sacks of PEG, from the containers. Because it was raining, they could not leave the sacks outside for even a single day. When some of the sacks fell, however, it was necessary to remove them by hand and carry them on their backs into a large exhibition room at the Allon Museum.

"The removal of the old PEG from the pool was exciting," Orna continued in her letter. The boat had not been visible for two years, and it was difficult to know what was taking place in the pool in the interim.

"To our delight," she noted, "the boat appeared a real beauty, much cleaner than when we had known her, and nothing had been harmed by the conservation process."

The PEG had also cleansed the last remaining mud from the hull, bringing out constructional details that had barely been visible when the boat had gone into conservation. Limber holes (openings cut through the bottom of the floors to permit bilge water to run freely back and forward) had been plugged with mud. During the conservation process, the mud had been absorbed into the PEG, and the limber holes were striking in their detail. The floors at the bow and stern each had a single limber hole in the center. The frames amidships had two holes, one on either side, with a large iron nail in the center of each frame holding them securely to the keel.

Most of the PEG used during the first phase was saved in eighty barrels which were stored in the museum. The boat and the pool were flushed out with fresh water for a day, with Orna using the opportunity to strengthen the framework supporting the boat and to have photographs taken by an Antiquities Authority photographer.

It was not easy to get the new PEG into the pool. To begin the treatment, the boat needed an initial dose of ten tons of PEG 4000 in the pool at startup. That meant melting down 400 25-kilogram (55-pound) sacks.

To no one's surprise, it was Moshele who provided the means. At the time, he was in charge of an ostrich ranch owned and run by Kibbutz Ginosar. The ostriches' stainless-steel water tank was commandeered and secured to a tractor. The first 30 sacks were emptied into the tank, which was then transported to the Nof Ginosar guest house, where boiling water was added and the whole brew was stirred. When the water melted the PEG, the tractor drove back to the boat, and the toddy was emptied into the pool. This process was repeated 13 times.

"As usual," Orna wrote, "it was cold and rained, and as usual, all the Lufan family and another member of the kibbutz, Bill Sheinman, worked until 10 PM, by which time we had succeeded in melting 400 bags, which was exactly the amount needed."

The entire process of changing the PEG in the pool was recorded on film by an Italian film crew. Yuvi and Moshele, noted Orna in her letter, were convinced that the pope would see the movie and immediately come to visit the boat.

This has yet to happen.

ᑫ ᑫ ᑫ

During the first phase of treatment, the PEG got progressively darker as additional amounts were added each day. Lamps were placed in the water at first, but soon the liquid turned opaque. Even so, tourists continued to visit the site where the vessel was being preserved and to view a 15-minute video about the boat. Now, during this second phase, the boat is not visible to the public—or, for that matter, to anyone else. The PEG 4000 is as dark as molasses, and getting darker; for as the water evaporates, more and more PEG is added. The temperature in the pool is now a constant, scalding 60 degrees centigrade (140 degrees fahrenheit), and sheets of white foam rubber cover the pool to prevent heat loss. Orna anticipates that the conservation will be completed in 1996 or 1997.

In ending her letter, Orna wrote, "Apart from all this, of course, we have problems with bacteria and with the pool's heating system, but we are used to such problems. I assure you that we will be able to overcome them. . . . I feel that we can see the end of the conservation process now."

For Orna to be that optimistic is something. Really something.

Chapter 10
Putting It All Together

For nothing is hidden that will not be disclosed, nor is anything secret that will not become known and come to light.

Luke 8:17

A fter inviting contributions to the excavation report by experts in the various research categories, there remained the problem of putting all the pieces together into a coherent whole and attempting to determine how the boat fit into the context of its times.

One of the main research issues to be addressed was comparing textual references to boats on the Sea of Galilee in the first century AD with the boat we had just excavated. Was the Kinneret boat representative of the type of boat used by the Apostles and disciples of Jesus as described in the Gospels? Was she the same type of boat as those used by the Jews against the Romans? What manner of inquiry, I wondered, would answer these questions?

Revealing the past, like many forms of problem solving, rarely follows a linear progression. Rather, discovery comes in fits and starts, in dead ends and reversals, in intuitions and hidden revelations. Just when one has given up ever reaching a resolution to an ancient enigma, one hears a knocking at an inner door, and a quiet voice asks, "Oh, by the way, is this what you've been looking for?"

ᕼᕼᕼ

One of the most memorable episodes for me during the entire excavation happened the day of Dick's first daylight encounter with the boat. For most of the morning, he had been busily poking here and measuring there. When he had probed enough to form a first impression of the hull, he came over to where I was supervising some volunteers and showed me a drawing he had made.

"This is what I think the boat would have looked like," he told me.

301

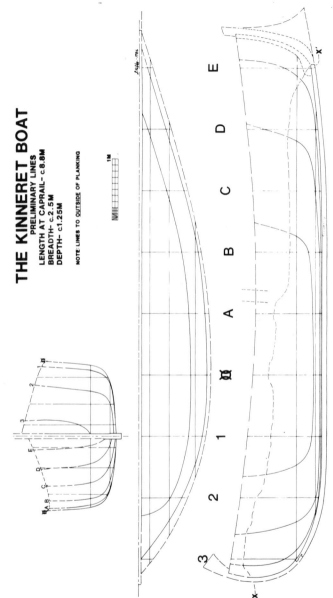

THE KINNERET BOAT
PRELIMINARY LINES
LENGTH AT CAPRAIL– c.8.8M
BREADTH– c.2.5M
DEPTH– c.1.25M

NOTE: LINES TO OUTSIDE OF PLANKING

1M

The sheer, or profile, view of Dick's lines drawings shows the boat's full recurving stern and pointed bow with cutwater.

Dick's sketch showed the sheer, or profile, of the boat, as he perceived it. He had drawn a vessel with a full, recurving stern and a fine, pointed bow with a cutwater.

"How many rowers would a boat this size need?" I asked.

Dick thought about this for a few moments. "Probably four— two on either side."

"Did the boat carry a sail?" I asked.

"It must have carried one," he said. "On a lake like the Kinneret, with its regular wind system, sailors must have taken advantage of the power of the wind. But I still haven't found a mast step."

This was curious. The boat would have needed something to support a mast. Otherwise the pressure of the wind against the sail would have put too much stress directly on the hull.

"How do you explain that?" I asked.

"At this point, I don't. But let me go back and take a closer look at the hull. This boat still has a great deal to teach us. Besides, if we had all the answers at the beginning, there wouldn't be any challenges, now would there?"

"I guess not."

"Actually, this is the fun part."

Right now I could do with fewer problems and challenges, I had thought at the time.

Under the bright sun and the blue sky, Dick and I continued our conversation for a short while, discussing other details that he had brought to light. Soon he went back to his recording, I to my supervising.

A short time later, I had a visit by two distinguished visitors, Fathers Stanislau Lofreda and Virgilio Corbo, Franciscan archaeologists who had excavated extensively at the nearby sites of Capernaum and Migdal. They had heard about the boat in the media and had come to see it with their own eyes. As I showed them about the site, they seemed to be totally absorbed in the boat.

As if not to be outdone, Father Corbo told me, with a twinkle in his eye, "You know, we, too, have discovered an ancient boat."

This caught me off guard. "Really? I thought this was the first

ancient boat found in the Sea of Galilee," I said, gesturing with a
wave of my hand in the direction of our boat.

The "boat" that Father Corbo referred to had never actually
"sailed" on the Kinneret. Rather, it was depicted in mosaic stones
(called *tesserae* in archaeological parlance) in a first-century AD
mosaic which they had uncovered in a private house during their
excavations at Migdal.

"Would you please draw it for me?" I asked, handing Father
Corbo the dog-eared field notebook I normally carried in the back
pocket of my jeans.

He took the little notebook, drew a rough sketch of the boat in
the mosaic, and handed it back to me. Looking at the drawing was
like being hit by a lightning bolt. It depicted a boat with a cutwater
bow and a stern that was high and curved. Except for the addition
of a mast, a yard, and a furled sail, it could have been a carbon
copy of the drawing that Dick just had shown me. Was this a
contemporaneous depiction of a boat like ours? If so, it could
supply some valuable clues to the parts of the boat and its accoutrements which were missing.

"How many oars does the boat in the mosaic have?" I asked.

Taking back the notebook, Father Corbo silently scratched
three slanting lines across the hull.

"I guess your 'boat' represents a larger type of watercraft than
ours," I said, disappointed. "We think our boat probably would
have had two oars to a side."

After the Franciscans had left the site, I showed Dick the
drawing.

"You're pulling my leg," he said.

It took me some time to convince Dick that I was not.

The mosaic that the Franciscans found at Migdal has been
removed from the house in which it was discovered and is at
present exhibited at the archaeological site of Capernaum. I visited it there, but time was too limited for detailed scrutiny. I asked
Danny to take some slides of the mosaic, particularly some close-
ups of the boat. It was only much later, long after the excavation
had been concluded, that I finally got around to studying the boat
depicted in the Migdal mosaic.

The boat in the mosaic from Migdal.

Late one hot and humid summer evening, I taped a fresh sheet of white paper to my refrigerator, placed my slide projector on a kitchen chair, and projected one of Danny's slides onto the paper. Kneeling on the cool linoleum floor in front of the refrigerator, with a pencil I began to trace each stone used in creating the illustration of the boat. Occasionally I interposed my body between the slide projector and the "screen," intentionally blocking the projection, to make sure I hadn't left out any lines.

I began from the top of the depiction, first drawing in the rigging and tackle, then the hull. Finally, I reached the oars. By this time my back was killing me.

I filled in the oar nearest the bow. It had originally consisted of a single line of ten stones, nine of which were light brown and one, apparently a repair, white. The oar was angled in a manner that made it clear that the artist intended to depict it at the end of the stroke, when the oar was pulled up against the rower's chest. The second oar was slanted in the same manner. It now contained nine stones, but there was a gap in the center of the line large enough for two additional stones.

I turned to the third, aftmost oar. Starting at its top, I began to trace slowly and monotonously the roughly square-shaped stones. As I was doing this, the lower part of the oar was projected onto the back of my hand and wrist, so I did not notice anything unusual about it until I was actually drawing in the final stones. Only then did I realize that the third oar, unlike the previous two, widened at the bottom into two courses of mosaic stones.

"Wait a minute. That's not a rowing oar," I said aloud to myself. "It's a quarter rudder!"

Moments later, the ramifications sank in.

"Ohmygod!"

The fact that the aftmost oar was a steering oar meant that the prototype of the boat depicted in the mosaic would have had only four rowers, as Dick had predicted for our boat. *That meant the boat in the mosaic had had the same crew as our boat and therefore must have been of the same size and type as our boat.* Such a vessel would have required a minimum of four rowers and a helmsman or captain at the quarter rudder: *a crew of five men.*

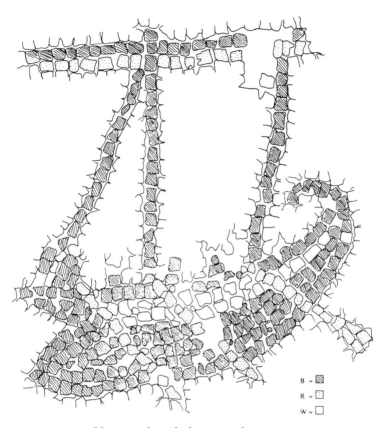

B = ▨
R = ▢
W = □

I began to draw the boat, stone by stone. . .

Crew sizes.

Of course. It was obvious. In fact, it was so obvious that my first thought was why I hadn't thought of that before. Crew size was a possible means of determining the relationship between the boats mentioned in the Gospels, those in the Battle of Migdal, and our boat. Now, if it were only possible to determine how many crewmen were in the boats mentioned in the written record.

I ran to my study, nearly tripping over the slide projector's electrical cord on the way, and yanked my Bible off the bookshelf. From my recent readings through the Gospels, I knew that there were references to only two *specific* boats. One boat had belonged to Zebedee, the father of James and John; the other was owned by Simon Peter.

Quickly flipping the pages to the Gospel of Mark, I read:[1]

> As he [Jesus] went a little farther, he saw James son of Zebedee and his brother John, who were in their boat mending the nets. Immediately he called them; and they left their father Zebedee with the hired men, and followed him.

Let's see. Grabbing a ballpoint pen and some scratch paper I translated the verses into an equation:

$$1 \text{ [Zebedee]} + 1 \text{ [James]} + 1 \text{ [John]}$$
$$+ 2 \text{ (or more?) } [\text{"hired men"}] = (5 + ?) \text{ men}$$

Gottcha. *A minimum crew of five men.* Zebedee's boat was apparently the same type as ours.

I quickly flipped the pages to the description of fishing in John:[2]

> Gathered there together were Simon Peter, Thomas called the Twin, Nathanael of Cana in Galilee, the sons of Zebedee, and two others of his disciples. Simon Peter said to them, "I am going fishing." They said to him, "We will go with you." They went out and got into the boat, but that night they caught nothing.

Presumably the boat referred to here is the one that belonged to Simon Peter.[3] Another equation:

$$1 \text{ [Simon Peter]} + 1 \text{ [Thomas called the Twin]} + 1 \text{ [Nathanael]}$$
$$+ 2 \text{ [sons of Zebedee]} + 2 \text{ [\"other disciples\"]} = 7\text{-man crew}$$

Again, a crew of five or more. As more hands were needed to man the nets than just the rowing and steering crew, the two additional men do not change the conclusion that Simon Peter's boat was also the same type of boat.

Excited, I scribbled down another equation:

Kinneret Boat (type) = Migdal mosaic boat (type) =
boat (type) of Zebedee = boat (type) of Simon Peter

Now, what about the boats used by the Jews in the Battle of
Migdal?

I turned to Josephus's account of the conflict. I must have read
the description of the battle at least twenty times that night looking for a clue to the number of people aboard the boats.

Nothing.

Nowhere does Josephus state how many persons were in any
of the boats. Furthermore, the circumstances of the battle indicate
that the situation was an extraordinary one, which might not
verify normal crew sizes. Even so, any specifics concerning the
number of people in the boats would have been valuable. But
there was nothing of substance in this regard. Josephus's description was simply too general. The closest he comes to intimating the
number of persons in the boats is this:[4]

> Thus pursued, the Jews could neither escape to land, where
> all were in arms against them, nor sustain a naval battle on
> equal terms. For their skiffs were small and built for piracy,
> and were no match for the rafts and the men on board each
> were so few that they dared not come to grips with the dense
> ranks of the Roman enemy.

I went to bed that night with mixed feelings. I was elated to
have found a "key" that finally related the boat to the Gospels. But
I was also frustrated that I had not been able to find the door that
the same "key" might unlock vis-à-vis the Battle of Migdal.

I lay there on my back for a long time with my arms crossed
behind my head and my eyes wide open, staring at the ceiling. I
was angry at Josephus—as much as anyone can be angry at
someone who has been dead for well over 18 centuries.

"Damn it. All it would have taken was one additional sentence, a few words," I said to Josephus. But the only response I

elicited was from a lonely owl somewhere in the distance outside my bedroom window.

To see a faint star you cannot stare directly at it; you must look *next* to it. As it turned out, such was also the case in drawing out information concerning the boats used by the Jews at the Battle of Migdal. I had been so intent on the battle that I had entirely ignored what was the single most crucial piece of evidence. It was Mendel who got me back on track.

A few days later I visited him at his home on the banks of the Kinneret at Kibbutz Ein Gev. I related to Mendel the fruits of my research and complained about my inability to take them any further.

"Try the story of Josephus's sham fleet," Mendel advised.

Few stories concerning the Kinneret are as bizarre as the one Josephus relates about his "sham fleet." And if his story needed another title, I guess you might call it "Cleitus Gives Josephus a Hand."

As we have already seen, at the outbreak of hostilities with Rome, the lakeside city of Tiberias teetered between those who wished to find an accommodation with the Romans and those who were intent on ridding the country of the hated Roman rule. Josephus, who had been appointed magistrate over the Galilee by the Jerusalem leadership, spent considerable time and energy keeping Tiberias from going over to the Romans.

Finally, the wavering Tiberians petitioned King Agrippa II, a supporter of Rome, to send troops, as they wished to come under his protection. Emboldened by the arrival of a contingent of Roman cavalry, the citizens applauded the horsemen, blessed Agrippa, and cursed Josephus.

Josephus had located his center of command at nearby Migdal, which, of all the cities bordering the Kinneret, most strongly supported the revolt. The turn of events in Tiberias caught him entirely offguard. He had just sent his troops home for a weekend of R & R, probably to prevent the good people of Migdal from being overly burdened during the Sabbath by masses of soldiers in the city. The only fighters that he had with him were seven soldiers and a few friends.

As the Sabbath, during which activity was forbidden, was fast approaching, it would be futile to try to recall his forces. The men of Migdal and their few allies inside the city, he realized, would be insufficient to subdue Tiberias. Yet, if Josephus delayed taking action, he ran the considerable risk of additional troops' entering Tiberias and reenforcing his enemies. Tiberias would be lost as an asset to the Jewish cause. Josephus was in hot water. Something had to be done immediately. But what?

When in doubt, use *chutzpah*.

Ever resourceful, Josephus devised a ruse to bring Tiberias back into the rebel fold. First, he placed trusted men at the gates of Migdal to prevent word of his scheme from reaching Tiberias. He then called together all the civilian "heads of families" who owned boats and instructed them to prepare their vessels to set sail immediately for Tiberias.

Josephus placed skeleton crews in each of the boats while he, together with the soldiers and a few of his friends, boarded one of the boats. The fleet sailed off to Tiberias.

Upon arriving opposite that city, Josephus instructed his fleet to ride at anchor far offshore. Only his boat, with the lone contingent of soldiers aboard, approached the shore.

The Tiberians were in a quandary. Suddenly, the lake was alive with what must have looked at that distance like a fleet full of combatants from Migdal who had come to wreak mayhem on the city.

Plans changed in Tiberias that day. Weapons disappeared. Waving olive branches (the ancient equivalent of a white flag), men, women and children rushed down to the shore. They beseeched Josephus not to destroy their fair city.

Josephus, still riding safely offshore in his boat, upbraided those on shore, on both a national and a personal level. First, he demanded to know, how could they be so foolish as to throw away the nation's strength in internecine warfare while the Roman wolf stood at the door? Furthermore, how dare they close the city to him? Was he not the one who had fortified it?

After many more recriminations, Josephus "magnanimously" agreed to receive a delegation of the city's most influential citizens to apologize for Tiberias's rash behavior toward him and to pledge its future loyalty. Soon, ten of the city's most influential men were standing on the shore. Josephus ordered one of the boats to approach the land. When it arrived, he had the delegation taken aboard and ordered the captain to return to Migdal. The Tiberian delegation had become Josephus's prisoners.

In this description, Josephus used the Greek term *mia ton haliadon*, which means "one of the *fishing boats*." That is another, perhaps obvious, clue that the large boats of Josephus's sham fleet consisted of vessels normally employed in fishing.

Next, Josephus required that members of the city council approach to apologize and to pledge future compliance with his orders. They, too, were shipped off to Migdal. In fact, Josephus claimed to have carted off 2,600 Tiberians to Migdal as hostages.

Needless to say, the Tiberians who remained in the city were exceptionally distraught. Still riding near shore in his boat, Josephus demanded to know who was responsible for the Tiberians' disloyalty. The crowd—among whom were those smarting at having seen their loved ones carted off to an uncertain future— informed Josephus that a young hothead named Cleitus had instigated the revolt against him.

As punishment, Josephus boldly ordered one of his soldiers, Levi, to go ashore and cut off Cleitus's hands. Fearful of the seething mass of humanity ashore, Levi refused. Josephus claims that he was about to carry out the deed himself when he was interrupted by the frightened victim. Cleitus petitioned the infuriated leader to permit him to retain one of his hands. To this Josephus agreed, but only on one condition: Cleitus had to sever his own left hand.

It speaks volumes for the spirit of the times in which these people lived that, upon hearing Josephus's judgment, *Cleitus drew his sword and cut off his own hand.* Apparently Cleitus thought he was getting a bargain.

In this manner, "with unarmed boats and seven guards," Josephus was able to subdue Tiberias. He released his captives the next day, hoping that this would ensure their loyalty. A few days later, however, Tiberias, together with the Galilean city of Sepphoris, again revolted against Josephus.

So it goes.

Josephus relates the story of his sham fleet twice, with minor variations: once in *The Jewish War* and then again in his later autobiography, *The Life of Josephus.*[5] Concerning the manning of the fleet, Josephus writes:[6]

> Then he [Josephus] collected all the boats that he could find on the lake—some two hundred and thirty, *with no more than four sailors in each*—and with this fleet made full speed for Tiberias.

But Josephus also makes repeated references to a helmsman or captain in each boat:[7]

> I then summoned the heads of families and ordered each of them to launch a vessel, bring the *steersman* with them, and follow me to Tiberias.

And:[8]

> As the boats were successively filled, he ordered the *captains* to make with all speed to Tarichaeae and to lock the men in prison.

Thus, the boats utilized by Josephus in his sham fleet also had crews of *four sailors in addition to a helmsman/captain.*

What was the relationship of the boats used by Josephus in his sham fleet to those that participated in the Battle of Migdal?

The 230 boats that Josephus mentions that he found on the lake must have been anchored at Migdal at the time. There is a problem in that the harbor which Mendel discovered at Migdal is far too small for such a huge fleet of fishing boats during normal times. If we are to give credibility to Josephus's story, this can only mean that these boats belonged to the fleet which, Josephus writes, had been prepared at Migdal for battle or retreat. In other words, the boats of the sham fleet were the same boats that the Jews were soon to employ in the Battle of Migdal.

Our boat was of that same type.

ℓℓℓ

"How many men could have got into the boat?"

"Could the boat have accommodated thirteen men?"

"Could Jesus and the 12 Apostles all have sailed in this boat?"

During the excavation the same question, in a variety of forms, kept popping up over and over again. It was only natural, therefore, that, when I began studying the Gospels to collect material on seafaring on the Kinneret in antiquity, I would search for the passages where Jesus is referred to as sailing with the Twelve. I read carefully through all four Gospels—and finished without finding a single reference. I reread them, convinced that I had missed something, but again to no avail.

I was surprised when I eventually realized that, although the concept of Jesus sailing with the twelve Apostles in a boat on the lake is a deeply ingrained popular Christian belief and sanctified in Christian art, nowhere do the Gospels specifically refer to Jesus sailing together with the twelve Apostles. What the Gospels do say is that Jesus was accompanied on various boat trips by his *disciples*. Jesus had many disciples, however, from among whom he chose the Apostles. Some of these disciples had been with him since his baptism by John.[9] How many disciples were in the boat with Jesus during the recorded boat trips? This the Gospels do not tell us.

For information on the capacity of these boats we have to return to Josephus and his sham fleet:[10]

> I myself, with my friends and the seven soldiers already mentioned, then embarked and set sail for the city.

If we assume that Josephus's boat also contained a skeleton crew, then we arrive at the following calculation:

1 [Josephus] + 7 [soldiers] + (2 + ?) ["friends"]
+ 4 [sailors] + 1 [helmsman/captain] = 15 (+ ?) men

Were there any doubt that these boats could support at least fifteen men, Josephus confirmed this calculation in his reference to the transportation of Tiberian captives in a single boat:[11]

> Ten citizens, the principal men of Tiberias, came down; these he took on board one of the vessels and carried out to sea.

As this boat must have had a crew, we may conclude:

10 [principal men of Tiberias] + 4 [sailors]
+ 1 [helmsman/captain] = 15 men

While the numbers of "230" boats and "2,600" prisoners in Josephus's story may be exaggerations, the ratio of boats to prisoners is compatible with 11 to 12 hostages per vessel. Including the five-man crews, this would have resulted in a total of 16 or 17 men in each boat.

I wondered if our boat could have supported the weight of 15 men. This led immediately to the question of how much men of the Galilee weighed at the time that the boat lived her life. I put this question to Joe Zias. Joe, an expatriate American, is a curator for the Antiquities Authority who specializes in physical anthropology, the study of human remains.

"We can't weigh anybody who lived then," Joe told me with a smile, "but I probably could calculate the weight based on the average height of skeletons of Galilean males. There's a general ratio between height and weight. Give me a while, and I'll work on it."

Several weeks later I went to visit Joe in his office, which is located in the bowels of the Rockefeller Museum in East Jerusalem. To get to the basement, I took the freight elevator, a relic left over from the British Mandatory period that looks like a refugee from an Agatha Christie novel. The lift is a metal cage with sliding mesh doors, a thick wooden floor, and no ceiling. This allows passengers a view of the heavily greased pulley system, which, as the cables slip through it, makes a sickly squishy sound. Like stepping on beetles.

A mutual acquaintance once described to me the topics which Joe studies. "He never does any research," she said, "unless it's totally disgusting."

True, I had thought at the time, Joe's research does run a bit to the macabre. One of his latest research topics, for example, is a study of head lice from ancient combs recovered in excavations. Eventually, he aims to extract human blood samples from the lice to learn more about the genetic makeup of people in antiquity.

Arriving at Joe's office, I found him busily studying several skulls from the Judean Desert.

"Look here," he said, carefully handing me one of the skulls to examine. As I held it up to the light, he pointed out a malformation in the bone structure.

"See this?" he said.

"Yes?"

"This man had leprosy."

In my rush to hand it back to Joe, I almost dropped the skull.

"Don't worry," he said, "it's not contagious."

"I'm happy to hear that."

Joe sat down. I sat down, careful not to touch anything else. Taking out some papers from his desk, Joe told me what he had found out concerning the weight of Galilean males.

"It's hard to calculate the weight of an individual," he explained, "but by studying the *average heights* of skeletons, it is possible to determine the average weight for a population."

"What was the average weight?" I asked.

Joe ignored my question. Instead, he continued slowly, "While nutritional stress has been recorded on skeletons in some marginal areas like the Judean desert, for example, such is not the case in the Galilee. There would have been a steady supply of protein there from fish caught in the lake, and the agricultural lands in the Galilee are among the most productive in Israel. The information I found on male skeletons from the Hellenistic to the

Byzantine periods shows that the average height for males was 166 centimeters [5 feet 5⅓ inches], and the average for females was 151 centimeters [4 feet 11½ inches]."

"Yes?"

"I then took a current copy of a listing of desired weights for men over 25 years old from an American insurance company. For someone with an average build, a man 166 centimeters tall should weigh between 62 and 67 kilograms [136.7 to 147.7 pounds]."

"Which end of that range would best fit the Roman-period Galilean population?"

Joe contemplated this for a long minute. "A society that based itself on fish, which is high in protein and low in fat, would probably result in a somewhat leaner individual than is the norm today. And apart from that, members of an ancient eastern-Mediterranean society would probably be of lighter build and less robust than the modern North American ones. I would judge that the low end of the scale would probably most closely approximate their average weight."

So, if I used a weight of 65 kilograms [143.3 pounds], I would probably be slightly over the actual average weight as you reconstruct it?"

"Correct."

I quickly calculated the weight of 15 men. It worked out to slightly less than a ton—a burden that our boat could have easily carried, even though the boat would probably have been a bit crowded.

Thus we had an answer to that most often posed question. Had Jesus wished to sail with only the twelve Apostles in a vessel like the Kinneret boat, yes, they could all have been easily accommodated.

And then some.

I thanked Joe, who went back to studying his skulls, while I headed for Agatha's elevator.

Sometimes textual evidence helped me clarify the boat. At other times the boat shed light on enigmatic historical or scriptural references. Take for example the boats in the Battle of Migdal.

Josephus emphasized that among the reasons for the defeat of the Jews was that their boats were "small and *built for piracy.*"[12]

Now piracy on a relatively small inland lake makes little sense. One of the prime requirements for pirates to be successful in their nefarious vocation is the ability to escape. In the Kinneret there was really no where to hide. Pirates simply could not escape detection.

Furthermore, what could they possibly want on the Sea of Galilee? There were no cargo-laden merchantmen here. What would they steal? Pottery going to market? A fisherman's catch?

"This is a stickup. Put your hands in the air and give me all the fish you've got!"

I don't think so.

And yet Josephus was certainly familiar with the lake from his experiences on and around it during his stint as governor of the Galilee. What then did he have in mind?

Josephus may be implying that the Jewish boats had something in common with vessels used by pirates on the Mediterranean. Indeed, pirates often used small craft for coastal piracy—to sneak up to a merchant ship slumbering at anchor in the night, for example.[13] To escape pursuit by larger craft and to facilitate beaching, a shallow draft on such boats was an absolute necessity. This allowed them to escape to shallow waters where pursuing vessels of deeper draft could not follow.

Josephus does not say that the Jewish boats were *used* for piracy, only that they were *made* for piracy. The hull of the Kinneret boat may explain his strange comment. One of the elements that had impressed Dick while he was studying the boat was the tight "turn of the bilge." This is the imaginary line along which a vessel's bottom joins its sides. Dick's section drawing across the hull of the Kinneret boat illustrates how boxlike the hull actually is.

"This is the tightest turn of the bilge that I have ever seen on a mortise-and-tenon-built vessel," Dick had told me during the excavation. "Any tighter than this, and the tenons would be sticking out of the sides of the strakes."

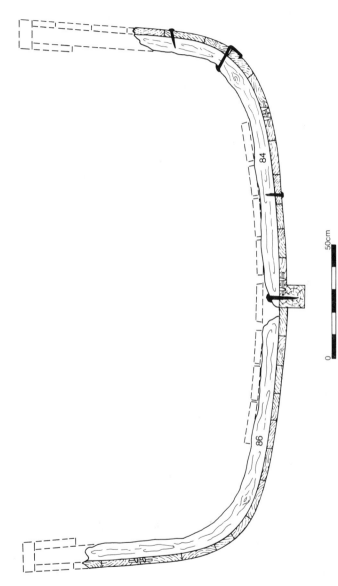

Dick's cross-sectional view of the boat amidships illustrates the tight turn of the bilge.

The manner in which the boat was built, with a shallow, only slightly curved deadrise, produced a hull with minimal draft, which would have been ideally suited for the shallow shores of the Kinneret—and for the purposes of pirates.

ℓℓℓ

Webster's defines *iconography* as "pictorial material relating to or illustrating a subject: a pictorial record of a subject."[14] Ship iconography, or representations, come in many forms: in paintings, carved on temple walls, perhaps incised or daubed in rough graffiti, or set in mosaics. As a group, these representations are a vital form of information—an important part of our metaphorical elephant, if you will—for learning about ships and boats in antiquity.

And not just for calculating crews. They are particularly valuable for learning about those parts of ships and boats which do not normally survive in shipwrecks.

The boat forever at sea in the mosaic found by the Franciscans at Migdal was important to our study because of its proximity in time and space to the Kinneret boat. Dick and I prepared a short study of the information to be derived from the Migdal boat mosaic for the excavation report. Several other mosaics uncovered in Israel, as well as in neighboring Jordan, bear depictions of ships. But for the most part, these mosaics were created much later, in the fifth and sixth centuries.

Dick's examination revealed that the Kinneret boat had a curving or "rockered" keel, deeper at the center of the boat than at the vessel's extremities. Although what appears to be a rockered keel sometimes is actually the result of the hull's settling and sagging after its deposition, this was not the case with our boat. The artist of the Migdal boat mosaic also gave it a rockered keel.

As I have related, Dick interpreted the bow of our boat as having had a ramlike cutwater based on the consideration that the keel ends in a tenon. Despite the later date of the other Israeli and Jordanian mosaics that depict ships, it is interesting that many of the boats and ships depicted in them have bows with a similar cutwater-like projection. This ramlike projecting forefoot appears frequently on the bows of ancient Mediterranean watercraft throughout antiquity, from tiny rowboats to seagoing merchant ships. The reasons for its popularity are unknown.

Across the length of the hull in the Migdal mosaic, in white tesserae, is a broad line, two stones wide in the bow, but narrowing to a single row aft of the quarter rudder. This line probably represents a wale, a strake thicker than the others, which encircled the hull and served to stiffen and strengthen it.

The Migdal mosaic also teaches us that boats on the lake used a single square sail that hung from a mast planted in the center of the hull. In the depiction, the sail has been furled up to the yard, the tapered spar used to spread the head of the sail. This type of "loose-footed" sail, which lacked a boom, or lower yard, is called a *brailed rig*.

The brailed sail had been introduced in the Mediterranean at the very end of the Late Bronze Age, over a millennium before our boat sailed the Kinneret. The sail worked in a manner similar to modern Venetian blinds. Lines, called *brails*, were attached to the foot of the sail and then were carried up the forward side of the sail through rings, usually made of lead, which were sewn in vertical rows onto the sail. This type of sail was reduced or furled by hauling on the brails. The brailed sail permitted greater maneuverability in sailing to windward than had previous rigs, thus opening new vistas for Mediterranean seafaring.

Not all of the boat's rigging is shown in the mosaic. To have included all of it at this scale would have made the picture incomprehensible. Therefore, the artist depicted only two lines of rigging. One runs from the top of the mast to the bow and must be a forestay, a line which supports the mast longitudinally forward. The one or possibly two backstays needed to support the mast aft are missing. The line that runs from one tip of the yard to the station of the helmsman is probably a brace, one of a pair of lines which allowed the helmsman to control the direction of the sail. The brails are not depicted.

Did the Kinneret boat have a mast and sail? This is one question that can be answered definitely and affirmatively. A few days into his visit, Dick discovered four nail *holes* and a slight discoloration on the upper surface of the keel, approximately amidships—all that was left of a mast step that had been yanked out in antiquity.

One important question is whether or not the artisan who created the mosaic at Migdal based his rendition on firsthand observation. At least in later times, we know that Byzantine artisans used documents with illustrations, called *pattern books* or *copybooks*, from which they derived their mosaic motifs. The naive manner in which the boat is depicted strongly suggests, however, that it was not copied from a pattern but was an original composition by a mediocre artisan.

The context of the boat within the mosaic itself is also important. Ronny Reich, the creator of the "boat in the bottle" cartoon, is an archaeologist with an astute eye for detail. In a recent publication, he studied the other elements depicted together with the boat in the mosaic.[15] These he shows to be diminutive objects. Above the boat are a pair of scrapers (*strigili*) used for removing oil and dirt after workouts in a gymnasium—an ancient form of soap. To the right of the boat are a *kantharos*, a type of vase often depicted in mosaics, and beneath the *kantharos* is a fish with seaweed in its mouth. On the upper right are two identical cylindrical objects, which may represent gaming pieces or perhaps a musical instrument. From this, Ronny concludes that because the "boat" is depicted in the same proportion as the other items in the mosaic, the mosaic "boat" is actually a depiction of a *model* of a boat like ours. What we may have here is an artist's still scene, not of flowers or a fruit bowl, but of objects that could fit on a tabletop nonetheless.

There may be one other depiction of the generic large-size Kinneret fishing boat typified by the boat found by the Lufan brothers. A coin minted in AD 220 at Caesarea Paneas (the former capital of Agrippa II), located just north of the Kinneret, has a representation of a tiny boat with a ramlike bow and a recurving

The mosaic from Migdal.

stern.[16] On the boat stand four figures. Yankele Meshorer identifies this as the ship of the Argonauts. Nevertheless, because the Kinneret is the nearest navigable body of water, one of its modest fishing boats may have served as a model.

Perhaps.

🌊🌊🌊

It seems sometimes that, the more things change, the more they stay the same. A type of vessel of approximately the same size as the Kinneret boat, although quite different in construction, continued to be used on the Sea of Galilee into the twentieth

century. These boats were used primarily for fishing with the large
and heavy seine net.

During his visit to the Kinneret in 1869, MacGregor recorded
that the largest boats that he saw on the lake were about 30 feet
(9.15 meters) long with a breadth of about 7 feet (2.14 meters). This
is almost identical to the presumed length of the Kinneret boat
before her bow assembly and sternpost were removed.

Intuitively, MacGregor concluded that these proportions
were the limits for larger-sized boats on the Sea of Galilee in
antiquity. He writes:[17]

> The boats now used in the lake by the fishers are all about the
> same size, rowing five oars, but very clumsy ones, and with a
> very slow stoke. Generally only three oars were in use, and I
> much regret that I failed to remark whether there was a
> rudder, but I think there was none. Their build is not on bad
> lines, and rather "ship-shape," with a flat floor, likely to be a
> good sea-boat, sharp and rising at both ends, somewhat re-
> sembling the Maltese. The timbers are close and in short
> pieces, the planks "carvel built," and daubed with plenty of
> bitumen which is readily obtained here. The upper streak
> [sic] of the boat is covered with coarse canvas, which adheres
> to the bitumen, and keeps it from sticking to the crew when
> they lean upon it. The waist is deep, and there are no stern
> sheets, but a sort of stage aft. As there appears to be no reason
> to suppose that the Turks should have altered, or at any rate
> improved, the Jewish boat on the lake, it is impossible not to
> regard the modern fishers' boat of Galilee with great interest
> and to people it at once with an Apostolic crew.

In the initial part of the twentieth century the British scholar
James Hornell carried out numerous studies on indigenous craft
that still continued in use in maritime cultures throughout the
world. His meticulous studies, published in scholarly journals
such as *Antiquity, Man,* and *The Mariner's Mirror,* and in his book
Water Transport, are a treasure of ethnological information which is
valuable in helping us understand ancient watercraft, their ac-

MacGregor's sketch of a fishing boat at Bethsaida.

coutrements, and their uses. This is particularly true as many of the types of watercraft that Hornell observed no longer exist.

Director of Fisheries in Madras for the British Mandatory government in the 1930s, Hornell was asked to carry out a survey of fishing in Mandatory Palestine. The result of this study was a slim volume in which Hornell reported on his findings.[18]

During his visit to the Sea of Galilee, Hornell did not miss the opportunity to examine the boats that plied the Kinneret. He noted that the boats he found were identical to those on the country's Mediterranean coast. None of the boats was built locally, but in Haifa or Beirut.

The largest type of boat that Hornell found on the Kinneret was called an *arabiyeh* and was used primarily for seine-net fishing. The largest *arabiyeh* seen by Hornell on the lake was 24 feet (7.2 meters) long with a beam of 8 feet (2.4 meters). It was a double-ended boat, one that had decks fore and aft, but it was open amidships. The deck located in the stern was the larger of the two and was needed for transporting the large and heavy seine net.

♪♪♪

The "calming of the storm" is one of the most cherished Gospel stories for Christians. Although all three of the Synoptic Gospels include a description of it, the Gospel of Mark includes two tantalizing bits of information that are lacking in both Matthew and Luke:

> But he was in the stern, asleep on the pillow. (Mark 4:38)

Why sleep in the stern? Although several interpretations have been put forward in the past, the Kinneret boat supplies an obvious and logical one.

The Kinneret boat, like the later *arabiyeh* boats, was apparently built for fishing with the large and heavy seine net. Boats used in this service required a stern deck on which to place the net. And although the Kinneret boat did not survive up to the level of a deck, it must have had one in the stern originally.

Now, sleeping *upon* the stern deck would have been precarious at any time, but particularly during a storm. In this location, a person would have been beneath the feet of the helmsman and open to the waves breaking over the boat. It is unlikely that anyone would have drifted off to sleep there. The area *beneath* the stern deck, however, would have been the most protected and closed part of the boat in such conditions.

And what of *the pillow*? As MacGregor pointed out long ago, the use of the definite article—"*the* pillow" (Greek: *epi to proskephalaion*), as opposed to "*a* pillow"—strongly suggests that this was part of the boat's equipment.[19]

But what is a boat's pillow?

I found no satisfactory answer for this question until one sunny day when I visited the small harbor at Jaffa. The modern port sits on one of the oldest and most venerable anchorages in the entire Mediterranean Sea. Occasionally, I would visit Jaffa in search of antiquities raised in fishermen's nets, or to examine sediments when the harbor was periodically dredged.

It was from Jaffa harbor that the prophet Jonah embarked aboard a ship to escape from the Lord, only to find himself washed up on the beach. It was also here that, according to Greek mythology, Perseus flew in to save the fair princess Andromeda, who had been chained to a rock in Jaffa harbor as a sacrifice to a sea monster. Andromeda is now among the stars, while Perseus is popular in Hollywood. I can assume only that there must have been someone from the press present in Jaffa that day to record the rescue, thus giving inspiration to generations of B-movie script writers.

Musa Shibli is an Arab Christian who has worked all his life as a fisherman out of Jaffa. As a youth he worked with the seine net—the *jarf*, as Musa calls it—on sailing boats in the Mediterranean. I put the question of the pillow to Musa.

"But the explanation is obvious," he said. His eyes sparkled at me as he handed me a tiny cup of dark Turkish coffee, so thick that it poured like chocolate syrup. "I'm surprised that you don't see it."

"See what?"

"When I was young, the boats that I worked on in the Mediterranean always carried a sandbag or two. There was either one large and heavy bag, of about 50 to 60 kilos [110–132 pounds], which we called a *kis zabura,* or two smaller bags, which we called *mechadet zabura.* These weighed *yaani* ["about"] 25 kilos [55 pounds] each. The bags were kept on board for ballasting the boat. But when they were not in use, we stored them under the stern deck. Then, if someone was tired, he would crawl in beneath the stern deck, use the sandbag as a pillow, and go to sleep. In fact . . ." Musa laughed.

"Yes?"

"In Arabic *kis zabura* means 'ballast bag,' but *mechadet zabura,*" and here Musa paused for a second, smiling broadly, "means 'ballast pillow.'"

I do not know whether or not Musa's explanation is right and that "the pillow" referred to in Mark's Gospel was simply a rough sandbag used for ballasting (imparting stability to) the boat. Indeed, Mendel informs me that such sandbags have not been used on the Kinneret in living memory.

I do know, however, that Musa's sandbags are the most sensible explanation I have heard yet.

ᘖᘖᘖ

In mid-April 1987, over a year after the conclusion of the excavation, I wrote to Dick Steffy suggesting a "working hypothesis" in which I proposed to him that the Kinneret boat represents a generic boat type used on the Sea of Galilee during the Roman period and that apparently it is the same type depicted in the Migdal mosaic, described by Josephus, and mentioned in the Gospels.

Dick responded:

> Your working hypothesis sounds OK, but may I make a further suggestion? Shell construction limited design possibilities, so there probably were not as many different boat designs on the Kinneret in antiquity as there are today. I suspect there were small boats—rowboats for one or two

fishermen—and big boats such as ours. They may have varied somewhat in appearance and size, but basically they must
have been limited to a couple of different hull forms in any
given period. Without propellers to push them along, it
seems unlikely that boats much larger than ours would have
been practical on such a small body of water.

As Dick had pointed out to me during the excavation, maritime cultures almost always have more than one size of boat, and
indeed apart from the *arabiyeh* boats, Hornell mentioned three
additional, smaller types of boats in use on the lake in the 1930s.
The *hassake*—a word that lives on in modern Hebrew as a flat
surfboardlike flotation device used by Israeli lifeguards, who maneuver them with a double-bladed paddle—was a lighter and
narrower version of the *arabiyeh*, which was used primarily in
fishing with trammel nets, called *mubattan* in Arabic. Smaller yet
than the *hassake* was the *sambuk*. The *keek* was different in design,
having a flat transom stern, and was used primarily as a passenger
transport.

Is there evidence "beyond a reasonable doubt" that smaller
types of boats were also used on the lake in antiquity? It seemed to
me that all the evidence I was finding pointed to one specific type
of boat, of which the Kinneret boat is a generic representative.

Two Greek terms are used in the Gospels to describe boats on
the Sea of Galilee. One is *ploion*, which literally means "boat," and
the other is *ploiarion*, which is a diminutive and might be translated "little boat." Although the general consensus among scholars
is that both terms refer to the same type of boat, I thought that this
dual use might be worth reexamining.

I took this question to Dr. Anson Rainey of the Institute of
Archaeology of Tel Aviv University. Anson is one of Israel's foremost linguists and is knowledgeable in a number of ancient languages; he has a gift with languages that I find truly phenomenal.
He is the kind of scholar whom one can well imagine reading a
cuneiform clay tablet propped up against his cereal box at the
breakfast table.

We sat in Anson's living room in a suburb of Tel Aviv, surrounded by his voluminous library. He reviewed the texts, and came to the generally accepted conclusion that the two terms are used interchangeably, and that they are synonymous.

Is there any evidence at all that smaller boats were used on the Kinneret in antiquity?

Perhaps.

Josephus, who always seemed to be having troubles with the Tiberians, related how he once escaped an attempt to murder him by a rival warlord and arch-enemy, John of Gishchala.[20] John had tried to turn the fickle citizens against Josephus, who had got wind of these goings-on, had rapidly advanced to Tiberias in an overnight march with two hundred of his soldiers, and had arrived in Tiberias at dawn. Josephus was met by the aroused citizens of the city. There—in the city's stadium, which was apparently located near the lake—he dismissed most of his bodyguards and, standing on a small mound, began to address the assembly.

Josephus relates that John had sent assassins to eliminate him in the midst of his oratory. When the attackers, apparently approaching Josephus from behind, drew their swords, the crowd gave out a shout. Josephus turned to face cold steel nearly at his throat. Without a moment to lose, he jumped down from the hill and hightailed it out of town, aided by a bodyguard named James and a Tiberian named Herod. The three men made their way down to the lake and escaped by commandeering a boat (Greek: *ploion*) moored nearby.

Presumably John's henchmen chased Josephus down to the beach. As getting a vessel the size of the Kinneret boat under way would have been difficult for three men to do speedily on their own, we may be permitted to assume that the three made their getaway in a smaller—rowboat-sized—vessel.

Perhaps.

Anson and I also discussed the Battle of Migdal.

"What word did Josephus use to describe the vessels built by the Romans for the battle?" I asked.

Anson thumbed through the text. "*Sxedia*," he said.

Sxedia. That word was to keep me busy for awhile.

In most translations the word is rendered as "rafts." In the *Odyssey*, however, Homer used the same term to describe the vessel that Odysseus built to escape from the island of the enchantress Circe.[21] Professor Lionel Casson, one of the foremost experts in the study of ancient ships, has shown that Homer was actually describing the shell-first construction of a hull with mortise-and-tenon joints.[22] Furthermore, Anson had pointed out to me that Herodotus, the fifth-century BC Greek historian, used the same term to describe the pontoon bridge built by the Persian king Darius over the Bosporus.[23] This was constructed of a platform supported by boats. Vegetius described the use of these floating bridges in his discussion on how the army should cross rivers:[24]

> But it has been found better for an army to carry around with it on carts "single timbers" [Greek: *monoxyli*], which are rather shallow canoes, hollowed out of single trunks, very light because of the type and thinness of the wood. Planks and iron nails are also kept with them in readiness. The bridge thus speedily constructed, tied together by ropes which should be kept for the purpose, provides the solidarity of a masonry arch in quick time.

This type of bridgework is commonly seen in art depicting Roman armies crossing water obstacles.

I gleaned as much as possible concerning the identity of these *sxedia* that Vespasian had built for the battle and derived the following list of attributes for them:

- They were made of wood.
- They were built by carpenters.
- They were completed in a relatively short time.
- They could carry quantities of soldiers.
- They were more massive and held more men than the Jewish boats.
- The Romans were able to leap into the Jewish boats; thus the caprails of the *sxedia* were either level with or higher than the Jewish boats.

I was convinced that Vespasian hadn't built simple log rafts. Ancient documents refer to the lashing of hulls together for various purposes from the fifth century BC onward. What if, I hypothesized, some of the boats in the Jewish fleet had been left at Migdal? The circumstances in which the Jews escaped onto the lake make it likely that not all the available boats had been used in their flight from the invaders.

By joining pairs of boats left behind at Migdal, the Romans could have quickly assembled *catamarans* (double-hulled vessels) joining the pairs of hulls with fighting platforms constructed of wood on which the legionaries and archers could stand and from which oarsmen could row the vessels.

As the hulls themselves already existed, it would not take long for the army carpenters to lash them together, using timber available locally. Such vessels would have been larger than the Jewish vessels and therefore could have carried considerably more fighting men. The addition of a fighting platform would have made them higher than the Jewish boats.

I proposed the catamaran idea to Professor Casson in a letter and asked for his opinion. Several weeks later I received his response. In it, he pointed out that simple rafts are usually slow and clumsy. Yet in Josephus's description of the battle the Roman vessels were maneuverable enough to hold their own against the Jewish boats, which were certainly quick and agile.

Unless one of these *sxedia* comes to light one day, we will probably never know for sure, but catamarans would have fulfilled all the conditions described by Josephus. So, did Vespasian have catamarans built for the battle?

A definite maybe.

Chapter 11

Like a Rock

We have this hope, a sure and steadfast anchor of the soul. . .

Hebrews 6:19

Ships and boats, whether they sail the deep blue sea or the shallow waters of an inland lake, require the ability to hold a firm position in the water. This is the purpose of an anchor, which is to a vessel what brakes are to a car.

True, on rivers and canals anchors are unnecessary. A simple stake, hammered into the shore with a mallet will suffice to secure the boat. Indeed, the ancient Egyptians, primarily river navigators, though certainly no slouches as seafarers (they sailed on both the Mediterranean and the Red Seas), never did create a term for *anchor* even though they obviously used anchors on their seagoing ships. Egyptian stone anchors have been found along the Egyptian Red Sea coast and on Levantine shores.

Today most anchors are made of metal and are attached to a ship with chains. But when humans first went down to the sea, metals were unknown. Stones, on the other hand, were readily available and could hold a ship by virtue of their weight alone. And so it was that the first anchors were made of stone, or of stone with ancillary wooden parts, and were attached to a boat with cables of rope, called *hawsers* in nautical parlance. In some parts of the world, such as the Indian Ocean, stone anchors continue in use to this day.

At first, a heavy rock used as an anchor may have simply been wrapped with rope or withies, which could be used to attach a rope. Eventually, however, seafarers realized that if they found a stone of the proper weight with a hole in it, they could tie the hawser directly to the anchor. The next stage was to chisel or to drill a hole through the anchor stone for the hawser.

Anchors had been used in our boat during her lifetime of work on the lake. Of that we can be certain. No anchors were found in the boat, however, nor were any found in her immediate vicinity. But after the excavation was over, Moshele did find two anchor stones in the general area. These were surface finds with no stratigraphical context and therefore could not be dated. Nor could they be related to the boat. Yet they prompted me to review the *types* of anchors that were commonly used on the lake in antiquity and that *may have been used* in our boat.

One of the anchors found by Moshele is made of basalt and weighs 19.3 kilograms (42.5 pounds). It is a simple stone, roughly rectangular in shape, with a hawser hole drilled through one of its narrow ends.

"Weight anchors," like this one found by Moshele, hold the vessel to the seabed by virtue of their mass. Some weight anchors are beautifully worked; others are simple rocks with a hole. The largest of those found in the Mediterranean weigh around a half ton.

Apparently weight anchors were not particularly dependable, were difficult to raise once lowered, or were considered expendable. For whatever reason, Mediterranean ships that used them went to sea with a complement of many anchors. This is beautifully illustrated by one of the major archaeological discoveries of this century: the Uluburun shipwreck. In 1983, the oldest known seagoing shipwreck, with a valuable cargo of trade items dating to the latter part of the Late Bronze Age (either late fourteenth or early thirteenth century BC), was discovered in deep waters off the southern coast of Turkey, near the city of Kaş. The wreck site has been excavated for the past decade by Dr. George F. Bass and Cemal Pulak for the Institute of Nautical Archaeology at Texas A&M University. The Uluburun ship, which is estimated to have been about 15–20 meters (50–65 feet) long, carried no less than *twenty-four* stone weight anchors with a combined weight in excess of four tons!

Stone weight anchors of varying shapes and weights have been found in and around the Kinneret. The first two to come out of the Kinneret—and to be identified as anchors—were found underwater by an American expedition in 1960, together with first-century AD pottery.

Moshele found two anchor stones.

The second anchor stone found by Moshele near the boat is quite different from the first. It is also of local basalt and weighs 31.3 kilograms (69 pounds). Rounded in shape, it has no hole; rather, it has a deep groove carved out of one side. This stone could have been tied directly to a rope. More likely, however, it served as a weight for a killick, a type of anchoring device composed of stone and wood.

There are numerous ethnological parallels for killicks, and they come in a variety of shapes. Killicks can be fashioned like a one-armed anchor, the crook of a tree being used as the shank and arm of the anchor, and the weight stone serving as a rudimentary

Stone anchors spill downslope from the Uluburun shipwreck.

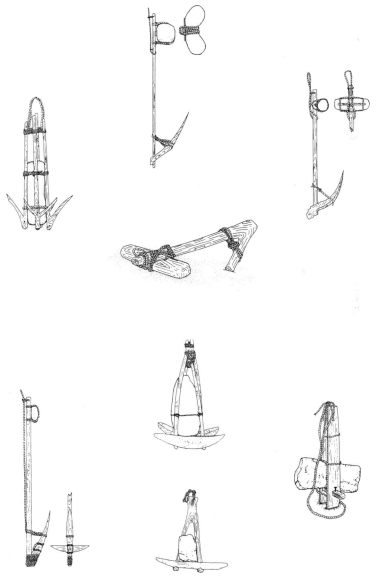

Killicks come in a variety of forms.

anchor stock. Such stones often have a slit or notch cut down their center to facilitate attachment to the wooden anchor shank, just like Moshele's second anchor stone.

One important difference—at least for an archaeologist— between other types of stone anchors and the killicks is that a stone used in a killick need not have any piercings. Indeed, a simple fieldstone of suitable shape and weight can be employed. This causes problems for the archaeologist, for once the wood has decomposed, there is nothing to identify the stone as ever having served as part of an anchoring device. Sometimes the most persuasive argument for the use of killicks by a maritime culture is not finding other types of anchors.

During his survey in the Kinneret with the *Rob Roy*, MacGregor recorded a stone at Capernaum shaped like "an oval, about four feet long and two feet broad. . . . In the middle is a deep cut a foot broad, and from two to six inches deep, leaving a sort of neck between two building ends."[1] The sketch which MacGregor appended to this description is reminiscent of the stone stocks of wooden anchors found in the Mediterranean. Since that time, additional examples of grooved stones suitable for killicks have been found in the Kinneret.

It was apparently such prototypes which led, toward the end of the seventh century BC, to the development of the full-fledged stone-stocked wooden anchor. Stone stocks flourished for only a short time, however. Stone is brittle, so it is a particularly unsuitable material from which to make a long and narrow anchor stock. As an anchor fell into the sea or was dragged along the bottom, stone stocks frequently broke. Indeed, their remains are often found on the Mediterranean seabed. One can well imagine the chagrin of an ancient mariner watching helplessly as his trusty wooden anchor, sans stock, floated to the surface while the winds and the waves tossed his ship onto a lee shore.

You might say that, with stone stocks, the ancient mariners had the right idea for an anchor, but they were using the wrong material. The stone stock was soon replaced by a wooden stock, into which had been poured four separate pieces of molten lead. With the increasing availability of lead—a by-product of the

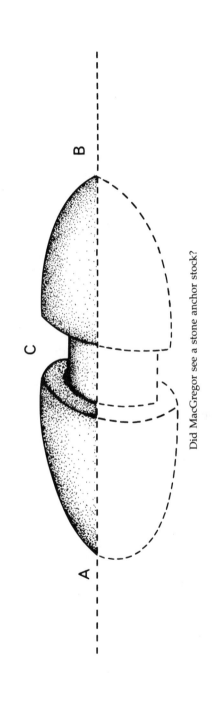

Did MacGregor see a stone anchor stock?

Iberian silver mines, which came under Roman control in the third century BC—lead-filled wooden blocks evolved into stocks made entirely of lead. These stocks were of two types: one was removable and the other fixed. Some of these lead-stocked wooden anchors reached truly enormous proportions.

Iron anchors were first mentioned by Herodotus, who lived during the fifth century BC. They did not become common on Mediterranean ships until the first century AD, however. Not surprisingly, wooden anchors appear to have served as the prototypes for the shape of early iron anchors, which soon evolved along a separate path. In the first century AD the arm segments on iron anchors took on a decidedly "unwooden" shape. The arms continued to straighten until, by the seventh century AD, the anchors became cruciform, which no doubt carried religious significance for Christian seafarers of the Byzantine Empire. Subsequently, the anchor arms continued to "droop" until, by the eleventh century, iron anchors had the shape of an upside-down Y.

From all the data I collected, I concluded that stone/wooden anchors continued in use on Kinneret boats long after they had been superseded on the larger Mediterranean ships by lead-stocked wooden anchors or by anchors made of iron. I could find no evidence supporting the use of iron anchors in the Kinneret in antiquity, perhaps because they were too expensive.

For every rule, however, there is bound to be an exception. And if there is one, then Yuvi and Moshele are bound to find it. During one of my frequent visits to Ginosar, I told the brothers about my research on the stone anchors.

"All in all," I said, "it looks as if only stone anchors and rudimentary wooden anchors with stone stocks were used on the Kinneret. I haven't found any evidence at all of the use of iron anchors on the lake in antiquity."

Moshele shook his head. "You archaeologists spend too much time with your heads in the books," he said. "We have an ancient iron anchor from the Kinneret right here in Ginosar."

"*Ain chaya k'zot* [There's no such animal]," was my immediate response.

But I was soon following Yuvi and Moshele through Kibbutz

A Brobdnignagian fixed lead-anchor stock found off Malta.

Ginosar until we arrived at one member's garden, which had an iron sculpture surrounded by weird-looking cacti. The "sculpture" actually consisted of an iron anchor to which had been appended modern metal items—including a bike wheel and a grapnel hook. The anchor had been welded to a stake buried in the ground, and someone had even attached a ball-bearing ring to its crown.

Moshele had been right, *it was an ancient iron anchor*. I learned that it had been raised in a net by fishermen from Ginosar over twenty years earlier near Capernaum. There were no signs of the salt corrosion which is characteristic of iron anchors from the Mediterranean Sea, a fact supporting the conclusion that the anchor had indeed come out of the Kinneret.

After removing all the "peripheries," it was possible to get a better view of the anchor. In its present form, it is 1.6 meters (5.25 feet) long, and the arms are 0.96 meter (3.2 inches) from tip to tip. It has a round stock hole but lacks an opening for attaching an iron ring. The arms are straight and then curve up toward their ends, which finish in chisel-shaped tips.

This anchor, of which even Mendel had not been aware, finds its closest parallel to iron anchors from two Roman-period shipwrecks found off Cape Dramont in France. The brothers convinced the kibbutz member to donate the anchor, and it is now exhibited near the boat.

An anchor of such large size and shape would have been both unwieldy and unnecessary on a vessel the size of the Kinneret boat, and we presume that this was the largest-size type of vessel which plied the lake in antiquity. One possible explanation is that we are wrong in our conclusion and there were larger boats on the lake. Of such hypothetical vessels we have no concrete evidence. This likelihood seems remote, although not impossible.

An iron anchor appears on coins of Tiberias minted under the emperor Trajan; however, this is best put in the same category as the porpoise that also appears on the coins of that city and that, obviously, never swam in the Kinneret.

When I wrote to Dick about the iron anchor, he suggested that it may have been inherited from a relative who had worked on the

The ancient iron anchor had been reincarnated as a garden decoration.

The iron anchor.

Mediterranean in larger ships by someone who worked on the Kinneret and chose to use it despite its awkward size. Alternately, it could have been used to moor floats or rigs. Even for this function, however, pierced stones would have made more sense. The anchor remains a mystery. How did it get to the bottom of the Kinneret?

I wish I knew.

℮℮℮

There is a Chinese saying that goes something like this: "He who has one watch knows what time it is; he who has two watches is confused." I now had three "watches" for determining the age of the boat. Each of these methods had its limitations. The chapter in the excavation report in which I proposed a date range for the boat is only two pages long. Despite its brevity, it was one of the most difficult parts of the report for me to write.

On the one hand, there were two forms of evidence from the hull itself: construction techniques and carbon 14 (^{14}C) dating. On the other, we had the artifacts found in proximity to the boat.

Dick's study of the boat's construction suggested to him that the boat lived its life sometime between the first century BC and the second century AD. But there were no other hulls to compare it to in the Kinneret.

Yisrael Carmi's ten ^{14}C tests had given a date of 40 BC ± 80. That meant there was a two-in-three chance that the timbers of which the boat was constructed had been cut down between 120 BC and AD 40, and a 19-in-20 chance of this having taken place sometime between 200 BC and AD 120.

The coins stretched over a time frame of 22 centuries. Although in some cases they evoked historical episodes, more than anything they simply illustrated the fact that the stretch of coast where the brothers had found the boat had been active over time. As the coins had not come from archaeologically secure contexts, they had no value at all in dating the boat.

Thanks to the reports by Varda and David, however, the ceramics turned out to be more promising than I had originally

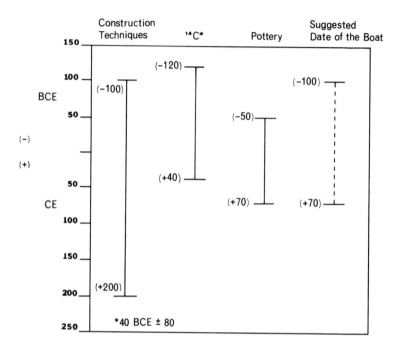

suspected. Varda gives the lamp a date range of about a century, from about 50 BC to about AD 50. David's study of the pottery shows that it was a particularly homogeneous group that included Kfar Hananya ceramic types that may date from the mid first century BC till the First Revolt in AD 66–70. While some of these pottery types continued after this, David notes that *none* of the identifiable pottery is from the types that began after that date.

From all these considerations we may create the above graph.

Despite the restrictions placed on us by the types of material available for dating the boat, the construction techniques, ^{14}C dating, and pottery do align well and suggest that the boat lived its life sometime during the first century BC or the early to mid-first century AD.

If we keep these considerations in mind, the *latest* date—or *terminus ad quem*, as archaeologists call it—that we are required to assign for the deposition of the boat at the site where it was found may reasonably be assigned to the Roman attack on Migdal in AD 67. The results of this event would have decimated the population of Migdal/Tarichaeae. If the site of the boat was an area of boatbuilding activity, which as we will see shortly seems to be the case, then its fate must have been irrevocably interconnected with that of the city, and work at the boatyard must have ceased for a time. Thus the ceramic evidence strongly argues for a date prior to this event.

The earliest date for the boat's deposition is not as clear-cut. The pottery, including the oil lamp, belongs to types that began around the mid-first century BC; however, a single standard deviation of the average of ^{14}C dates and the earliest reasonable dating for the construction techniques used in the hull's construction push this back by a half century or more to around 100 BC.

Thus, in the end, I proposed in the report a range for this period during which the boat lived her life from about 100 BC to AD 67. At present I do not believe that it is possible to be more accurate than that. It is my hope that, once the boat's conservation is completed, it will be possible to have some of her timbers dated by dendrochronology.

One of my greatest disappointments is that I was unable to submit timbers from the hull for dendrochronological examination. This is an archaeometric method which was not available to us before the beginning of the conservation treatment, and now, with the boat undergoing conservation, it is not possible to select samples for study.

In this dating method, timbers are dated by studying the series of tree rings and comparing them to a scientifically established series of tree rings. If all factors are favorable, it is possible to date the sample down to the year—and to the season of the year—in which it was cut. We hope that, when the boat comes out of conservation, this can be done and may supply us with a more accurate determination of the boat's age.

It is not clear how long the boat was in use on the lake. Boats, like cars, eventually wear out. The repairs noted by Dick on our boat indicate a long work life.

But how long is long?

This question is difficult to answer. The only parallel material that I have found for the lifetime of boats in freshwater environments in the Middle East is a reference to a type of boat called a Dongola *markab*, which was described by James Hornell.[2] Writing in 1940, he notes that these vessels, employed on the Nile between the Third and Fourth Cataracts, had a normal life expectancy of about eight to nine years. Mendel tells me that he knows of some wooden boats that are still working after 20 years of service. But these must be exceptional.

Thus, if we assign to the Kinneret boat a work life of a decade or two between 100 BC and AD 67, we would presumably not be far from the mark.

It is now time to address two remaining questions.

🌊🌊🌊

Both the life of Jesus and the Battle of Migdal fell within the time range to which I had assigned the boat. I had also been able to demonstrate "beyond a reasonable doubt" that our boat was of the same large type employed by the disciples of Jesus and mentioned in the Gospels. It was on this same type of vessel that the Jews had done battle with the Romans on the lake.

Could our *specific* boat have taken part in one or the other of these episodes? Could this boat have been the one owned by the Zebedee family? Or by Simon Peter? At our present stage of knowledge, the answer to that questions is this: Yes, it could have, but for the present at least, there is no archaeological evidence to support such an identification.

How probable is it that this specific boat is one of the two mentioned in the Gospels? To answer that question, we must first determine how many boats might have existed on the lake during the 170-year period to which the boat is assigned. Needless to say, this is not easy.

Josephus mentions 230 boats on the lake in connection with his sham fleet. He makes it clear, however, that all these boats must have been moored at Migdal that day. And while this number must have included the boats of other communities around the lake, it was unlikely to include all of the boats on the lake. It certainly did not include the boats from the pagan cities of Hippos and Gadara, for example, nor all of the boats of Tiberias. We are probably safe in assuming that, during the entire period under consideration, there were at least that number of vessels working on the lake at any given time, and probably many more.

The lifetime of boats on the lake was unlikely to have been more than a decade on the average and was probably much less than that. But let us be ultraconservative and assign to them an average lifetime of about 20 years. Thus:

$$170 \text{ [years]} \div 20 \text{ [years]} \times 230 \text{ boats} = 1{,}955 \text{ boats}$$

This very conservative estimate suggests that the statistical likelihood of our boat's belonging to the Zebedees or to Simon Peter is about one in a thousand (that is, 0.1 percent). If we lower the average age of boats on the lake to the more reasonable span of a decade, then the likelihood goes down to 0.051 percent.

Not likely.

In making this statement, however, the first thought that comes to my mind is that of the proverbial statistician who drowned in a lake that was, on the average, only a foot deep.

Furthermore, it would be unwise to limit Jesus's use of watercraft on the lake to those two boats alone. Remember, the information contained in the Gospels concerning the period of Jesus's ministry refers to a relatively few incidents and sayings. It does not cover all the events during this time, a fact of which the Gospel writers themselves were only too well aware. Jesus may have come in contact, in one way or another, with numerous vessels during the time he spent on the Kinneret's shores. But here we leave behind archaeology and enter the realm of conjecture.

The Gospels are concerned with the exceptional. They do not deal with the mundane. In this sense, the written word, by lighting up specific events, serves only to make the darkness surrounding them—the day-to-day life that went unrecorded—all the more impenetrable.

For example, we have no way of knowing how many boat trips—of which there is no extant memory—were made, and how many boats were used in them during the period of Jesus's ministry. *We tend to forget how much we do not know.* For example, when the listeners to his sermons arrived by water, as they did at times, might Jesus have blessed their boats?[3]

Jesus's arrival on the shores of the Kinneret after he left Nazareth suggests a certain familiarity with the region and its inhabitants. Some men of the Kinneret—Simon Peter, his brother Andrew, and Philip—Jesus had already met when he was with John the Baptist across the Jordan River at Bethany.[4]

But might there be another link between a carpenter and the lake? Perhaps Jesus was drawn to the lake because he had already spent time on the Kinneret during the missing years of his young adulthood. If so, might Jesus have worked as a carpenter, perhaps building boats on the lake during that time?

We have no yardstick with which to measure the plausibility of these scenarios.

Let us turn now to the Battle of Migdal. At first glance, it would seem that a stronger case can be made for the boat being one of the many vessels that washed ashore in the aftermath of that terrible conflict. The boat's site of discovery, close to Migdal, seems to support such a conclusion. And then there is the tantalizing arrowhead, possibly shot during the battle, which was found inside the boat.

A judicious reading of the evidence, however, suggests that this particular boat did not participate in the battle. Reflect on the following considerations:

- This is an old boat, and not just for us. She was an old boat when she found her way to the seabed in antiquity, as is amply demonstrated by the many repairs that Dick was able to identify on her hull.

- Prior to her deposition in the lake, all reusable timbers had been removed, presumably for use on other craft. Who would have been left to work on boats after the local population had been decimated in the Battle of Migdal?
- The boat was not alone at the site. She was found in what appears to be a graveyard of boats that were deposited over a considerable period of time.

Dick pointed out in his report that such a situation is reminiscent of boatyards where old vessels are kept around as a source of used parts—not unlike the modern practice of keeping old cars around a garage for the same purpose. Thus it would seem that, following a long and productive work life, the old hull was brought ashore near an area of boat-building activity (boatyard?) located on the outskirts of Migdal, there to be stripped down. And once she had rendered up all that she could, the useless hull was pushed into the lake to be forgotten as she snuggled into the seabed.

The identification of the assembly found beneath the boat remains to be determined. It might have been a cradle to support the boat, part of a dock, or perhaps a makeshift boarding ladder that somehow ended up beneath the boat. The truth is, we do not know.

One might argue that the timbers could have been removed by Vespasian's carpenters for use on the *sxedia*. This seems improbable, however, for the care taken in removing the timbers— particularly the stem assembly and sternpost—suggests that the wreckers intended these timbers for specific positions on future vessels. In the rush to build the *sxedia*, Vespasian's carpenters would have had neither the time nor the need to be so careful.

Josephus's reference to the abundant quantities of wood available to Vespasian seems to be at odds with the seeming situation of "timber starvation" indicated by our boat. But remember, a Roman general leading three legions in the field could easily appropriate any timber available, whether it was stored up at a boatyard or had to be cut down from the groves of fruit and nut trees that grew in the Valley of Gennesaret. Such definitely was not the case for the average Sea of Galilee fisherman.

~~~

Two and a half years after the completion of the excavation, in the summer of 1988, I delivered the entire manuscript to Ayala Sussmann, the editor of 'Atiqot. After much editorial TLC, the report was published in 1990 as Volume 19 of the English series under the title *The Excavations of an Ancient Boat in the Sea of Galilee (Lake Kinneret)*.

Many questions raised by the boat's discovery remain to be answered. And if Dick was only half-joking, many more will be raised after conservation is completed and the reconstruction phase begins. In looking at the completed excavation report, however, I was surprised to discover how much we had learned. Even though many of the pieces of the puzzle are missing, it is still possible to paint a coherent picture of the boat's history.

That story follows.

Chapter 12

Once upon a Boat

Phantom ships are on the sea, the dead of twenty centuries come forth from the tombs, and in the dirges of the night wind the songs of old forgotten ages find utterance again.

From *The Innocents Abroad*
MARK TWAIN[1]

About 2,000 years ago, give or take a century, a master boat-wright set about building a boat on the shores of the Sea of Galilee. He had considerable experience in his trade. Perhaps he had gained it building ships on the Mediterranean or had learned it from someone, possibly a relative, who had. In any event, he brought to his task on these inland shores a knowledge and an understanding of Mediterranean hull construction techniques and traditions.

He may have built the vessel at a boatyard located north of Tarichaeae-Migdal Nunya, although there probably were other boat-building locations on the lake. It is unlikely that he built the ship on speculation; this boat's creation presupposes a need. We would probably not be incorrect in assuming a transaction between the boat builder and a customer. One important consideration in determining the vessel's price was the quality of the materials used in its construction. Whether by choice or, more probably due to a lack thereof, the future owner chose to purchase a vessel in which many of the timbers used in its construction had already seen better days in the hulls of other boats and ships. In fact, many of the timbers were of such poor quality that they would have been tossed aside as worthless on the Mediterranean coast. But here, on the inland lake, they would suffice.

Alternately, wood may have been so scarce that a condition of "wood starvation" existed in the region. We have no evidence of such a situation, however, in other sources. Indeed, Vespasian was able to commandeer "an abundance of wood" near or at this boatyard for use in the construction of his attack fleet prior to the Battle of Migdal.

Perhaps the future owner of this specific boat was too poor to be able to afford timber of higher quality. If so, this also is peculiar. Boats of this type were family ventures, and the owner of a boat could *hire* men to work in the boat. Thus the owner of a fishing boat on the lake should not be considered as at the bottom of the economic ladder. The Galilee at this time was economically depressed, however; the timbers used in the boat's construction are perhaps a physical expression of this overall economic situation.

After the parties agreed on a price, the boatwright set to work. He began by laying the keel. Supports were set up near the lake. Although the keel was to be only 8.27 meters (27 feet) long, the boatwright chose to construct it from two timbers, forming a slightly rockered keel. For the forward part, he selected a used timber of Lebanese cedar, on which mortise-and-tenon joint scars were still visible, while the after timber was of jujube. This latter choice of wood is peculiar. The two pieces were locked together by a wooden linchpin, or by wedges inserted from one or either side into the scarf.

At the stem, the keel ended in a tenon, while a second hook scarf finished it off at the stern. There, the boatwright now joined the keel to a recurving sternpost, into which had been cut the opposing end of a scarf, and again, he locked them in place. At the bow, our boatwright probably added a ram-shaped timber.

Had the boatwright been building a plank-and-frame wooden boat today, he would have next added the frames directly to the keel and then attached the planking (strakes) to the frames with nails. Instead, consistent with the shipbuilding practices of his time on the Mediterranean, he first began to attach the strakes. The lowest strakes, or garboards, he attached directly to the keel. The remaining strakes were attached to each other. In all this construction, mortise-and-tenon joints were used. As each strake was put in place, it was cut to the correct shape so that the edges set flush. The boatwright probably did this, for the most part, by eye, depending for accuracy on long years of experience. Among his tools, however, he may have had one that he employed for determining correct curvatures.

Perhaps he used a wooden compass, like those that were still in use in our century among boat builders on the Nile for exactly this purpose. These compasses have one long, and one short arm. The long arm is run along the upper edge of the strake already in place on the hull, while the shorter arm, which has been dipped in blue paint, runs along the inner side of the plank to be added, thus marking the desired curvature. The upper plank is then dubbed with an adz.

The planks used in the boat's hull were, for the most part, of Lebanese cedar. But the boatwright used anything that was at hand. Planks that had been removed from older boats required preparation before being attached to the hull. This meant plugging holes with wooden pegs and narrowing each plank to remove the old and now useless mortise-and-tenon-joint scars. This process resulted, in at least some cases, in unusually narrow planks. Rather than attach them directly to the hull, the boat builder may have first built up planks of reasonable width by attaching two or more of these narrow planks together with mortise-and-tenon joints before connecting the reconstructed plank to the hull. The planking edges were smeared with pine resin in an attempt to prevent rot, which, the boatwright knew from experience, was a particular problem for wooden boats working in a freshwater environment like the Kinneret. He used no driven caulking to seal the seams, however, a fact that would have surprised a modern shipwright.

Each plank, as it went onto the hull, was attached to its neighbors with closely spaced mortise-and-tenon joints. The boatwright, or perhaps one of his apprentices, spent hours and days doing nothing else but monotonously cutting mortises (slots) into the plank edges with a chisel and mallet. Into each mortise, a flat oak tenon (dowel) was inserted to half its length. Then opposing mortises (matching slots) were cut in the next plank to be applied to the hull. As soon as the planks were attached to each other and carefully tamped into place, holes were bored through the planks and tenons with a bow drill. Multisided tapered oak pegs, whittled down by hand, were then driven into the holes from inside the hull.

The boatwright's tool kit was modest, but sufficient for his needs. It must have held an ax, a measuring device, an awl or race knife for marking the timbers, and probably a drawknife and brushes. It definitely contained several sizes of saws, adzes of varying shapes and proportions, a bow drill with bits of at least two sizes, and various chisels, hammers, and mallets. Most of these tools left evidence of their use on the ship's timbers.

The boatwright gave the vessel a bottom with a shallow, curved deadrise, a tight turn of the bilge, and sides with a gentle outfall. These imparted to the boat a minimum draft, which was ideally suited to the Kinneret's shallow shores. The boat shared this feature with the small pirate boats that plied their trade on the Mediterranean, perhaps leading at least one contemporary observer to describe boats of this type as "built for piracy."

The hull was widest well astern of amidships. Thus the hull shape had a fine bow and a full stern, well suited for the work for which the boat was intended. Perhaps the boatwright raised the first six or seven strakes before he inserted the frames. These the builder attached to the planking with iron nails, which he hammered in from the outside of the hull. Before attaching the frames, he carved into them small rectangular limber holes, to allow the inevitable bilge water to spill back and forth unhindered beneath the ceiling planking.

In securing the frames to the hull, the boatwright deviated from normal practice on the Mediterranean coast and did not clench the nails. Perhaps he felt that clenching was not necessary for a boat that would ply the usually quiet waters of the Kinneret. Alternately, clenching would have required longer nails, which meant more iron. This would have been an added expense which the boat's future owner may have been unwilling, or perhaps unable, to pay.

For the frames, most of which were fashioned from oak, the boatwright again used timbers of questionable quality. The bark was left on many of them. These timbers were chosen for their curvatures, but again, their selection suggests a lack of availability. Most are twisted and gnarled.

The boatwright then completed the sides up to the caprail and attached the remaining futtocks. Decks were then added at the stern, and probably in the bow also. The ceiling planking probably consisted of little more than a few loose-fitting boards, laid longitudinally over the frames. Slightly forward of amidships, the boatwright attached a small block of wood with four iron nails to the keel. This would serve as the vessel's mast step.

The hull was smeared inside and out with a thick cover of pitch or bitumen, probably brought from the Dead Sea. This coating was applied with brushes, trowels, or perhaps boards.

When the hull was completed, the boatwright and his helpers launched her into the lake, where she lay quietly, slowly taking on water through the open seams. A casual observer, watching the water accumulate in the bilge until the boat seemed as if she was about to sink, no doubt would have shaken his or her head in dismay and concluded that the boat builder had erred terribly in his creation.

But the casual observer would have been wrong. This dunking was the final step of the building process, for it was specifically this contact with water which swelled the wood, sealed the seams, and created a watertight fit. Once the seams had closed, the hull was ready for delivery to its new owner.

When the boatwright had finished his work, he could well be proud of the result. Although the boat was no beauty, from inferior materials he had crafted a simple, sturdy hull which was well suited to the needs of the future owners.

The prospective owner made his living from the lake. Of this at least we can be sure. No doubt other male members of his family were employed with him in this work, for a boat was a family enterprise. When family members were insufficient to man the boat or to assist in fishing operations, the family head would hire additional workers. These perhaps received a percentage of the catch as in-kind payment for their work.

Presumably the family was Jewish. At the time the boat was built and lived her life, the Kinneret could well be termed a "Jewish" lake, virtually surrounded on all sides by predominantly Jewish settlements; many of these had their own small fishermen's harbors to accommodate the numerous fishing boats that plied the lake's waters. Only on her southeastern flank, where the cities of Hippos (Sussita) and Gadara (Hammat Gader) were situated, was the lake bordered by pagans.

Upon receiving their "new-old" vessel from the boatwright, the owner and his family rigged it with the necessary accoutrements. To sail, the boat would require oars, quarter rudders, a mast, a yard, a sail, and rigging. They furnished it with four rowing oars and a pair of steering oars which hung at the quarters. A full crew would have consisted of five men: four rowers and a helmsman or captain. The boat's captain need not have been her owner, although in the case of the boat which concerns us this would have been likely.

It is not clear if the boatwright supplied the rigging, oars, and sail. Perhaps the buyer had saved these items from an earlier boat, or had purchased them from a chandler. We can only conjecture about these accoutrements, for none of them have come down to us.

The boat's anchor would have been little more than an unshaped stone of limestone or basalt, which was pierced with a hole to take the hawser. Alternately, the anchoring device may have been of composite construction, a killick-like device fashioned out of a tree crook with a heavy, roughly hewn stone employed to weigh it down.

The single square sail was carried from a mast, which was stepped into the small mast step, actually little more than a chock. The mast was supported longitudinally by fore and aft stays and perhaps also by shrouds. The yard was raised and lowered by means of one or two halyards and was controlled by a pair of

Texas A&M University graduate student Bill Charlton puts the final touches on a
1:10 display model of a generic Sea of Galilee first-century AD fishing boat.

braces attached to the extremities of the yards. The sail was probably made from pieces of linen sewn together. And if the vessel's
hand-me-down hull is any indication, the boat's sail was also
likely to have been of a dingy, oft-repaired patchwork design.

The crew spread and took in the sail by working the brails.
These ropes were attached to the foot of the sail and then rose
vertically, perhaps through wooden rings sewn to the fore side of

the sail. Hauling on the brails caused the sail to rise in a manner similar to a modern Venetian blind.

When the winds were contrary, or absent altogether, the boat could be rowed. The oars had another use also, one which can still be observed today on the Kinneret. Crew members sometimes used them to slap the water in order to scare fish into a spread net.

This boat appears to have belonged to the largest boat type commonly in use on the lake. It was employed primarily for fishing with the seine net; indeed, this net appears to have been the primary raison d'être for the existence of this type of boat, the maximum size of the hull being dictated by the weight and size of the seine net. The net was an expensive piece of equipment and was therefore carefully maintained. Stones were used as weights to sink the foot of the net to the lake bottom.

During the days of fishing, the net was loaded onto the vessel's stern platform. The boat needed to be able to support the considerable weight of this net after it was loaded, wet from use in the lake. This may have been the motive for a boat such as this having her greatest breadth well astern of amidships.

After the net had been spread, the boat would lie quietly, anchored near shore or grounded upon it, while the crew pulled their catch to land, collecting the fish into baskets—that is, with the notable exception of any stray catfish which may have been caught up in the net. These fish, lacking scales and therefore not allowed for food according to the strict Jewish dietary laws, were of no monetary value and were therefore simply tossed back into the lake.

The seine net, thus, had two profound influences on the architecture of boats of the type under consideration. First, the net defined the maximum size of boat required on this inland lake to carry a seine net on her stern deck and to transport a crew capable of working her to the fishing site. This ideal length, about 7–9 meters (23–30 feet), continued on the lake into the present century. Second, the net required a large stern deck, where it could be stored on the boat. And although this particular type of vessel was ideally suited to work with the seine nets, it could also have been employed with the other types of nets commonly used on the lake.

Occasionally, a crew member or a passenger, seeking a place to rest, would crawl in beneath the stern deck, on the few loose boards that served as ceiling planking, and go to sleep. There, out of the way of the captain and crew, he might find some peace and quiet, as well as a certain measure of solitude in the darkened space. As he rested there, he would hear through the planks the sounds of the water gurgling and splashing against the hull as it cut through the lake's waters. Above him and about him, the boat and its rigging would creak, but this creaking would become a soft and welcome litany. Below him, bilge water would scurry back and forth through the limber holes. Perhaps a rough sandbag, kept in the boat for ballast, served as his pillow. The air might be a bit stale. The smell of fish would also permeate the air, but his nostrils would have been well accustomed to it. Loose scales left behind by previous catches were likely to be found clinging to his clothing.

The Kinneret was a vital source of food, and fishing was a significant industry for the settlements that grew up around the lake. Although we are probably right in inferring that fishing was the main source of the family's income, any other services which the boat could render, and which could put a few more coins into the family purse, were not to be ignored. And as the lake was an important transportation hub, currency could be made in other ways also. Thus, on any given day, the boat might be found transporting supplies—ceramics from the pottery shops at Kfar Hananya, for example, or foodstuffs—between the cities and the settlements that surrounded the lake. At other times, the boat may have served as a waterborne taxi, transporting paying passengers from one side of the Kinneret to the other, as well as along her shores. At such times, if business was good, as many as ten passengers could be taken on board at once. Together with a full five-man crew, however, the boat would have been quite crowded. Of course, the passengers themselves may have helped to row. In

times of military emergencies, boats could be hired—or drafted—
as rapid troop transports.

Thus, at one time or another during its work life on the lake,
the boat probably called at most, if not all, of the small harbors that
surrounded the lake. In search of schools of fish, the boat would
also have visited many of the less inhabited shores.

We do not know if the boat changed ownership during its
relatively long lifetime. We do know, however, that she lived a
long work life on the lake as evidenced by the many repairs made
to her hull. She probably lived a decade or two—a long life for a
work boat.

As time passed, however, the hull began to weaken. Fungi
and bacteria had been attacking and weakening the boat's timbers
from before the moment she was placed in the water. Now these
agents, along with the inevitable wear and tear of constant use,
began to take their toll on the hull. Joints weakened and lost their
integrity. Seams opened.

Some repairs were made by simply hammering in large iron
staples to hold the planking together. For more complex repairs,
however, the boat was probably brought to a boatwright. Frames
and planking were removed and replaced, perhaps on more than
one occasion. The substituted frames were nailed to the keel. In its
final days, the boat contained frames of hawthorn, redbud, and
willow, as well as a plank made of Aleppo pine. Some, if not all, of
these may have been replacements.

If ownership of the boat had not changed hands, it appears
that the owner's financial conditions had not improved in the
interim. The replacement timbers are of no better quality than the
interior pieces which had been utilized in the boat's original construction.

Eventually the day came when the boat's owner realized that
his boat would not make it through another winter storm. It must
have seemed to him that no matter how much she was repaired, a
leak would spring up somewhere else. Her work life had come to
an end.

The nets were unloaded from the boat for the last time, and the boat was sailed, or rowed, to a boatyard located on the shore of the Kinneret in the Valley of Ginosar, just north of Tarichaeae, there to end her days. Perhaps the boatwright purchased the old hull outright, paying the owner a pittance for the timbers in her that could be salvaged. Alternately, the boat may have been the ancient equivalent of a "trade-in," the boatwright agreeing to lower the price for the construction of a new boat on condition that he could utilize timbers from her hull.

Either way, the boat was stripped of all her gear. The mast was unstepped, and all the rigging, the oars, beams, oar thole pins, and ceiling planks were removed. Decks may have been dismantled.

At the bow, the stem construction was removed, care being taken to ensure that this valuable timber would not be harmed, so that it could be reused. Someone ungraciously removed the two forward frames, yanking them out. The nails that had secured them were laid bare, protruded starkly like fingers through the planking. These frames were particularly valuable to the boatwright because of their sharp angles. Amidships the small mast step was removed, leaving behind only a slight discoloration and the holes that had been pierced by the nails that had held it securely to the keel.

At the stern the post was removed. First, someone carefully pulled out the nails holding the planks' ends to the post. They took care not to put any pressure on the planks in doing this, to avoid cracking the sternpost. Then the wooden wedge in the scarf holding the sternpost to the keel was carefully knocked out, and the post was removed, with its half of the scarf still intact. A saw, which left its mark in two places on the keel, was employed to facilitate the post's removal.

All that remained were worn-out timbers, tired and of little use to the wreckers. Still smeared with pitch, these timbers could not even have been used for kindling.

Waterfront space in the yard was valuable and not to be taken up with a useless old hulk. At this time, if our understanding of events is correct, the boat was floated out into the lake, perhaps to keep her from blocking the shore. The buoyancy of the remaining timbers assisted the wreckers in moving the hull into the water, even though it was now full of water, which rushed in through the open stem and stern.

Whether by intent or by chance, the boat's bow came to rest on a loose tree trunk, a common enough commodity along the shores of the Kinneret. Perhaps the stump was intended to facilitate future access should additional parts be desired for use. If so, this never took place. Instead, the tree stump continued to support the hull at the bow, while the stern settled into the mud. The boat, perhaps nudged by the current, came to rest with a distinct list to port.

In time, the hull was forgotten by those ashore. Soon the lower parts of the hull became enveloped in a soft, silty mud. As time passed, the soft sediment became hard-packed clay, supporting a hull which progressively weakened as its timbers became waterlogged. The hull rested in the anaerobic embrace of the Kinneret's bed, which limited greatly the ability of microorganisms to continue their ongoing attack on the hull.

The upper parts of the remaining hull—the strakes and futtocks which shared the misfortune of remaining above the sediment—slowly succumbed to the ravages of time. They disintegrated in oxygen-rich water, leaving behind only small piles of the iron nails that had previously held them together.

At some point after the boat's arrival on the lake bed, an arrowhead, perhaps shot from a bow during a bloody battle on the lake, came to rest inside the boat and was entombed with the hull. The region where the boat rested subsequently continued to serve as a center for boat building. Additional hull fragments, and perhaps hulls, joined the boat and became buried in the mud alongside her.

Time passed. This could be measured first in years, then in centuries, and finally in millennia. Armies clashed. Kingdoms and empires rose and fell. Cultures came and went. Battles and wars were won and lost. Continents were discovered, rediscovered, and colonized. Humankind flew through the air in machines and even landed on the moon. Through all this, the boat continued to slumber peacefully.

Occasionally, during times of drought, the waters of the Kinneret receded. Trees and brush grew on the former lake bed, and their roots penetrated the wood of the abandoned hull. Many times the waters rose and receded again, as they did in 1985 and 1986. It was then that two brothers who had gone on a quest to find an ancient boat in the lake happened upon a few iron nails and the curving outline of a wooden strake in the mud . . .

Epilogue

The cat only grinned when it saw Alice. It looked good-natured, she thought: still it had *very* long claws and a great many teeth, so she felt that it ought to be treated with respect.

"Cheshire Puss," she began, rather timidly, as she did not at all know whether it would like the name: however, it only grinned a little wider. "Come, it's pleased so far," thought Alice, and she went on. "Would you tell me, please, which way I ought to go from here?"

"That depends a great deal on where you want to get to," said the Cat.

"I don't much care where—" said Alice.

"Then it doesn't matter which way you go," said the Cat.

"—so long as I get somewhere," Alice added as an explanation.

"Oh, you're sure to do that," said the cat, "if you only walk long enough."

From *Alice's Adventures in Wonderland*
LEWIS CARROLL[1]

S ome might feel a certain sense of disappointment in the inability to provide a definitive identification for the boat. While this might be a natural and understandable response, we are forced to think further. Although the boat cannot be linked scientifically to the Gospel stories or the Battle of Migdal, she speaks volumes on both these subjects. She is, as best we can ascertain, an anonymous traveler from the past: a generic Sea of Galilee fishing boat that lived her humble life—one of effort and toil—on the lake during an era of great events.

Though this is the last chapter of the book, in truth, I have barely begun to tell the story. The previous pages dealt with a view of the past, imparted to us by the boat. There is, however, another view, one that faces the future.

In 1988, I was invited to the United Kingdom to deliver a series of slide lectures about the excavation. By that time, the boat had been in the pool at the Yigal Allon Centre for two years, submerged in plain water. This, remember, was merely first-aid treatment. Never far from my thoughts was the knowledge that those parts of the boat not covered by the lake's protective sediment had not survived. The conservation process needed to get under way as soon as possible, but it was far from clear how we would pay for the heating and circulation system, without which the PEG treatment could not begin.

At Nitsa's request, Karen had spent considerable time and effort submitting grant proposals to numerous agencies for funding the boat's conservation. Our hopes especially rested on approval from a prominent foundation known for its interest in the conservation of antiquities.

To our dismay, we were informed politely that the project did not fall within the parameters of the organization's giving, as the boat was neither a "historic building" nor a "work of art." This response was a severe blow to us all. It was not only that we did not get the funding. It was also the idea that an agency that supported conservation did not consider the boat a worthy recipient.

What were we doing wrong?

Nautical archaeologists working in the Mediterranean do not often have the opportunity to meet their compatriots who work on Northern European ships. So I was pleased that my lecture trip gave me the chance to visit with two veteran North European nautical archaeologists. Dr. Ole Crumlin-Pedersen is responsible for the excavation and exhibition of an outstanding group of five Viking ships found at Roskilde in Denmark, and Dr. Peter Marsden is a curator at the Museum of the City of London and has carried out considerable work on shipwrecks found in the Thames and elsewhere in England.

I knew that both Peter and Ole were knowledgeable about the museum aspects of ship archaeology, and I therefore solicited their thoughts on how we might go about raising funds to conserve and exhibit our boat. I must have made it sound as if the boat had become a burden. When I explained the problem we were having, the two archaeologists looked surprised. They did not understand why I considered it a problem.

Peter enlightened me. "Understand that each ancient—or even old—ship or boat has a specific group of people who have an interest in preserving that particular hull," he said. "You might call it a *constituency.*

"There are those who would be interested in and support the reconstruction of the *Mayflower*, for example, but care little about Viking ships. Others would support Nelson's *Victory* or Henry VIII's *Mary Rose*. In each case, the interest group is relatively small.

"So for the Galilee boat, the potential constituency is immense. It *could* include the entire Judeo-Christian world. Your boat simply cannot be beaten for worldwide public appeal."

If managed and exhibited properly, Ole and Peter went on to

explain, not only would our boat be able to cover her own expenses, but she could also generate revenue.

Hmmmm. Now that was something to think about.

I was considerably cheered by that discussion, but it was only later that something clicked. When it did, I was strapped into the seat of a little puddle jumper, winging my way over the Irish Sea to Dublin, there to give a lecture at Trinity University.

I pulled out my yellow legal pad, and ideas, concepts, and dreams began to flow. I decided to look beyond the immediate funding problems. Those would be solved (and indeed have been). I wanted to look further ahead, to imagine a potential future reality: a final home for the boat.

That would be a museum, and it would contain only one artifact: the boat. The building would be very much alive, and the story of the boat and her milieu would be related as an experience.

I decided that my imaginary museum would have at least four major themes. The first thread in the tapestry would deal with the boat's discovery, and the story of the excavation would be related here. With a judicious use of audiovisual exhibits, visitors to the museum could be transported back to those days and share in our adventure.

In the next room, the relationship of Galilean seafaring to the Gospels would be presented.

From here, the visitors would move on to a tableau depicting the Battle of Migdal. A battle, all but forgotten, would be returned to memory as the story was related to the accompanying sounds of the clash of arms.

Visitors would then walk into a fourth and final room with dark walls. After they entered the room, the doors would be closed and the visitors would be, momentarily, in total darkness. Then, slowly, lights would begin to glow, and the boat would appear, behind glass, as if from nowhere.

Oh, and on their way out, there would be a tiny fragment from the boat. So that visitors could touch the past. Literally.

There would be one more component to my dream museum: It would support with its revenue continuing nautical archaeological research in the Kinneret. In this way, the museum would continually renew itself rather than remaining static. The research would include the final study of the boat's construction, the construction of an authentically built 1:1 scale replica—like the *Kyrenia II*—of the boat for sea trials, the search and study of other ancient boats that surely exist beneath the Kinneret's seabed, perhaps even some that took part in the Battle of Migdal. And that was only the beginning.

When you know where you want to go, it is a lot easier to get there. I was excited. In those short scribbled notes, there was a target at which to aim. As the plane began its descent and I stowed my notes, I decided that upon my return to Israel, I would plant the seeds for the boat museum.

The museum would not happen overnight. We were in for the long haul.

♪♪♪

After the plane landed in Dublin, I took a taxi to the university. The cabby stopped at the university's main gate. I paid the fare, added a tip, collected my bags, and got out.

Only then did I notice that I was standing opposite a large, wall-sized advertisement. The notice sang the praises of a well-known and large company that manufactures electronic equipment. In no uncertain terms, it promised a steady stream of remarkable products to make life easier and more pleasant.

But it was the large multicolored rainbow cascading down the center of the announcement that caught my attention—as rainbows tend to do these days. As I followed the rainbow down, my eyes came to rest on the short one-liner written across it. Chills ran up and down my spine. In letters big enough to be read at night under the light of a new moon it said:

YOU AIN'T SEEN NOTHING YET

"What the . . . ?" I said out loud to myself, oblivious of the fact that I was standing on a busy thoroughfare. Passers-by stared at me strangely. I barely noticed.

And then, with a chuckle, I said, "Well, actually, why not?" and, shouldering my bag, I headed for the university.

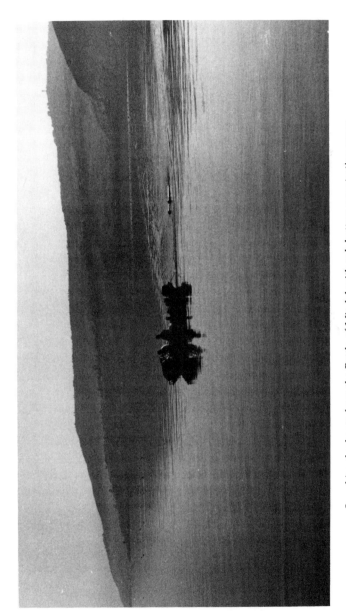

Searching for boats from the Battle of Migdal with sub-bottom-penetrating sonar.

Notes

Prologue

1. *SFAC*: 92.

Chapter 1. The Boat That Made Rainbows

1. Bibby 1969:31.
2. See Rabinowitz 1994.

Chapter 2. A Sea of Legends

1. Twain 1870:507.
2. *The Jewish War* III:516–518.
3. MacGregor 1870:113.
4. MacGregor 1870:249.
5. MacGregor 1870:253.
6. Twain 1870:512.
7. Vilnay 1978:126–127.
8. Albright and Mendenhall 1942; Sukenik 1947.
9. Barton 1940:217–218; Ullendorff 1962:342–343; Margalit 1976:172–177; 1981.
10. Margalit 1981:134.

11. Hirschberg 1954:215.
12. Exodus 17:1–7.
13. Numbers 21:16.
14. Numbers 21:17–18.
15. Vilnay 1978:128–130.
16. Vilnay 1978:130–131.
17. Pococke 1745:70.
18. Vilnay 1978:168–169.
19. Ecclesiastes 2:8.

Chapter 3. The Excavation from Hell

1. *Annotated Alice*:233–234.

Chapter 4. Galilean Seafaring in the Gospels

1. Luke 1:1–4.
2. See, for example, Pagels 1979.
3. Matthew 11:20.
4. Twain 1870:502.
5. Vilnay 1978:127.
6. Matthew 4:19; Mark 1:17; Luke 5:10.
7. Matthew 13:1–3; Mark 3:9; 4:1.
8. Nun 1989a:16–22; 1993.
9. Ezekiel 26:5; 26:14; 47:10.
10. Schürer 1979(II):271–272.
11. Matthew 8:28; Mark 5:1; Luke 8:26.
12. There were two demonics according to Matthew (8:28).
13. Tzaferis 1983; 1989; Nun 1989b.
14. Nun 1989c.
15. Matthew 9:9–13; Mark 2:13–17; Luke 5:27–32.

Chapter 5. "Yep, It's an Old Boat"

1. The younger Pliny, *Letters* VI:16.3.
2. Grant 1971, 1990:121–124; Gore 1984; Deiss 1985.
3. Grant 1971:215.

Notes 381

4. The younger Pliny, *Letters* VI:16.8–9.
5. The younger Pliny, *Letters* VI:16.20.
6. The younger Pliny, *Letters* VI:16.20.14–15, 17.
7. The practice of placing a hull in water to close the seams is mentioned by Theophrastus as well as the Talmud (*Enquiry into Plants* V.VII.4; Sperber 1986:32). I thank Professor Michael Katzev for bringing my attention to the quote from Theophrastus and for the photo of the *Kyrenia* II sinking on page 153.
8. Katzev and Katzev 1986:8–10; Katzev 1989:170–171.

Chapter 6. The First Jewish Naval Battle

1. *The Jewish War* III:522, 525.
2. Matthew 22:15–22; Mark 12:13–17; Luke 20:20–26.
3. Acts 25:13–27; 26.
4. Acts 26:31–32.
5. Vegetius I:10.
6. *The Jewish War* III:466.
7. *Life of Josephus* LXXIII:406.
8. Vegetius I:16.
9. *The Jewish War* I:3.
10. *The Jewish War* II:572–576.
11. Tacitus, *The Histories* V:13; Seutonius, *The Twelve Caesars* X:4.
12. *The Jewish War* VII:143–148.
13. Hart 1952; Barag 1978; Meshorer 1982:190–197.
14. Two other battles in which ships took part are mentioned by Josephus in the context of the First Revolt. In one, the Jewish fleet at Jaffa—which had been attacking Roman shipping—put out to sea in an attempt to escape the Romans but were destroyed by a storm which Josephus called "the Black Norther"; during mop-up operations near the Dead Sea, some Jews who had taken refuge in boats on the Dead Sea were captured (*The Jewish War* III:414–427; IV:439).

Chapter 7. The Impossible We Do Immediately; Miracles Take a Little Longer

1. *Annotated Alice*:67–68.

Chapter 8. A Pride of Scholars

1. Translation from Fitzmeyer 1986:716.
2. Sussman 1985.
3. Stager 1991.
4. Sussman 1982.
5. Proverbs 31:18.
6. Exodus 27:20.
7. Adan-Bayewitz 1993.
8. Matthew 27:29; Mark 15:17; John 19:2, 5.
9. Judges 9:14–15.
10. Zohary 1982:154–155.
11. Liphshitz and Biger 1991.
12. *Jewish War* V:36.
13. Leviticus 23:40.

Chapter 9. Good Night, Sleeping Beauty

1. Vilnay 1978:134–135.

Chapter 10. Putting It All Together

1. Mark 1:19–20.
2. John 21:2–3.
3. Luke 5:3.
4. *Jewish War* III:522–523.
5. *Jewish War* II:632–646; *Life of Josephus* (XXXII–XXXV:155–178).
6. *Jewish War* II:635. My italics.
7. *Life of Josephus* XXII:163. My italics.
8. *Jewish War* II:641.
9. Acts 1:15, 21–22.
10. *Life of Josephus* XXXII:164. In the parallel reference in *The Jewish War* (II:636), Josephus does not mention his friends being in the boat.
11. *Jewish War* II:639.
12. *The Jewish War* III:523.
13. Ormerod 1978:26–28.
14. *Webster's: s.v. iconography.*

15. Reich 1991.
16. Meshorer 1984–1985:46–47, 56, No. 56, Pl. 15:56.
17. MacGregor 1870:357–358.
18. Hornell 1935.
19. MacGregor 1870:358, fn. 14.
20. *The Jewish War* II:614–619; *Life of Josephus* XVII–XVIII:87–96.
21. *Odyssey* 5.244–257.
22. Casson 1971:217–219.
23. Herodotus, *History* IV:88, 97.
24. Vegetius III:7.

Chapter 11. Like a Rock

1. MacGregor 1870:341.
2. Hornell 1940:127.
3. John 6:23–24.
4. John 1:35–43.

Chapter 12. Once upon a Boat

1. Twain 1870:512–513.

Epilogue

1. *Annotated Alice*: 87–88.

Glossary

1. The nautical terms are derived from Steffy 1994:266–298 and Hocker, in press.

Bibliography

Josephus

Quotes from Josephus are taken from the following translations:
The Jewish War   *Josephus: The Jewish War.* Ed. G. Cornfeld. Grand Rapids. 1982.
Life of Josephus   *Josephus I: The Life against Apion.* Trans. H. St. J. Thackeray. (Loeb Classical Library.) Cambridge. 1976.

Prologue

SFAC   *Stories from Ancient Canaan.* Ed. and trans. M. D. Coogan. Philadelphia. 1978.

Chapter 1. The Boat That Made Rainbows

Bibby, G., 1969. *Looking for Dilmun.* New York.
Rabinowitz, A., 1994. Inside the Israel Antiquities Authority. *Biblical Archaeology Review* 20/2:40–45.

Chapter 2. A Sea of Legends

Albright, W. F., and G. E. Mendenhall, 1942. The Creation of the Composite Bow in Canaanite Mythology. *Journal of Near Eastern Studies* 1:227–229.

Barton, G., 1940. Danel, a Pre-Israelite Hero of Galilee. *Journal of Biblical Literature* 60:213–235.

Hirschberg, J. W., 1954. The tombs of David and Solomon in Moslem Tradition. *Eretz Israel* 3:213–220. (In Hebrew.)

MacGregor, J., 1870. *The Rob Roy on the Jordan, Nile, Red Sea & Gennesareth &c. A Canoe Cruise in Palestine and Egypt, and the Waters of Damascus.* London.

Margalit, B., 1976. Studia Ugaritica: II. Studies in *Krt* and *Aqht. Ugarit-Forschungen* 8:137–192.

Margalit, B., 1981. The Geographical Setting of the AQHT Story and Its Ramifications. In: *Ugarit in Retrospect: Fifty Years of Ugarit and Ugaritic.* Winona Lake, pp. 131–158.

Pitard, W. T., 1994. The Reading of *KTU* 1.19:III:41: The Burial of Aqhat. *Bulletin of the American Schools of Oriental Research* 293:31–38.

Pococke, R., 1745. *A Description of the East and Some Other Countries.* II, Part I: *Observations on Palaestine or the Holy Land, Syria, Mesopotamia, Cyprus, and Candia.* London.

SFAC   *Stories from Ancient Canaan.* Ed. and trans. M. D. Coogan. Philadelphia. 1978.

Sukenik, Y., 1947. The Composite Bow of the Canaanite Goddess Anath. *Bulletin of the American Schools of Oriental Research* 107:11–15.

Twain, M., 1870. *The Innocents Abroad, or the New Pilgrims Progress; Being Some Account of the Steamship Quaker City's Pleasure Excursion to Europe and the Holy Land; With Descriptions of Countries, Nations, Incidents as They Appeared to the Author.* San Francisco.

Ullendorff, E., 1962. Ugaritic Marginalia, II. *Journal of Semitic Studies* 8:339–351.

Vilnay, Z., 1978. *Legends of Galilee, Jordan and Sinai: The Sacred Land III.* Philadelphia.

Chapter 3. The Excavation from Hell

Annotated Alice   *The Annotated Alice: Alice's Adventures in Wonderland and Through the Looking Glass,* by Lewis Carroll. Illus. J. Tenniel. Introduction and notes by M. Gardiner. New York. 1960.

Chapter 4. Galilean Seafaring in the Gospels

Nun, M., 1989a. *The Sea of Galilee and Its Fishermen in the New Testament.* Ein Gev.

Nun, M., 1989b. *Gergesa (Kursi): Site of a Miracle Church & Fishing Village.* Ein Gev.

Nun, M., 1989c. *Sea of Galilee: Newly Discovered Harbors from New Testament Days.* Ein Gev.

Nun, M., 1993. Cast Your Net upon the Waters: Fish and Fishermen in Jesus' Time. *Biblical Archaeology Review* 19/6:46–56, 70.

Pagels, E., 1979. *The Gnostic Gospels.* New York.

Schürer, E., 1979. *The History of the Jewish People in the Age of Jesus Christ (175 B.C.–A.D. 135)* I–III. New English version, rev. and ed. G. Vermez, F. Millar, and M. Black. Edinburgh.

Twain, M., 1870. *The Innocents Abroad, or the New Pilgrims Progress; Being Some Account of the Steamship Quaker City's Pleasure Excursion to Europe and the Holy Land; With Descriptions of Countries, Nations, Incidents as They Appeared to the Author.* San Francisco.

Tzaferis, V., 1983. *The Excavations of Kursi—Gergesa.* ('Atiqot 16) (English Series). Jerusalem.

Tzaferis, V., 1989. A Pilgrimage to the Site of the Swine Miracle. *Biblical Archaeology Review* 15/2:44–51.

Vilnay, Z., 1978. *Legends of Galilee, Jordan and Sinai: The Sacred Land.* III. Philadelphia.

Chapter 5. "Yep, It's an Old Boat"

Deiss, J. J., 1985. *Herculaneum: Italy's Buried Treasure*, rev. and updated. New York.

Gore, R., 1984. The Dead Do Tell Tales at Vesuvius. *National Geographic Magazine* 165/5 (May):557–573.

Grant, M., 1971. *Cities of Vesuvius: Pompeii and Herculaneum.* New York.

Grant, M., 1990. *The Visible Past: Greek and Roman History from Archaeology 1960–1990.* New York.

Katzev, M. L., 1989. "Kyrenia II": Building a Replica of an Ancient Greek Merchantman. *Tropis* I:163–175.

Katzev, M. L., and S. W. Katzev, 1986. Kyrenia II: Research on an Ancient Shipwreck Comes Full Circle in a Full-Scale Replication. *INA Newsletter* 13/3:1–11.

Kinneret Boat   Wachsmann, S., et al. *The Excavations of an Ancient Boat in the Sea of Galilee. ('Atiqot* 19). English Series. Jerusalem. 1990.

Sperber, D., 1986. *Nautica Talmudica.* Ramat Gan.

Steffy, J. R., 1985a. The Herculaneum Boat: Preliminary Notes on Hull Details. *American Journal of Archaeology* 89:519–521.

Steffy, J. R., 1985b. The Kyrenia Ship: An Interim Report on Its Hull Construction. *American Journal of Archaeology* 89:71–101.

Steffy, J. R., 1987. The Kinneret Boat Project. II: Notes on the Construction of the Kinneret Boat. *International Journal of Nautical Archeology* 16:325–329.

Steffy, J. R., 1989. The Role of Three-Dimensional Research in the Kyrenia Ship Reconstruction. *Tropis* I:249–261.

Steffy, J. R., 1990. The Boat: A Preliminary Study of Its Construction. In *Kinneret Boat,* pp. 29–47.

Steffy, J. R., 1994. *Wooden Ship Building and the Interpretation of Shipwrecks.* College Station, TX.

Tropis I   *Proceedings of the First International Symposium on Ship Construction in Antiquity.* (Piraeus, August 30–September 1, 1985). Ed. H. Tzalas. Athens. 1989.

Younger Pliny, *Pliny: Letters and Panegyricus* I. Trans. B. Radice. (Loeb Classical Library.) Cambridge. 1972.

Chapter 6. The First Jewish Naval Battle

Albright, W. F., 1923. Contributions to the Historical Geography of Palestine: The Location of Taricheae. *Annual of the American School of Oriental Research* 2–3:29–46.

Barag, D., 1978. The Palestinian "Judaea Capta" Coins of Vespasian and Titus and the Era of the Coins of Agrippa II Minted under the Flavians. *The Numismatic Chronicle* 18:14–23, pls. 3–5.

DRBE   *The Defence of the Roman and Byzantine East* I. (Proceedings of a Colloquium held at the University of Sheffield in April 1986). Eds. P. Freeman and D. Kennedy. (*BAR International Series* 297:I).

Evans, R. F., 1986. *Soldiers of Rome: Praetorians and Legionnaires.* Washington, DC.

Gichon, M., 1986. Aspects of a Roman Army in War According to the *Bellum Judaicum* of Josephus. In: *DRBE*: 287–310.

Gracey, M., 1986. The Armies of the Judean Client Kings. In *DRBE*, pp. 311–328.

Grant, M., 1970. *The Roman Forum*. London.

Hart, H. St. J., 1952. Judaea and Rome: The Official Commentary. *Journal of Theological Studies*, N.S., 3/2:172–198, pls. I–VI.

Jones, B. W., 1984. *The Emperor Titus*. London.

Meshorer, Y., 1982. *Ancient Jewish Coins* I–II. New York.

Payne, R., 1962. *The Roman Triumph*. London.

Rajak, T., 1983. *Josephus: The Historian and His Society*. Philadelphia.

Schürer, E., 1973. *The History of the Jewish People in the Age of Jesus Christ (175 B.C.–A.D. 135)* I–III. New English version rev. and ed. G. Vermes and F. Millar. Edinburgh.

Seutonius, *Gaius Suetonius Tranquillus: The Twelve Casears*. Trans. R. Graves. Revised with an Introduction by M. Grant. Harmondsworth. (Reprint)

Thackeray, H. St. J., 1967. *Josephus: The Man and the Historian*. New York.

Vegetius   *Vegetius: Epitome of Military Science*. Trans. with notes by N. P. Milner. Liverpool. 1993.

Williamson, G. A., 1964. *The World of Josephus*. Boston.

Chapter 7. The Impossible We Do Immediately; Miracles Take a Little Longer

Annotated Alice   *The Annotated Alice: Alice's Adventures in Wonderland and Through the Looking Glass*, by Lewis Carroll. Illus. J. Tenniel. Introduction and notes by M. Gardiner. New York. 1960.

Chapter 8. A Pride of Scholars

Adan-Bayewitz, D., 1990. The Pottery. In: *Kinneret Boat*: 89–96.

Adan-Bayewitz, D., 1993. *Common Pottery in Roman Galilee*. Ramat Gan.

Amos, E., and D. Syon (Friedman), 1990. Photomosaics of the Boat's Interior. In: *Kinneret Boat*: 57–64.

Carmi, Y., 1990. Radiocarbon Dating of the Boat. In: *Kinneret Boat*: 127–128.

Feig, N., 1990. Burial Caves at Nazareth. *'Atiqot* (Hebrew Series) 10:67–79. (In Hebrew.)

Fitzmeyer, J. A., 1986. *The Gospel According to Luke (I–IX): Introduction, Translation and Notes by Joseph Am Fitzmeyer, S. J.* (The Anchor Bible). Garden City, NY.

Gitler, H., 1990. The Coins. In: *Kinneret Boat*: 101–106.

Kinneret Boat   Wachsmann, S., et al. *The Excavations of an Ancient Boat in the Sea of Galilee.* (*'Atiqot* 19). English Series. Jerusalem. 1990.

Liphshitz, N., and G. Biger, 1991. Cedar of Lebanon (*Cedrus libani*) in Israel during Antiquity. *Israel Exploration Journal* 41:167–175.

Nir, Y., 1990. Sedimentation in Lake Kinneret and the Preservation of the Boat. In: *Kinneret Boat*: 23–28.

Rosenthal, R., and R. Sivan, 1978. *Ancient Lamps in the Schloessinger Collection.* (*Qedem* 8). Jerusalem.

Siegelman, A., 1988. An Herodian Tomb near Tell Abu-Shusha. In: *Mishmar Ha'Emeq*: 13–42. Ed. B. Mazar. Jerusalem. (In Hebrew.)

Stager, L. E., 1991. Eroticism and Infanticide at Ashkelon. *Biblical Archeology Review* 17/4:34–53, 72.

Sussman, V., 1982. *Ornamented Jewish Oil-Lamps.* Warminster.

Sussman, V., 1985. Lighting the Way through History: The Evolution of Ancient Oil Lamps. *Biblical Archaeology Review* 11/2:42–56.

Sussman, V., 1990. The Lamp. In: *Kinneret Boat*: 97–98.

Syon (Friedman), D., 1990. The Arrowhead. In: *Kinneret Boat*: 99–100.

Werker, E., 1990. Identification of the Wood. In: *Kinneret Boat*: 65–75.

Zevulun, U., and Y. Olenik, 1979. *Function and Design in the Talmudic Period.* (Haaretz Museum Publication). Tel Aviv.

Zohary, M., 1982. *Plants of the Bible.* Cambridge.

Chapter 9. Good Night, Sleeping Beauty

Cohen, O., 1990. Conservation of the Boat. In: *Kinneret Boat*: 15–22.

Kinneret Boat   Wachsmann, S., et al. *The Excavations of an Ancient Boat in the Sea of Galilee.* (*'Atiqot* 19). English Series. Jerusalem. 1990.

Vilnay, Z., 1978. *Legends of Galilee, Jordan and Sinai: The Sacred Land* III. Philadelphia.

Chapter 10. Putting It All Together

Casson, L., 1971. *Ships and Seamanship in the Ancient World.* Princeton.

Hornell, J., 1935. *Report on the Fisheries of Palestine.* London.

Hornell, J., 1970. *Water Transport*. Newton Abbot. (Reprint 1946.)

Kinneret Boat   Wachsmann, S., et al. *The Excavations of an Ancient Boat in the Sea of Galilee*. (*'Atiqot* 19). English Series. Jerusalem. 1990.

MacGregor, J., 1870. *The Rob Roy on the Jordan, Nile, Red Sea & Gennesareth: A Canoe Cruise in Palestine and Egypt, and the Waters of Damascus*. London.

Meshorer, Y., 1966. Coins of the City of Gadara Struck in Commemoration of a Local Naumarchia. *Sefunim* 1:28–31, pl. II.

Meshorer, Y., 1984–1985. The Coins of Caesarea Paneas. *Israel Numismatic Journal* 8:37–58, pls. 7–15.

Ormerod, H. A., 1978. *Piracy in the Ancient World*. Oxford. (Reprint.)

Rainey, A. F., 1990. Appendix B: The Skiff and the Boat in John 6:22–24. In: *Kinneret Boat*: 126.

Reich, R., 1991. A Note on the Roman Mosaic at Magdala on the Sea of Galilee. *Liber Annuus* 41:455–458.

Steffy, J. R., and S. Wachsmann, 1990. The Migdal Boat Mosaic. In: *Kinneret Boat*: 115–118.

Vegetius   *Vegetius: Epitome of Military Science*. Trans. with notes by N. P. Milner. Liverpool. 1993.

Wachsmann, S., 1990a. First Century CE Kinneret Boat Classes. In: *Kinneret Boat*: 119–124.

Wachsmann, S., 1990b. Literary Sources on Kinneret Seafaring in the Roman-Byzantine Period. In: *Kinneret Boat*: 111–114.

Webster's   *Webster's New Collegiate Dictionary*. Springfield, MA. 1977.

Zias, J., 1990. Appendix A: Anthropological Observations. In: *Kinneret Boat*: 125.

Zias, J., 1991. Death and Disease in Ancient Israel. *Biblical Archaeologist* 54/3:146–159.

Chapter 11. Like a Rock

Hornell, J., 1940. The Frameless Boats of the Middle Nile, II. *Mariners Mirror* 26:125–144.

Kinneret Boat   Wachsmann, S., et al. *The Excavations of an Ancient Boat in the Sea of Galilee*. (*'Atiqot* 19). English Series. Jerusalem. 1990.

MacGregor, J., 1870. *The Rob Roy on the Jordan, Nile, Red Sea and Gennesareth: A Canoe Cruise in Palestine and Egypt, and the Waters of Damascus*. London.

Nun, M., 1993. *Ancient Stone Anchors and Net Sinkers from the Sea of Galilee.* Ein Gev.

Wachsmann, S., 1990. The Date of the Boat. In: *Kinneret Boat*: 129–130.

Chapter 12. Once upon a Boat

Twain, M., 1870. *The Innocents Abroad, or the New Pilgrims Progress; Being Some Account of the Steamship Quaker City's Pleasure Excursion to Europe and the Holy Land; With Descriptions of Countries, Nations, Incidents as They Appeared to the Author.* San Francisco.

Epilogue

Annotated Alice   *The Annotated Alice: Alice's Adventures in Wonderland and Through the Looking Glass,* by Lewis Carroll. Illus. J. Tenniel. Introduction and notes by M. Gardiner. New York. 1960.

Glossary

Hocker, F., in press. Glossary of Nautical Terms. In: S. Wachsmann, *Seagoing Ships and Seamanship in the Bronze Age Levant.* College Station, TX.

Steffy, J. R., 1994. *Wooden Ship Building and the Interpretation of Shipwrecks.* College Station, TX.

Glossary

I have attempted throughout this book to avoid technical terms when possible. Some terminology is unavoidable, however, particularly when one is talking about details of ship and boat construction.[1] This glossary will hopefully aid in clarifying those terms.

Adz Woodworking tool with the blade set at right angles to the handle.

Aft Toward the stern.

Akkadian Semitic language written in a cuneiform script.

Amidships In the middle of the vessel.

Amphora Ceramic jar, used in antiquity primarily for the transport of liquids.

Anchor Any device employed to hold a vessel to the sea floor by means of a cable.

Anchor shank The shaft of an anchor.

Anchor stock A weighted crosspiece designed to cant the anchor so that one of its arms will dig into the seabed.

Aramaic The predominant (Semitic) language spoken by Jews in their homeland during the Second Temple period.

Auxilia Foreign troops that augmented the Roman legions.

Backstay Line running from the mast aft.

Ballast Heavy material placed low in a vessel to improve its stability.

Bitumen   Natural hydrocarbon substance, such as asphalt, used as pitch.

Boatwright   Master craftsman skilled in the construction and repair of boats.

Boom   Yard or spar to which the foot of a sail is attached.

Bow   (a) The forward portion of a ship; (b) a weapon used to cast an arrow in archery.

Braces   Pair of lines attached to the ends of the yard and used to control the direction of the sail.

Brails   Lines employed to control the area of sail exposed to the wind.

Brailed rig   A sail system that employs brails.

Caprail   Timber attached to the top of a vessel's frames, which is also normally the upper edge of the vessel's side.

Cataphract (armor)   Scale armor or coats-of-mail.

Caulk   To drive fibrous material into the seams of planking and to cover it with pitch to make a vessel's seams watertight.

Ceiling planking   A vessel's internal planking placed over the upper surface of the frames.

Clastic sediments   Sediments that contain stone fragments.

Cuirasse   Armor that protects the body from neck to waist.

Cutwater   Forwardmost part of the stem that parts the water.

Deadrise   The amount of elevation, or rising, of the floor above the horizontal plane.

Deck   A horizontal platform placed across the interior of a hull.

Dendrochronology   The study of tree-ring patterns that can be used to determine the age of timber.

Draft   The depth to which a hull is immersed.

Dutchman   American shipwright's slang term for a wooden patch or insert let into a damaged or rotted plank; also called a *graving piece.*

Edge joinery   A form of hull construction prevalent in the Mediterranean region during antiquity, in which individual planks or timbers are joined to adjacent ones at their narrow edges.

Essenes   One of the three main forms of first-century AD Judaism;

the Essenes ceased to exist after the First Jewish Revolt in AD 66–70.

Floor (timber) A frame timber that crosses the keel and spans the bottom of the hull.

Forestay Line running from the mast forward.

Frame Transverse timber which supports or reinforces the hull planking.

Furl To bundle or roll up a sail when it is not in use.

Futtock A framing member that extends the line of a floor timber or a half frame.

Garboard strake The first strake on either side of the keel.

Half frame A frame whose heel, or bottom, begins near one side of the keel and spans part, or all, of one side of the hull; half frames were normally used in pairs on either side of the keel.

Halyards Lines employed in hoisting and lowering the sail.

Hanukkah The Jewish Feast of Dedication (of the Holy Temple) commemorating the Maccabees' rededicating of the Holy Temple in Jerusalem in 165 BC.

Hook scarf Attachment of two planks or timbers, the angular ends of which are offset to lock the joint; hook scarfs are sometimes locked with wedges or keys.

In situ In its original place.

Keel The main longitudinal timber in most hulls; a vessel's "backbone."

Killick Primitive anchoring device generally made of wood and stone.

Kosher Food that conforms to Jewish dietary laws.

Lee The direction away from the wind.

Levant The lands bordering the eastern Aegean and Mediterranean Seas, especially Israel, Lebanon, and Syria.

Lines drawings A set of geometric projections, usually arranged in three views, that illustrates the shape of a vessel's hull.

Loose-footed sail A sail that lacks a boom, or lower spar.

Maccabees Name given to a group of Jewish partisans led by Judas Maccabaeus and his brothers, who defeated the Seleucid king Antiochus IV and rededicated the Temple in Jerusalem in 165 BC after it had been desecrated.

Mast   Spar used to support a sail and associated rigging.

Mast step   Wooden block placed above the keel into which the mast is stepped, or secured.

Merchantman   Trading ship.

Mortise-and-tenon joinery   One of several methods for attaching planks or timbers to each other by means of a projecting piece that is fitted into one or more cavities (mortises) of corresponding size.

Neutron Activation Analysis (NAA)   A technique that allows the "fingerprinting" of certain type of artifacts.

Pharisees   One of the three main forms of first-century AD Judaism, from which modern Judaism evolved.

Pithos (pl. pithoi)   Large amphora.

Port   (a) Harbor; (b) left.

Procurator   Roman official governing a minor province such as Judea.

Quarter   The after part of a vessel's sides.

Quarter rudder   Rudder affixed to the side of a hull at the stern.

Rabbet   Groove or cut made in a piece of timber so that the edges of another piece can be fitted into it to form a tight join.

Rigging   General term for the lines (ropes) used in conjunction with masts, yards, and sails.

Sadducees   One of the three main forms of first-century AD Judaism; the priestly class which ceased to exist following the destruction of the Second Temple in AD 70.

Scarf   An overlapping joint used to connect two planks or timbers without increasing their dimensions.

Second Holy Temple   The Babylonian king Nebuchadnezzar destroyed the First Holy Temple, built by Solomon in Jerusalem, and exiled the Jews to Babylonia in 586 BC. King Cyrus of Persia, who defeated the Babylonians, allowed the Jews to return to Jerusalem in 538 BC, after which they built the Second Temple. The Second Temple was repeatedly enlarged, notably by King Herod the Great (37–4 BC). It was destroyed by the Romans under Titus in AD 70.

Seleucid Greeks Greek dynasty (ca. 312–64 BC) founded by one of Alexander the Great's generals; at its greatest extent, the Seleucid Empire included all of modern Israel, Lebanon, and Syria, as well as much of Iraq, Iran, and Turkey.

Sharkia Strong winter easterly wind in the region of Israel.

Sheer The longitudinal sweep of a vessel's sides or decks; the profile view of a vessel.

Sherd A fragment of a broken ceramic vessel.

Shipwright Craftsman expert in the construction and repair of ships.

Starboard Right side.

Stem The forwardmost timber, which is scarfed into the keel.

Stern The after end of a vessel.

Sternpost Vertical or upward-curving timber attached to the stern end of the keel.

Strake A continuous line of planks extending from bow to stern.

Succoth Jewish religious festival celebrating the harvest and the period of wandering after the exodus from Egypt.

Talmud Collection of Jewish law and tradition, consisting of the Mishna and the Gemara.

Tenon Wooden projection either cut from the end of a timber or being a separate wooden piece that was shaped to fit into a corresponding mortise.

Timbers All wooden hull members.

Tophet Hell; originally a location in the Valley of Hinnom, south of Jerusalem, where children were sacrificed to the Molech (Jeremiah 7:31).

Treenail A round or multisided piece of hardwood driven through planks and timbers to connect them.

Turn of the bilge The portion of the lower hull where a vessel's bottom curves toward its sides.

Ugaritic A cuneiform alphabetic script that evolved in the city of Ugarit in Syria during the Late Bronze Age.

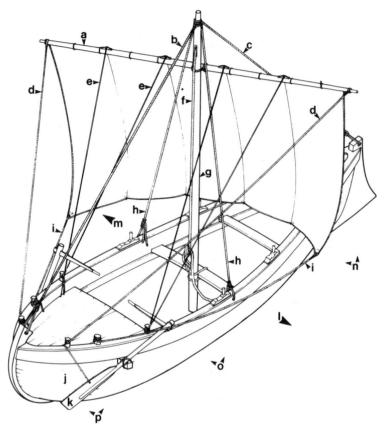

Rigging (brailed rig) and general terms pertaining to ships and boats. Key: a—
yard; b—backstay; c—forestay; d—braces; e—brails; f—halyard; g—mast; h—
shrouds; i—sheets; j—quarter; k—quarter rudder; l—starboard (right); m—port
(left); n—bow; o—amidships; p—stern.

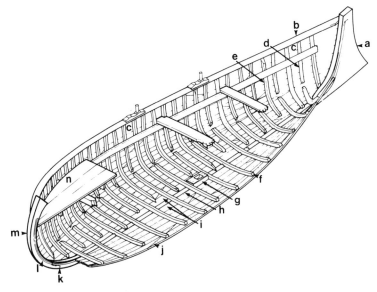

Nautical terms for a vessel's parts. Key: a—cutwater stem; b—caprail; c—strake; d—futtock; e—half-frame; f—floor timber; g—mast step; h—keel; i—garboard strakes; j—diagonal scarf; k—hook scarf; l—rabbet (apparently not present on the Galilee Boat's now-missing stem and sternpost); m—sternpost; n—deck.

Waterline ram A metal fixture at the bow of an oared warship which transformed the vessel into a rowed torpedo used in ramming enemy ships with the intention of incapacitating them; the nautical weapon *par excellence* in the Mediterranean from about 900 BC to the sixth-century AD.

Yard A spar employed to spread a sail.

Zealots Jewish sect that advocated armed opposition to all foreign rule.

Illustration Credits

Acknowledgments

p. xiv. Photo courtesy Israel Antiquities Authority.

Chapter 1. The Boat That Made Rainbows

p. 17. Drawing: D. Johnson. Courtesy Institute of Nautical Archaeology. **p. 18.** Drawing: D. Johnson. Courtesy Institute of Nautical Archaeology. **p. 19.** Drawing: R. Reich. Courtesy Israel Antiquities Authority. **p. 20.** Photo: S. Wachsmann. Courtesy Israel Antiquities Authority. **p. 23.** Courtesy Israel Antiquities Authority. **p. 24.** Courtesy Israel Antiquities Authority.

Chapter 2. A Sea of Legend

p. 43. From MacGregor 1870:287. **p. 45.** From MacGregor 1870:255. **p. 46.** From MacGregor 1870:frontispiece. **p. 48.** From Twain 1870:497.

Chapter 3. The Excavation from Hell

p. 64. Photo: D. Syon. Courtesy Israel Antiquities Authority. **p. 66.** Photo: D. Syon. Courtesy Israel Antiquities Authority. **p. 67.** Photo: D. Syon. Courtesy Israel Antiquities Authority. **p. 69.** Photo: D. Syon. Courtesy Israel Antiquities Authority. **p. 71.** Photo: D. Syon. Courtesy Israel Antiquities Authority. **p. 72.** Photo: D. Syon. Courtesy Israel Antiquities Authority. **p. 73.** Photo: D. Syon. Courtesy Israel Antiquities Authority. **p. 75.** Photo: D. Syon. Courtesy Israel Antiquities Authority. **p. 76.** Photo: D. Syon. Courtesy Israel Antiquities Authority. **p. 78.** Photo: D. Syon. Courtesy Israel Antiquities Authority. **p. 79.** Photo: D. Syon. Courtesy Israel Antiquities Authority. **p. 82.** Photo: D. Syon. Courtesy Israel Antiquities Authority. **p. 87.** Photo: D. Syon. Courtesy Israel Antiquities Authority. **p. 88.** Photo: D. Syon. Courtesy Israel Antiquities Authority. **p. 90.** Photo: D. Syon. Courtesy Israel Antiquities Authority. **p. 91.** Photo: D. Syon. Courtesy Israel Antiquities Authority. **p. 92.** Photo: D. Syon. Courtesy Israel Antiquities Authority. **p. 95.** Photo: D. Syon. Courtesy Israel Antiquities Authority. **p. 96.** Photo: D. Syon. Courtesy Israel Antiquities Authority. **p. 101.** Drawing: R. Reich. Courtesy R. Reich. **p. 102.** Drawing: D. Berg. Courtesy D. Berg. **p. 103.** Drawing: D. Berg. Courtesy D. Berg.

Chapter 5. "Yep, It's an Old Boat"

p. 127. Courtesy Institute of Nautical Archaeology. **p. 139.** After Steffy 1994:46 Fig. 3–26. **p. 140.** After Steffy 1990:42 Fig. 5.13. **p. 144.** After Steffy 1994:48 Fig. 3–30b. **p. 145.** After Steffy 1994:48 Fig. 3–30a. **p. 146.** Drawing: J. R. Steffy. Courtesy Institute of Nautical Archaeology. **p. 149.** Courtesy Israel Antiquities Authority. **p. 150.** Courtesy Israel Antiquities Authority. **p. 151.** From Steffy 1990: Foldout 1. Courtesy Israel Antiquities Authority. **p. 153.** Photo: M. L. Katzev. Courtesy Kyrenia Ship Project. **p. 154.** Photo: D. Syon. Courtesy Israel Antiquities Authority. **p. 157.** Drawing: J. R. Steffy. Courtesy Institute of Nautical Archaeology. **p. 158.** Photo: D. Syon. Courtesy Israel Antiquities Authority. **p. 159.** Photo: D. Syon. Courtesy Israel Antiquities Authority. **p. 161.** Photo: D. Syon. Courtesy Israel Antiquities Authority. **p. 162.** Drawing: J. R. Steffy. Courtesy Institute of Nautical Archaeology.

Chapter 6. The First Jewish Naval Battle

p. 184. After Syon (Friedman) 1990:99, Fig. 13.1. **p. 186.** Photo: S. Wachsmann. **p. 193.** Courtesy Israel Museum.

Chapter 7. The Impossible We Do Immediately; Miracles Take a Little Longer

p. 200. Photo: S. Wachsmann. Courtesy Israel Antiquities Authority. **p. 205.** Photo: D. Syon. Courtesy Israel Antiquities Authority. **p. 207.** Photo: D. Syon. Courtesy Israel Antiquities Authority. **p. 208.** Photo: D. Syon. Courtesy Israel Antiquities Authority. **p. 210.** Photo: D. Syon. Courtesy Israel Antiquities Authority. **p. 212.** Photo: D. Syon. Courtesy Israel Antiquities Authority. **p. 213.** Photo: D. Syon. Courtesy Israel Antiquities Authority. **p. 215.** Photo: D. Syon. Courtesy Israel Antiquities Authority. **p. 217.** Photo: D. Syon. Courtesy Israel Antiquities Authority. **p. 218.** Photo: D. Syon. Courtesy Israel Antiquities Authority. **p. 220.** Photo: D. Syon. Courtesy Israel Antiquities Authority. **p. 221.** Photo: D. Syon. Courtesy Israel Antiquities Authority. **p. 222.** Photo: D. Syon. Courtesy Israel Antiquities Authority. **p. 223.** Photo: D. Syon. Courtesy Israel Antiquities Authority. **p. 224.** Photo: D. Syon. Courtesy Israel Antiquities Authority. **p. 225.** Photo: D. Syon. Courtesy Israel Antiquities Authority. **p. 226.** Photo: D. Syon. Courtesy Israel Antiquities Authority. **p. 227.** Photo: D. Syon. Courtesy Israel Antiquities Authority. **p. 228.** Photo: D. Syon. Courtesy Israel Antiquities Authority.

Chapter 8. A Pride of Scholars

p. 243. After Sussman 1990:98 Fig 12.1. **p. 245.** After Adan-Bayewitz 1990:91 Fig. 11.1. **p. 257.** From Nir 1990:24 Fig. 4.1. **p. 259.** Photo: D. Syon. Courtesy Israel Antiquities Authority.

Chapter 9. Good Night Sleeping Beauty

p. 265. Photo: D. Syon. Courtesy Israel Antiquities Authority. **p. 266.** Photo: D. Syon. Courtesy Israel Antiquities Authority. **p. 268.** Photo: D. Syon. Courtesy Israel Antiquities Authority. **p. 269.** Photo: D. Syon. Courtesy Israel Antiquities Authority. **p. 272.** Photo: D. Syon. Courtesy Israel Antiquities Authority. **p. 273.** Photo: D. Syon. Courtesy Israel Antiquities Authority. **p. 274.** Photo: D. Syon. Courtesy Israel Antiquities Authority. **p. 277.** Photo: D. Syon. Courtesy Israel Antiquities Authority. **p. 284.** Photo: D. Syon. Courtesy Israel Antiquities Authority. **p. 290.** After Cohen 1990: 22.

Chapter 10. Putting It All Together

p. 302. Drawing: J. R. Steffy. Courtesy Institute of Nautical Archaeology. **p. 305.** Photo: D. Syon. Courtesy Israel Antiquities Authority. **p. 307.** Drawing: S. Wachsmann. Courtesy Israel Antiquities Authority. **p. 319.** Drawing: J. R. Steffy. Courtesy Institute of Nautical Archaeology. **p. 323.** Photo: D. Syon. Courtesy Israel Antiquities Authority. **p. 325.** From MacGregor 1870:371.

Chapter 11. Like a Rock

p. 337. Photo: S. Wachsmann. Courtesy Israel Antiquities Authority. **p. 338.** Photo: D. Frey. Courtesy Institute of Nautical Archaeology. **p. 339.** After van Nouhuys 1951:23 Fig. 3; 30 Figs. 14–15, 19; 33 Fig. 20; 38 Figs. 27–29. **p. 341.** After MacGregor 1870:341. **p. 343.** Photo: H. Frost. Courtesy H. Frost. **p. 345.** Photo: S. Wachsmann. Courtesy Israel Antiquities Authority. **p. 346.** Photo: S. Wachsmann. Courtesy Israel Antiquities Authority.

Chapter 12. Once upon a Boat

p. 363. Photo: J. Lyle. Courtesy Institute of Nautical Archaeology.

Epilogue

p. 377. Photo: W. H. Charlton. Courtesy Institute of Nautical Archaeology.

Glossary

p. 398. Drawing: F. Hocker. Courtesy Institute of Nautical Archaeology.
p. 399. Drawing: F. Hocker. Courtesy Institute of Nautical Archaeology.

Index